Zen Cosmology
Dogen's Contribution to the Search for a New Worldview
By Ted Biringer

Zen Cosmology
Dogen's Contribution to the Search for a New Worldview

Ted Biringer

© 2016 Ted Biringer

All rights reserved.

No part of this book may be reproduced or transmitted in any form or by any means, electronic or mechanical, including photocopying, recording, or by any information storage and retrieval system or technologies now known or later developed, without permission in writing from the copyright owner, except in the case of brief quotations embodied in critical articles or reviews.

ZazensatioN
Fellowship for the Transmission of Wisdom
12232 Abbott Lane
Anacortes, WA 98221
The United States of America
tedbiringer@gmail.com

Zen Cosmology: Dogen's Contribution to the Search for a New Worldview

Library of Congress Cataloging-in-Publication Data

Biringer, Ted
   Zen Cosmology: Dogen's Contribution to the Search for a New Worldview/Ted Biringer
     Includes bibliographical references and index.
     ISBN: 1537187309
1. Dogen, 1200-1253. 2. Zen/Buddhism—Doctrines. 3. Zen/Buddhism Methodology

10 9 8 7 6 5 4 3 2 1

For Donna Rachelle Biringer – God bless her!

Acknowledgements

My sincere thanks to Dr. Hee-Jin Kim for the several reviews and suggestions he provided during various stages of this project. Of even greater value to me than his expert criticism and guidance were his encouraging words. This work would not have been possible without him.

Special thanks to Alex Jonusas for providing continuous support and excellent guidance through every phase of this work from the very beginning.

Heartfelt thanks to my wife, Donna Biringer, for her ever inspiring encouragement and infinite patience.

Thanks also to author Steven Conifer for his expert advice and inspiring words.

And as always my gratitude to the community of friends and wise counselors without which any pursuit would be impossible: Nils, Jack, 'Een, Rusty, Rae, Jim, Rune, Bill, and Bill's friends.

In fact, I would suggest, by following Friedrich Schleiermacher's wise counsel, that it is our obligation—whether we are Zen practitioners or not—to understand Dogen's insights better than he did himself. From this perspective, his religio-philosophical groundwork not only offers a new direction in Zen praxis but also opens up new possibilities for creative dialogue between Zen and contemporary thought, especially regarding social ethics, to which modern Zen by and large has been sadly impervious.
Hee-Jin Kim[1]

Contents

Preface

Introduction
Neglecting the Facts
Buddhism and Right Views
Buddhism and Wrong Views
Dualism in Cosmology and Zen
Obstacles on the Path to a Reliable Worldview
The Zen Perspective

Part 1 Outline of Zen Cosmology
Key Terms and Fundamental Propositions

Key Terms
Dharma and Dharmas
Dharma-Positions
Dori: The Reason, Rationality, and Rationale of Zen
Existence-Time
Genjokoan: Actualizing the Universe
Kensho and Kenbutsu
Nonduality
Normality

Fundamental Propositions
The Verifiability of Knowledge Concerning the Nature of Reality
Nonduality
The Nonduality of Enlightenment and Delusion
The Nature and Dynamics of Enlightenment and Delusion
The Doctrine and the Experiential Verification of Emptiness
Dharmas: The Fundamental Constituents of Reality
The Universal Normality of Dharmas
Dharmas: The Constituents of Existence and Experience

Consciousness is Dharmas
Zen Practice-Enlightenment
Language, Thinking, and Reason
The Zen of Words and Letters
Self is the root metaphor of Zen expression
Self-Expressions
The Normality of Buddhas and Ordinary Beings
Emptiness and the Reason (dori) of Total Exertion/Self-Obstruction
Self and Spirit
Iconoclasm
The Nobility of Suffering

Clarifications
Concerning Dharmas
Great Delusion and Great Enlightenment
Authentic Zen, Authentic Culture
The Normality of Dharmas
Two Modes of Self-Actualization (Soul-Making); Genjokoan

Part 2 Zen and Contemporary Thought
Science and Zen in Light of Dogen and Shobogenzo

Contemporary Cosmology and its Flaw
Epistemology
The Representative Nature of Dharmas in the Prevailing Cosmology
Irrational Rationality
The Nature of Subjectivity in Contemporary Cosmology
The Fundamental Flaw of the Representational Theory of Knowledge
Science and Contemporary Cosmology
Summary: Contemporary Cosmology is Fundamentally Flawed

Part 3 Zen Form, Zen Reason
The Appearance of Reality and the Reality of Appearance

Clear Seeing and Emptiness
Emptiness
The Sentient Nature of Reality
The Emptiness of the Self is the Emptiness of Other Than Self

This Sutra: Zen Expressions, Expressions of Zen

Zen Cosmology
Zen and Epistemology
The Mental Nature of Reality – The Real Nature of Mentality
Existence is Experience
Objects of Consciousness
The Consciousness of Dharmas
Dharma Transmission

The Language of The Self
The Mythopoeic Nature of Zen Expression
Something That Can Be Metaphoric
Seeing is Fashioning
The Double-Edged Sword: Killing and Giving Life, Truth and Falsity

Continuous Actualization of Sole-Sitting – The Keystone of Zen

Fashioning a Moon and Fashioning a Rice Cake
Consciousness, Speculation, and Actualization
Experience As It Is: Existence As It Is
Consciously Actualizing the Universe (genjokoan)
Nonthinking
This Goes Along With That

Zen Cosmology: Summary Expression

Notes

Bibliography

Index

Preface

Our world view is not simply the way we look at the world. It reaches inward to constitute our innermost being, and outward to constitute the world.
Richard Tarnas[2]

Not many people have clearly understood that cosmology is a literary art form, not a religious or scientific one.
Northrop Frye[3]

The limits of my language mean the limits of my world.
Ludwig Wittgenstein[4]

Insofar as my aim is to present a *cosmology*, my task is to present an accurate and comprehensive vision of the true nature of reality. Insofar as my aim is to present a *Zen* cosmology, the medium of my expression must be the mythopoeic language of Zen; specifically, the metaphorical framework provided by the classic literature of Zen/Buddhism.

Because I consider *Shobogenzo* (True Dharma-Eye Treasury), the magnum opus of Zen Master Eihei Dogen (1200-1253), to be the clearest, most comprehensive presentation of Zen in the classic literature, it is my primary source. In my view *Shobogenzo* not only presents a unique *culminating vision* of Buddhist thought, it presents the most accurate, most accessible vision of reality available to the modern mind. More than a treasure trove for Zen students then, I am convinced *Shobogenzo* has much to offer in the way of humankind's urgent need for a new worldview.

As I hope to clarify, the reasons for my conviction are many and various. Among the more significant reasons are *Shobogenzo's* unique vision of the nature of existence and time (*uji*; existence-time), the dynamic of impermanence (*mujo*) in the context of Buddha-nature (*bussho*), the significance of the unity of practice and enlightenment (*shusho*), and most importantly, the liberating potential of language, thinking, and reason, particularly in light of Zen's insight into the nonduality of experience and existence (epistemology and ontology).

In opposition to many popular views about Zen's aloofness from or even disdain of language, *Shobogenzo* reveals how and why language, thinking, and reason are our greatest capacities – more, vital organs of the universe itself. In short, Dogen presents a vision that elucidates and verifies the accuracy of Valery's assessment about cosmology being a literary art. To summarize one major implication of this; *Shobogenzo* itself is a cosmology, complete with a clear and simple methodology for making Zen's universally appealing (if widely misunderstood) vision of reality immediately accessible and verifiable.

Shobogenzo presents a cosmos wherein each and all things, beings, and events are spatial-temporal phenomena – particular *forms* manifest at particular *times*. These phenomena constitute the totality of reality (i.e. besides such phenomena nothing exists). Further, the *appearance* (in space and time) of phenomena and their *origin* are not different things (i.e. phenomena are autochthonous; they inhabit the realm they originate in). Moreover, each and all phenomena are *interdependent* – coessential and coextensive – with each and all other phenomena. These phenomena, often referred to in Zen/Buddhist literature as 'dharmas', actualize existence-time (*uji*) in an ever-advancing creation – a ceaseless 'advance into novelty', to borrow a phrase from A. N. Whitehead.[5] This advance is presented by *Shobogenzo* as an ever-ongoing self-generation wherein each unique particularity and the whole universe cooperate to simultaneously ever-realize and ever-transcend a universe constituted of particular location-moments (or space-times) of here-now.

Dogen's view of phenomena (*dharmas*) as the primary *and* primordial constituents of existence-time (*uji*), characterized by Hee-Jin Kim as 'radical phenomenalism',[6] informs every aspect of his Zen. One object of this study is to elucidate the reason intrinsic to this view of reality. For experience has shown that to attain a clear understanding of this reason is to attain personal certainty of its accuracy. More specifically, to truly grasp this reason is to recognize the indisputable truth of the nonduality of experience and existence (epistemology and ontology). The other object of this study is to clearly outline the methodology presented by *Shobogenzo*. That is, to provide readers with a working knowledge for the practical application of the Zen techniques proscribed in *Shobogenzo*. In sum, I am convinced an accurate grasp of the reason and methodology of *Shobogenzo* can empower anyone with the ability to *verify* the *phenomenal* nature of (all) dharmas – that is to awaken (realize direct personal certainty) to the true nature of reality itself.

After Dogen's own writings, the works of Professor Hee-Jin Kim, essential to any serious study of Dogen, are far and away my most essential source. Hee-Jin Kim's insights into Dogen and Zen are central to the whole of this book. Dr. Kim is frequently cited throughout, therefore the nature and depth of his influence speaks for itself.

Among other sources, my influences range widely within the various fields of science, philosophy, psychology, religion, history, and literary criticism. Beside the universally recognized masters of these realms (e.g. Plato, Dante, Blake, Freud, Einstein, etc.), James Hillman, 'the father of archetypal psychology', is probably my most influential source. Archetypal psychology and Zen share many similarities and I believe each has much to offer the other. Probably of most significance is Hillman's view of the *phenomenal nature* of archetypal images – the trait that most sharply distinguishes 'archetypal psychology' from the 'analytical psychology' of C.G. Jung. Dr. Hillman's excursions into the nature of images are rich with implications concerning Zen's view on the nature of dharmas and vice versa.

Other significant contemporary influences include; philosophers Alfred North Whitehead and Alva Noe, mythologist Joseph Campbell, literary critic Northrop Frye, cultural historian Richard Tarnas, linguists George Lakoff and Mark Johnson, physicists N. Lee Swanson and David Bohm, biologists Bruce H. Lipton and Rupert Sheldrake, and geneticist Robert Lanza.

Truth is inherently fluid – open, alive, metaphorical, and inclusive; dogma is inherently rigid – closed, fixed, literal, and exclusive. Acknowledging this means acknowledging that maintaining authority within any institution *depends on* maintaining allegiance to dogma – thus perpetuating fallacies. Recognizing, then, that sectarianism, which continues to thrive within the Zen community, is a matter of *self-preservation*, I have attempted to maintain a certain tolerance for it herein. While its role in obscuring the truth of Zen deserves censure, the sectarian rivalry waged throughout most of Zen's history also merits gratitude. Without it *Shobogenzo*, secreted away in Soto sect treasuries scattered across Japan for centuries, might have been lost long ago.

Finally, to bring Zen's vision forward and westward to observe it within the accumulated insights of humankind's 'grand discussion' – which does continue despite appearances – means also to extend it back and eastward to its origins. This work, then, makes every effort to harmonize with the mythopoeic vision of the Zen Ancestors as descendents from the Seven Ancient Buddhas to the Historic Shakyamuni Buddha and his Indian successors from Mahakayshyapa to Bodhidharma and his Chinese successors from Huike to Huineng and his successors through the five ancestral lines to Dogen and beyond.

According to Dogen reality is actualized by 'Buddha alone together with Buddha' (*Yui Butsu Yo Butsu*). Huike, the second ancestor of Zen in China, described the experience of this vision in these words:

> For those who find this body of reality [dharmakaya], the numberless sentient beings are just one good person: the one person who has been there in accord with This through a million billion aeons.
> Huike [7]

Introduction

[Zen]...currently confronts an extraordinarily chaotic and fragmented world borne of the inexorable forces of science, technology, and global capitalism that have become increasingly misguided and dehumanizing... We in the Northern Hemisphere—in sharp contrast to those in the Southern Hemisphere—are so affluent, so technologically advanced, and yet so morally and spiritually disoriented that we are at a profound loss as to how to manage such pressing issues as world peace, economic, social, and ecological justice, cultural and religious diversity, and the possibility of living authentically in today's world. Like other religious traditions, Zen cannot escape the exigency of this worldwide crisis.

Zen now stands at a crossroads. I submit that in such a contemporary context, Dogen as meditator and Dogen as thinker challenge us as much as we challenge him and his Zen. In this respect, we live in one of the most intellectually challenging and exciting periods in the history of the Zen religion and of Dogen studies.
Professor of Religious Studies Hee-Jin Kim[8]

The notion that all these fragments are separately existent is evidently an illusion, and this illusion cannot do other than lead to endless conflict and confusion. Indeed, the attempt to live according to the notion that the fragments are really separate is, in essence, what has led to the growing series of extremely urgent crises that is confronting us today. Thus, as is now well known, this way of life has brought about pollution, destruction of the balance of nature, over-population, world-wide economic and political disorder and the creation of an overall environment that is neither physically nor mentally healthy for most of the people who live in it. Individually there has developed a widespread feeling of helplessness and despair, in the face of what seems to be an overwhelming mass of disparate social forces, going beyond the control and even the comprehension of the human beings who are caught up in it.
Physicist David Bohm[9]

In recent decades our knowledge of the cosmos as well as our knowledge of Zen has greatly improved – and greatly *altered* – our understanding of both. New discoveries, advances in technology and methodology, and more extensive research have revealed much in both realms that was formerly unsuspected. As a result, whole new avenues of study have opened up. For example, new discoveries in cosmology led to the introduction of theories about dark energy and dark matter; and the recent confirmation of the continuity between the Zen koan literature of China and the works of Eihei Dogen (until recently explicitly denied) has led to new understandings of both.

While new facts established by recent discoveries are crucial, of even greater significance are fallacies that have been toppled – some of which had been sustained for centuries. For example the whole world of science was shaken to its very core when experimental evidence shattered the basic scientific tenet that 'objects' separated by space are and must be *independent* realities. As physicist and author Brian Greene writes:

> We used to think that a basic property of space is that it separates and distinguishes one object from another. But we now see that quantum mechanics radically challenges this view. *Two things can be separated by an enormous amount of space and yet not have a fully independent existence*. A quantum connection can unite them, making the properties of each contingent on the properties of the other. Space does not distinguish such entangled objects. Space cannot overcome their interconnection. Space, even a huge amount of space, does not weaken their quantum mechanical interdependence.
> Brian Greene[10]

The fact that 'distinct objects' far distant from each other in space can be so interconnected that the very existence of each is utterly *dependent on* the existence of the other flies in the face of a multitude of basic 'scientific facts.'

At least as significant an upheaval occurred within the Zen community with the obliteration of the nearly universally accepted fallacy of Zen's anti-literary, anti-philosophical stance. In direct contradiction to the longstanding notion that Zen was aloof from, or even disparaging of literary and philosophical pursuits, scholarship has shown that such pursuits are actually considered to be essential elements of authentic Zen practice. Learning and study, it turns out, is as integral to Zen practice as is meditation (zazen). In the words of Hee-Jin Kim:

> The issue was not so much whether or not to philosophize as it was *how* to philosophize... [The] philosophic enterprise was as much the practice of the bodhisattva way as was zazen.
> Hee-Jin Kim[11]

Despite having been thoroughly repudiated by the scholarship for decades, the anti-literary fallacy continues to prevail. The pernicious tenacity of this particular false view is seen in the fact that it not only continues to prevail outside the Zen community, but within it as well. As we shall touch on again, in advocating a disdain for learning and study, this fallacy fosters the veneration of anti-intellectualism. By deliberately cultivating a disdain for knowledge and a distrust of language, those that ascribe to such views effectively bar themselves from its only remedy: reason.

Neglecting the Facts

The biggest scientific delusion of all is that science already has the answers. The details still need working out but, in principle, the fundamental questions are answered.
Rupert Sheldrake[12]

If we take something to be the truth, we may cling to it so much that when the truth comes and knocks on our door, we won't want to let it in.
Thich Nhat Hạnh[13]

As just observed, many of the new revelations and overthrown fallacies are not acknowledged, much less assimilated, even within their respective spheres. The significance of this neglect in regard to cosmology is clear. Our cosmology functions as the very foundation of our conduct. We think, speak, and act in the world in accordance with what our understanding of the world is. The more *our view of* reality diverges from the way reality *actually is*, the more unreliable our thoughts, words, and deeds in reality will be. One does not need to be a scientist to recognize we would do well to establish a more reliable cosmology – and sooner rather than later. As if the unprecedented levels of social injustice and environmental destruction worldwide were not reason enough, evidence confirming the accuracy of various forecasts predicting global extinction has long surpassed any rational arguments for denial.

The results of this neglect in the realm of Zen may not be as obvious as it is in cosmology, but the profundity of its consequences certainly is. For, as Zen contends, knowledge (epistemology) and existence (ontology) are not two different things – our 'cosmology' is not simply how we *see* the universe it is how the universe is *actualized*. The significance of this point is succinctly illustrated in the following observation by Hee-Jin Kim concerning Dogen's (hence Zen's) view of the unity of knowledge and reality:

> To Dogen, mind was at once knowledge and reality, at once the knowing subject and the known object, yet it transcended them both at the same time. In this nondual conception of mind, what one knew was what one was—and ontology, epistemology, and soteriology were inseparably united.
> Hee-Jin Kim[14]

Kim's consistent attention to the crucial importance of accurate knowledge (epistemology), commonly treated in terms of the Buddhist notion of 'right views', has been a defining characteristic of Buddhist thought since its very beginning.

Before exploring this further I want to clarify that I do not mean to give the impression that positive progress is completely absent in contemporary spheres of cosmology and Zen. There continues to be steady growth among the minority within both calling for an unbiased consideration of the evidence. The efforts of these minorities are having a positive influence; bringing attention to new evidence, as well as to the dangers of scientific rationalism (or 'scientism') in the one and of dogmatic formalism and sectarianism in the other. Unfortunately, such progress continues to be hard-won and slow-going.

Buddhism and Right Views

I do not feel obliged to believe that the same God who has endowed us with sense, reason, and intellect has intended us to forgo their use.
Galileo Galilei[15]

For there is but one essential justice which cements society, and one law which establishes this justice. This law is right reason, which is the true rule of all commandments and prohibitions. Whoever neglects this law, whether written or unwritten, is necessarily unjust and wicked.
Marcus Tullius Cicero[16]

After the Socratic aphorism, we might say that an unexamined Zen is not worth living—but then, in the same breath, add that an unlived Zen is not worth examining.
Hee-Jin Kim[17]

Above I cited the central role epistemology has held in Buddhist thought from the beginning. Its emphasis on the importance of accurate knowledge harmonizes with the great insight from which Buddhism developed. This is the insight, crystallized in Buddhism's *Four Noble Truths*, that bondage to suffering (*dukkha*)[18] has its cause in ignorance and delusion about the nature of reality (i.e. cosmology). To be ignorant or deluded about reality is to be *inherently* incapable of thinking, speaking, or acting in a manner *harmonious with* reality. To think, speak, or act in conflict with reality naturally results in suffering. Therefore, to be ignorant or deluded is to be *in bondage to* suffering. Accordingly, enlightenment – seeing the true nature of reality – is the Buddha Way or Way of Zen; the Way to *liberation from* suffering.

Ignorance, of course, is the *absence of knowledge*. Delusion is the *presence of distorted knowledge*. Now, ignorance is relatively easy to remedy – the ignorant need only be acquainted with right knowledge. Delusion, however, is another story – the deluded must recognize the fallibility of their current views before they can even be *receptive to* right knowledge. Accepting that one's own beliefs are invalid is inherently difficult. The measure of difficulty is proportional to the depth of attachment with which a view is held. No beliefs are prone to deeper attachment than those concerning one's own knowledge about reality.

It is only natural, then, that a vast amount of Zen/Buddhist literature concerns 'right' and 'wrong' views, theories, and systems of thought. Critiques of certain Brahmanic views appear in the earliest Buddhist records. Refutations of 'wrong' views also constitute a considerable bulk of the writings attributed to Avaghosa (80-150 CE), Nagarjuna (150-250 CE), and other major figures of Indian Buddhism. Early Chinese Zen texts reference 'great debates' over 'right' and 'wrong' views between 'northern' and 'southern' schools. The records of Bodhidharma (470-543?) and Huineng (638-713), the two greatest figures of Chinese Zen, and the writings of Dogen (1200-1253) and Hakuin (1689-1769), the two giants of Japanese Zen, largely involve differentiating 'right' and 'wrong' views. Whether in terms of 'shaved headed fools' denounced by Linji (died 866), 'shit-eating flies' lamented by Yunmen (864-949), 'demons and wild beasts' disparaged by Dogen or 'know-nothing bonzos' reviled by Hakuin, false views, teachers, doctrines, and methods have been constant examples of ignorance and delusion throughout the history of Zen.

In sum, the presence of fallacious knowledge (delusion) is the greatest barrier to enlightenment; liberation from suffering. Accordingly, the great Zen masters devoted much time and energy refuting and criticizing fallacies. The fact that such refutations and criticisms were inevitably leveled at fallacies expressed in *doctrinal* and *literary* forms has not been inconsequential.

Buddhism and Wrong Views

It is useless to attempt to reason a man out of a thing he was never reasoned into.
Jonathan Swift[19]

Do not misunderstand Buddhism by believing the erroneous principle 'a special tradition outside the scriptures.'
Shobogenzo, Bukkyo[20]

The criticism of *specific* doctrines and literary expressions has frequently been superficially interpreted as denouncing doctrinal and literary pursuits *generally* – not excepting the doctrines and literature of Zen/Buddhism itself!

Although, as already noted, the various critiques in the classic literature cannot be ascribed to Zen's disparagement of literary or doctrinal activities generally, their appearance is not without any general significance. For example, two significant general truths clearly demonstrated by the variety of criticisms in the classic literature are that:

- Zen recognizes *some* views and doctrines as 'right' and *others* as 'wrong.'
- Zen recognizes dualism – the 'wrong' view most often and most fervently disputed – as a seriously pernicious disease.

The reason for Zen's rejection of dualism is most comprehensively presented by the corollary Buddhist teachings of emptiness (*sunyata*) and interdependence (dependent origination; *pratitiya-samutpada*). The primary insight of these teachings is the nondual nature of reality – that is the interdependence of all things, beings, and events in and of space and time (existence-time; *uji*). Of the many insights revealed by these teachings, three of particular relevance here are:

- There is no independently existent objective reality.
- There is no independently existent subjective reality.
- The world (objective reality) and the self (subjective reality) are coessential elements of a single unified reality.

Dualism in Cosmology and Zen

Man's general way of thinking of the totality, i.e. his general world view, is crucial for overall order of the human mind itself. If he thinks of the totality as constituted of independent fragments, then that is how his mind will tend to operate, but if he can include everything coherently and harmoniously in an overall whole that is undivided, unbroken and without border (for every border is a division or break) then his mind will tend to move in a similar way, and from this will flow an orderly action within the whole.
David Bohm[21]

In short, *total existence* is *the Buddha-nature,* and the perfect totality of *total existence* is called *'living beings.'*
Shobogenzo, Bussho[22]

With this, then, we are ready to notice another characteristic shared by the prevailing cosmology and the prevailing views in contemporary Zen – both are grounded in, and severely distorted by dualism. More specifically, while Zen asserts the nondual nature of reality, and the evidence of contemporary science confirms the nondual nature of reality, the current prevailing forms of both inherently presuppose tenets of dualism.

While the general scientific community has yet to truly accept it, the actual evidence from diverse fields of science confirms the nondual nature of reality. Like the findings of Copernicus, Galileo, and other great scientific figures of the past, after having repeatedly met the highest scientific standards of verification the true significance of the evidence has hardly been recognized, much less assimilated in the various spheres of science.

I want to be clear, the actual evidence of the nondual nature of reality is no less 'scientifically valid' than that affirming the chemical compound of water (H_2O); and its actual implications have been clear for almost a century. For example, the nondual nature of objective and subjective reality was already recognized by the founders of quantum mechanics – the 'new physics' established by 1926:

> There is obviously only one alternative, namely the unification of minds or consciousnesses. Their multiplicity is only apparent, in truth there is only one mind.
> Erwin Schrodinger[23]

> There is a fundamental error in separating the parts from the whole, the mistake of atomizing what should not be atomized. Unity and complementarity constitute reality.
> Werner Heisenberg[24]

> An independent reality in the ordinary physical sense can neither be ascribed to the phenomenon nor to the agencies of observation.
> Niels Bohr[25]

Nevertheless, other than paying 'lip service' to the facts and exploiting technical applications that were already apparent in its earliest formulations, the greater implications of quantum physics continues to be all but ignored by the majority of scientists. Those scientists that have sincerely attempted to discover what this knowledge tells us about the nature of the universe and of ourselves constitute a very small minority indeed. Of the various individuals of particular importance among this minority, I would note the physicist David Bohm (1917-1992). Bohm's importance rests not only in his contribution to science itself, but in the accessibility of some of his presentations – specifically, his ability to communicate the significance of quantum mechanics to non-scientific readers. For example:

> We have reversed the usual classical notion that the independent "elementary parts" of the world are the fundamental reality, and that the various systems are merely particular contingent forms and arrangements of these parts. Rather, we say that inseparable quantum interconnectedness of the whole universe is the fundamental reality, and that relatively independent behaving parts are merely particular and contingent forms within this whole.
> David Bohm[26]

The nondual nature of reality revealed by quantum mechanics has in recent decades been greatly reinforced and supplemented by evidence from a number of other scientific realms, particularly the biological and cognitive sciences. Indeed, the accumulated evidence has long surpassed any point where the interdependent nature of reality can be ignored by any field and still be considered authentic science. The fact that the 'scientist' and the 'science' constitute a single unified reality is obviously relevant in every field. As Robert Lanza,[27] the pioneering scientist and stem-cell researcher affirms:

> Our external and internal perceptions are inextricably intertwined. They are different sides of the same coin and cannot be separated.
> Robert Lanza[28]

Fortunately, the evidence is so overwhelming that any claiming legitimate membership in the scientific community, whatever their actual beliefs, are compelled to recognize at least some of the nondual facts, for example, that 'distinct objects' in and of our universe are *nondually united*, as noticed above in the citation of Brian Greene. Nevertheless, the contemporary worldview – whether of the 'scientific' or 'common' version – remains firmly grounded in dualism. The untenable proposition that our universe is constituted of *separate*, *independent* realities continues to be nearly universally accepted as all but self-evident.

Such dualism is especially apparent in our prevailing views (thus conduct) concerning the nature of 'objective' and 'subjective' reality. The scientific and common view alike regards and treats objective reality and subjective reality as two entirely different realms. Moreover, both presuppose objective reality to be *realer*, thus *more reliable* than subjective reality. Clear evidence of this can be seen, for example, in how 'verified truths' or 'matters of fact' are commonly spoken of in terms of *objective* knowledge, while *subjective* knowledge is commonly understood to mean 'questionable,' 'inherently unreliable,' or even 'misleading.'

Obstacles on the Path to a Reliable Worldview

When we survey the subsequent course of scientific thought throughout the seventeenth century up to the present day, two curious facts emerge. In the first place, the development of natural science has gradually discarded every single feature of the original commonsense notion. Nothing whatever remains of it, considered as expressing the primary features in terms of which the Universe is to be interpreted. The obvious commonsense notion has been entirely destroyed, so far as concerns its function as the basis for all interpretation. One by one, every item has been dethroned.
Alfred North Whitehead[29]

Granted, our usual reluctance to let go of old ideas has a part in our failure to assimilate the new facts, the greatest factor, however, is probably the nature of specialization central to the very framework of our society. Typically, by the time scientific findings are assimilated by the masses – or even the general scientific community – they have since been usurped by newer findings. In short, a great many of the 'facts' that constitute the prevailing scientific cosmology, not to mention the common worldview have long been discredited. Indeed, many of the most basic, most widely accepted 'scientific' assumptions, about space, time, light, mass, and energy for example, have long been disproved by the actual scientific evidence.

The words of the philosopher Alfred North Whitehead quoted above are as true today as they were when he spoke them in the 1930s Whitehead's observations in the following passages are illuminating and to the point of this discussion:

> Indeed, even when we confine attention to natural science, no special science ever is grounded upon the conciliation of presuppositions belonging to all the various sciences of nature. Each

science confines itself to a fragment of the evidence and weaves its theories in terms of notions suggested by that fragment. Such a procedure is necessary by reason of the limitations of human ability.
Alfred North Whitehead[30]

Every special science has to assume results from other sciences. For example, biology presupposes physics. It will usually be the case that these loans from one specialism to another really belong to the state of science thirty or forty years earlier. The presuppositions of the physics of my boyhood are today powerful influences in the mentality of physiologists. Indeed we do not need even to bring in the physiologists. The presuppositions of yesterday's physics remain in the minds of physicists, although their explicit doctrines taken in detail deny them.
Alfred North Whitehead[31]

The state of modern thought is that every single item in this general doctrine is denied, but that the general conclusions from the doctrine as a whole are tenaciously retained. The result is a complete muddle in scientific thought, in philosophic cosmology, and in epistemology. But any doctrine which does not implicitly presuppose this point of view is assailed as unintelligible.
Alfred North Whitehead[32]

Anyone that has ever tried to reason with a fanatic (of any species) will understand the kind of exasperation intimated by the phrases 'tenaciously retained' and 'assailed as unintelligible.' Yet obstinacy is certainly not the only challenge we need to meet if we are ever to establish a truly reliable worldview. While acknowledging that our present cosmology is obsolete is challenging, adequately envisioning a more reliable one is more challenging still.

It is one thing to *recognize* that a cosmology based on dualism is untenable; it is another to *envision* a nondual cosmology. Despite having successfully 'discarded every single feature' of the common worldview, the scientific community has 'tenaciously retained' *the fundamental basis* upon which those 'features' were established. In short, the prevailing scientific worldview is, at best, only marginally less obsolete than the common worldview. For both worldviews are grounded on the same untenable basis – dualism. This is where we meet the most formidable challenge.

Because our worldview is the very perspective *from which* we see, understand, and reason about reality, we are *inherently obstructed* from envisioning a worldview that is fundamentally different from our own. In short, the greatest challenge to establishing a reliable cosmology is making a nondual worldview intelligible from a dualistic perspective – the nature of nonduality must somehow be made discernible to those whose *abilities to discern* are grounded in dualism. The philosopher and cultural historian Richard Tarnas addresses this issue in terms of 'the larger Copernican revolution' the 'first principle and foundation' of the prevailing worldview:

> For all the notable strides made in deconstructing the modern mind and moving towards a new vision, whether in science, philosophy, or religion, nothing has come close to questioning the larger Copernican revolution itself, the modern mind's first principle and foundation. The very idea is as inconceivable now as was the idea of a moving Earth before 1500. That most fundamental modern revolution, along with its deepest existential consequences, still prevails, subtly yet globally determining the character of the contemporary mind.
> Richard Tarnas[33]

So it seems we face a massive paradox, a cosmic catch-22 so to speak. The forces that have propelled us to the brink of self-knowledge – as well as self-destruction – are the very forces that we must now see through, not only to advance but to survive. The accumulated discoveries and insights that have actually *qualified* the civilized world *as civilized*, have, in the very process of their realization, produced a subtle but vastly powerful obstacle to civilization's own longevity. As Tarnas goes on to observe:

> No amount of Revisioning philosophy or psychology, science or religion, can forge a new world view without a radical shift at the cosmological level. As it now stands, our cosmic context does not support the attempted transformation of human vision. No genuine synthesis seems possible. The enormous contradiction that invisibly encompasses the emerging paradigm is precisely what is preventing that paradigm from constituting a coherent and effective world view.
> Richard Tarnas[34]

In short, time to take action is running out, while a reliable source to determine *what action* to take – an accurate cosmology – is practically unavailable.

The Zen Perspective

Reality is in the observations, not in the electron.
Werner Heisenberg[35]

A physicist is just an atom's way of looking at itself.
Attributed to Niels Bohr[36]

Here, then, is the reason for the present study. As I hope to show, Zen possesses certain attributes, some of which have been largely neglected, that have proven to be uniquely effective for meeting the specific obstacles presently hindering us from realizing a more reliable worldview, particularly that concerning our ability to envision a nondual reality. The key attribute Zen has in this regard is an ability to activate a normal human capacity for not merely envisioning the nondual nature of reality, but for seeing it directly. The nature of this human capacity concerns Zen's fundamental insight that *seeing* reality and *creating* reality are not two different things. Again I defer to the words of Hee-Jin Kim:

> The vision of 'things as they are' is never of a fixed reality/truth; the power for self-subversion and self-renewal is inherent in the vision itself. Thus 'things' seen as they are are transformable. Every practitioner's task is to *change* them by seeing through them. From Dogen's perspective, this is the fundamental difference between contemplation (*dhyana*) and zazen-only. To him, seeing was changing and making.
> Hee-Jin Kim[37]

What kind of a miraculous concurrence of events is Dr. Kim talking about here? How could seeing things *as they are* 'change' them or 'make' them? Aren't 'things as they are' necessarily, and by definition, *as* they *are*? If seeing things '*makes* them' what does it make them *from*; if they are not things in the first place, how can seeing even occur? And, if *seeing* things '*changes*' them, is it not a violation of reason to call it seeing things 'as they are'?

As I hope to show, in the light of Zen reason (*dori*), it is impossible to see reality in any way *contrary to* Dr. Kim's account here. In short, the reason of Zen opens a way, accessible to all, to clearly see the true (nondual) nature of the self and the world, thus a way to a truly reliable cosmology.

Part 1 Outline of Zen Cosmology
Key Terms and Fundamental Propositions

Key Terms

Words and letters, however socially constructed, are never mere signs in the abstract, theoretical sense, but alive and active "in flesh and blood." Contrary to the conventional view that language is no more than a means of communication, it is profoundly internal to an individual's life as well as to the collective life. Language flows individually and collectively through the existential bloodstream, so much so that it is the breath, blood and soul of human existence. Herein lies the essence of Dogen's radical phenomenalism. Thus knowledge becomes *ascesis*, instead of *gnosis* or *logos* — "seeing things as they are" now means "*making* things as they are." In this light the indexical analogy of "the finger pointing to the moon" is highly misleading, if not altogether wrong, because it draws on a salvifically inefficacious conception of language.
Hee-Jin Kim[38]

Clarifications concerning terminology in this study are generally confined to endnotes. However, clarifications are provided in the main text wherever terms are unusual, of crucial import, or their meaning diverges significantly from common usage. To minimize the frequency of digression, therefore, I here introduce certain key terms that meet one or more of these qualifications which appear frequently in this study.

Dharma and Dharmas

In Zen/Buddhism the term 'dharma' has many meanings; the intended meaning of a particular instance depends on its context. 'Dharma' is commonly used as a synonym for 'Buddhism' itself, as in 'the Buddha-Dharma' or simply 'the Dharma.' In this usage, 'Dharma' or 'Buddha-Dharma' often connotes the whole cosmos itself (i.e. reality, the universe). I occasionally use the term in this sense. When I do, 'Dharma' is always capitalized and applied in an unambiguous context.

In another common use, 'dharma' denotes 'phenomenon' a *distinct particularity*. As such, dharma can refer to any specific thing, being, or event; anything that can be singled out, identified, or distinguished. In this sense 'dharma' is similar to the English word 'thing' excepting the latter's limitations for denoting living beings; birthdays, flowers, and picnics can be called 'things,' but referring to teachers, children, or penguins as 'things' is awkward if not inaccurate. The term 'dharma,' then, is more general then 'thing' – it is applicable to *any* particularity; a *person* is a dharma, so is a *minute*, a *century*, a *unicorn*, a *phone call*, a *universe*, and a *friend*. I use the term 'dharma' and 'dharmas' (capitalized only at the beginning of sentences) to denote 'phenomenon' and 'phenomena' – *particular* things, beings, and events – very frequently throughout this study.

Because specific phenomena (dharmas) are recognized by Zen as the most fundamental elements of reality itself – the very fabric of space and time – understanding the nature of dharmas is crucial to an accurate understanding and application of Zen doctrine and methodology. The vast significance of dharmas in Zen cosmology is clear when we consider the fact that in Zen, 'the myriad dharmas' is synonymous with 'the whole universe' (i.e. all things, beings, and events throughout space and time). Because of its singular importance, elucidating the true nature of dharmas is regarded as a primary task throughout this study.

If there are any key elements or images within the symbolism of Zen it is that 'the myriad dharmas' and 'the whole universe' are the same thing, and 'a dharma' and 'a particular reality' are the same thing. Whenever Zen speaks of the universe, reality, (all) space and time, (the totality of) self and other, Buddha (in the universal sense), or similar terms that refer to the cosmos, Zen means 'the myriad dharmas.' Likewise, 'a dharma' is what Zen means by a thing, a being, an event, an image, and any other particular reality.

In relation to this, the terms, 'form,' and 'appearance' are especially noteworthy. Both 'form' and 'appearance' are *literally* concerned with 'visual sensation,' and like other mythopoeic (mythical, metaphorical, poetic, or figurative) forms of expression, Zen literature commonly uses them as root metaphors. That is, 'form' and 'appearance' serve as 'umbrellas' or 'abbreviations' for the whole category or mode to which they belong. For example, variations of the term 'see' are commonly used as references to our capacities for 'knowledge,' 'experience,' or 'understanding' in general (e.g. 'he saw the point,' 'taste it and see for yourself,' etc.). Similarly, variations of 'form' and 'appearance' are used for 'objects of consciousness' (e.g. 'an idea formed in my mind,' 'a new form of music,' 'the sound appeared to come from behind me,' 'the pain appears when I least expect it,' etc.).

Further, the term 'form' in Zen is not only commonly used to denote any 'object of consciousness' generally (i.e. sights, sounds, smells, tastes, tactile sensations, and thoughts), but all manner of phenomena whatsoever. This includes, significantly, each and all of the 'five skandhas' or 'five aggregates' – the elements that constitute the human 'body-mind' according to the Buddhist tradition. In short, 'form,' in context of individual human beings, is an abbreviation for all 'five skandhas' – form, sensation, perception, mental formulation, and consciousness.

In sum, 'form' and 'appearance' (and variations thereof) are common synonyms of 'dharma.' Accordingly, all particular sights, sounds, smells, tastes, tactile sensations, and thoughts are dharmas, and all particular manifestations of form, sensation, perception, mental formulation, and consciousness are dharmas.

Dharma-positions

A 'dharma-position' is the *place* (location, existence, space) and *time* (moment, duration, temporal period) of a dharma's appearance or manifestation. The notion of 'dharma-positions' is one way Zen accounts for and communicates about the intrinsic characteristic of reality to be simultaneously 'one' (singular, unified) and 'many' (plural, differentiated). The notion of dharma-positions provides an effective means to accurately understand and discuss the interdependent nature of reality, particularly how dharmas *interact* and *coordinate,* yet do not *interfere* with or *alter* one another in the process. Briefly, a 'dharma-position' is the inherent quality of a dharma's simultaneous *connection to* and *separation from* each and all other dharmas; dharma-positions connect-and-separate each dharma to-and-from all dharmas *and* to-and-from each (other) dharma. Thus, dharmas – as unique, particular instances of reality – are *interconnected* (connected/separated) via their 'place-and-time' in-and-of the totality of space-and-time.[39]

Dori: The Reason and Rationale of Zen

Reason, rationality, rationale and related terms and notions are vital to an accurate understanding of Zen cosmology. More specifically, I mean the significance of the reason or rationality indicated in Zen/Buddhist literature, particularly Dogen's writings, by the Japanese term '*dori*.'[40]

The term *'dori,'* which is commonly translated into English as 'reason,' 'rationality,' etc., is a compound term that combines *'do'* (Chinese, *tao*; way, path; also, speak, express) and *'ri'* (Chinese, *li*; principle, pattern, order; also, arrange, manage, regulate). The significance of *'dori'* (reason) in Zen/Buddhism is profoundly subtle and wide ranging. Fortunately Dr. Hee-Jin Kim has consistently emphasized and eloquently illumined the central importance and profound significance of *dori* in Dogen's Zen. Therefore, to convey the significance of 'dori' in Dogen's writings – hence 'reason' in this study – I can do no better than cite some key passages from the grand-master himself.

> Another important idea that bore deeply upon Dogen's thought was the concept of reason, in the sense of the nature or intrinsic logic of things—not the reasons for them, but the principle, meaning, or truth behind them. In the Buddhist tradition, the concept of reason was a common subject. Dogen in particular favored this word and used it in practically all the subjects with which he dealt... The Buddhist tradition in general advocated the fourfold reason of the *Samdhinirmocana sutra* and the *Yogacarabhumi*—namely the reason of relation *(kandai-dori),* the reason of causation *(sayu-dori),* the reason of recognition *(shojo-dori),* and the reason of naturalness *(honi-dori).* However, Dogen's usage was much wider and more comprehensive; in fact, the whole spectrum of his thought and practice was permeated without exception by his search for reason in all aspects of life.
> Hee-Jin Kim[41]

> At each moment of existence, reason *(dori)* went hand-in-hand with expressions and activities so as to exert totally.
> Hee-Jin Kim[42]

> As we have reminded ourselves so often, Dogen's philosophical and religious thought revolved around his search for the meaning and reason *(dori)* of existence, specifically of human existence in the context of impermanence and ultimately of death.
> Hee-Jin Kim[43]

> It is noteworthy that the notion of *do* in the East Asian traditions has a single common thread, namely, the meaning of walking, journeying, or movement along a path. The Way is never extricated

from the processes of phenomena themselves. As such, it is neither a metaphysical principle, not a moral law external to phenomena, nor a fate dictated from without, nor a God of absolute transcendence...

In line with such a worldview, the *do* in East Asian Buddhism is closely associated with specifically Buddhist practices as precepts, rules, and disciplines... In contrast to the cognate word *ho* (*dharma*; *fa*), meaning "law," "truth," and "teaching," *do* strongly connotes the praxis orientation. In this latter context we should remember that *do* also means "to speak"; in relation to this, Dogen provided deep insights into Zen language...
Hee-Jin Kim[44]

All things considered, the *li* constitutes those patterns, rhythms, and regularities which humans discern as meaningful in carrying out their day-to-day activities, by participating in the dynamics of the natural, and according to their personal, historical, and cultural conditions and forces. Rationality is never regarded as an immutable, self-contained truth or essence transcendentally existent in a hierarchical, teleological world order, but is grasped in an ever-shifting process of human affairs in relation to nature, history, and culture.

Considered in the Buddhist context, *li*, like *tao*, attains enormous complexity in its significance: The word is employed to denote *siddhanta* (fundamental principle/law) and, hence such Buddhist notions as thusness, emptiness, equality... On the other hand, *li* is also used to signify, for example, *pramaha* (to arrange, to regulate, to rectify). It is particularly noteworthy that in Hua-yen thought *li* ("principle") is paired with *shih* ("phenomena"), and their relationship is conceived in such a way that the non-obstruction of *li* and *shih* (*li-shih wu ai; rigi muge*) is further refined as "the nonobstruction of *shih* and *shih*" (*shih-shih wu ai; jiji muge*)—in other words, the interpenetration and harmony of all phenomena...
Hee-Jin Kim[45]

...*Dori* is broad and fexible enough in its capacity to embrace *logos, mythos, ethos*, and *pathos*; cognition, affection, and conation; nature and culture; fact and value; *theoria and praxis*; the self and the universe. ...*dori* is practically oriented, enabling humans to participate in its countless configurations, rhythms, and regularities

in life and the world as they discern meaningful ...*dori* regulates, arranges, and manages, as much as it challenges, surmounts, and subverts.
Hee-Jin Kim[46]

Existence-Time (uji)

In Zen cosmology time and existence are not two different things; time is always existence-and-time, existence is always existence-and-time. This view is most clearly and comprehensively demonstrated in *Shobogenzo's* development and use of the term 'uji.' Dogen fashioned this term by combining two terms; 'u' (existence) and 'ji' (time) into the single term 'uji' (existence-time, or time-being).[47] The significance of the unity of existence and time will become clearer as this study progresses. The point I want to stress here is that existence and time are *never* separate from each other; each is an *essential element* of the other – no dharmas exist independent of time, and there is no time independent of dharmas. This notion of existence-time is central to Zen's vision of reality, thus is presupposed in all Zen expressions.

Hee-Jin Kim brings the crucial significance of this notion to light in a comment from his discussion of the aptly titled '*Uji*' fascicle of *Shobogenzo*:

> Dogen's whole thesis in this regard was crystallized in the following: "As we realize with the utmost effort that all times *(jinji)* are all existence *(jin'u)*, absolutely no additional dharma remains." In other words, existence-time subsumed space and time totally and exhaustively.
> Hee-Jin Kim[48]

The most significant implication of this point (i.e. the unified nature of existence and time) is that each and every particular thing, being, and event (i.e. dharma) is an intrinsic and essential element of total time, and each and every moment or duration of time is an intrinsic and essential element of total existence – hence each and every particular dharma is a manifestation of the whole universe, and the whole universe is manifest in and as each and every particular dharma. In Dogen's words:

> Let us pause to reflect whether or not any of the whole of existence or any of the whole universe has leaked away from the present moment of time.
> *Shobogenzo, Uji*[49]

Accordingly, throughout this study the terms 'existence,' 'time,' and 'existence-time' are synonymous.

Genjokoan: Actualizing the Universe

Zen cosmology recognizes the universe as a continuous, creative activity – a ceaseless, dynamic 'advance into novelty.' In fact, Zen practice-enlightenment itself is understood to be a mutually coordinated process between objective and subjective reality in a continuous 'actualization of the universe' (*genjokoan*).

'Genjokoan,' (*genjo*; realization, and *koan*; public case, dharma, also, yin-yang or universe) translates as 'manifesting the universe,' 'actualizing the fundamental point,' or 'realizing the koan.' Unlike the scientific and common worldviews, Zen cosmology is thoroughly nondual; objective reality and subjective reality *are not two different things*. 'Actualizing the universe' (*genjokoan*), according to the vision of Zen, is only and always actualizing an objective world *and* a subjective self *simultaneously*. The actualization of objective reality is inherently inclusive of the actualization of subjective reality – the objective universe is actualized through 'putting our self in order':

> We put our self in order, and see [the resulting state] as the whole universe.
> *Shobogenzo, Uji*[50]

The actualization of subjective reality is inherently inclusive of the actualization of objective reality – actualizing the subjective self by 'putting the self in order' (thus *seeing* the objective universe) we see what the self is:

> Putting the self in order, we see what it is.
> *Shobogenzo, Uji*[51]

Kensho and Kenbutsu

According to Zen, enlightenment, liberation, or Buddhahood – the supreme aim of Zen – is realized by 'seeing one's own true nature,' awakening to our 'true self' or 'Buddha-nature.' Zen literature often refers to this realization as *kensho,* particularly when referring to an *initial* awakening. Literally, 'kensho' means, 'seeing (one's own) true nature'; '*ken*'; seeing, knowing, experiencing (epistemology), and '*sho*'; true nature, essential being, real existence (ontology).[52]

Dogen used the term '*kensho*' only rarely; he was even critical of it, pointing out that 'seeing' and 'true nature' are nondual, thus 'seeing true nature' smacked of dualism by suggesting 'seer' and 'seen' were two different realities. However, Dogen often used the term '*kenbutsu*' (even using it as the title of a fascicle in *Shobogenzo*) – '*ken*' here is the same as in 'kensho' (epistemology) and '*butsu*' is 'Buddha.' Now, since Zen recognizes 'Buddha' as our 'true nature,' '*kenbutsu*' ('seeing Buddha') is more or less synonymous with '*kensho*.'

In an attempt to recognize the validity for Dogen's disfavor of the term 'kensho' while nevertheless giving due credit to the essential place in Zen practice-enlightenment of the 'awakening experience,' I use the term 'kensho' as specific to an 'initial awakening' and 'kenbutsu' to more generally address the same condition or experience.

Nonduality

'Nondual' means 'not two,' which is *not* the same as 'one.' While 'one' can be used to denote the self-same identification of two (or more) *apparently* distinct or separate entities, 'nondual' only and always denotes two (or more) *actual* distinctions (apparent or not) inherent (thus essential) to a particular entity – thus essential to each other. The *head* and the *tail* of a coin are 'one' in that both constitute a single coin. The *head* and the *tail* are 'nondual' insofar as *each* is an essential attribute of the *other* – the existence of the head is integral to the existence of the tail (and vice versa). Where 'one' indicates an *undifferentiated unity*, 'nondual' indicates a *differentiated unity*.

That a pair is 'nondual' means that the appearance and reality of *each* aspect of the pair is *dependent on* the existent presence of the other. Because Zen cosmology recognizes each and every particular reality (i.e. dharma) as a nondual element of every other particular reality, as well as all particular realities, this quality of dependence applies to each and all things, beings, and events, not only to commonly recognized 'pairs' like 'heads and tails,' 'up and down,' 'existence and non-existence,' 'inside and outside,' etc. Therefore, while 'nonduality' is most commonly treated and analyzed in terms of 'nondual pairs,' its fundamental reality and reasoning applies universally. In a sense, then, 'nondual,' literally 'not-two,' might be accurately rendered as 'non-multiple' or 'non-many,' at least in some cases.

The main point here is that the Zen notion of 'nonduality' is concerned with reality's universal characteristic of being *simultaneously* diverse *and* unified, *instantaneously* many *and* one. The most crucial implication of this being that *each* and *every* particular existent (i.e. dharma) is *essential* to the existence of *every other* particularity *and* of *all* particularities. The *existence of* each dharma is *dependent on* the *existence of* each *other* dharma *and* the *existence of all* dharmas, and the *existence of* all dharmas is *dependent on* the *existence of* each dharma. The most comprehensive treatment of this quality of reality in Zen appears in the corollary Buddhist doctrines of 'emptiness' and 'interdependence.'

Contemporary works on Zen/Buddhism commonly treat the notion of nonduality almost exclusively in terms of 'polarities' or 'opposites.' In neglecting the wider ramifications of nonduality – which are its most significant ramifications – such accounts tend to foster distorted, antithetical notions of nonduality. Hee-Jin Kim realized some success in mitigating this tendency by opting for the term 'foci' (plural of 'focus') over terms associated with opposition or polarity. 'Foci' denotes *particular* points or aspects *of* a larger reality, and unlike 'opposite' and 'pole,' 'focus' is not *defined* as (hence *confined to*) 'one of *two*' but as 'one of *any*-multiple.' In sum, 'foci' more accurately describes nondual aspects or elements than 'opposite' or 'pole,' and is thus less prone to misunderstanding. In this study I gratefully follow Kim's lead and adopt this term where it is appropriate.[53]

While all aspects of Zen cosmology need to be understood in light of the reason (*dori*) of nonduality, certain notions warrant special attention due to their propensity for misunderstanding or to the nature of the consequences of a particular misunderstanding. Of all distortions concerning nonduality, the antithetical polarization of 'duality' and 'nonduality' is the most common and most pernicious. This antithetical polarization results from mistaking *coessential* foci of nonduality (i.e. nonduality/duality) as *independent* entities (or unrealities), and thereby seeing them as two distinct, exclusive positions within the milieu of Zen doctrine and methodology. Such distortions can, and often do, *result from* misunderstanding 'duality' *as* 'dualism,' and or *result in* identifying 'duality' *with* 'dualism.' 'Dualism' is a view that *presupposes the existence of independent realities* (e.g. 'objective reality' existing independent of 'subjective reality,' 'mind' existing independent of 'matter,' etc.); 'duality' is the foci of the 'nonduality/duality' unity that is exemplified as the inherent diversity of reality.[54]

Normality

I use the terms 'normal' and 'normality' throughout this study in the specific sense epitomized by the Zen saying, 'The normal mind is the Tao' (*byodoshin-zedo*). This is commonly translated into English as, 'The ordinary mind is the Way,' or 'The everyday mind is the Way,' which is why I want to stress the term 'normal' in this saying denotes *healthy, true, accurate, right, harmonious*, etc., and *does not* denote *average, ordinary, common, mundane, routine,* etc.

To clarify, 'normal,' in the Zen sense, is equivalent to the Zen/Buddhist notion of 'thusness' or 'as it is-ness.' 'Thusness' is the Sanskrit; *tathata* (Japanese; *shin-nyo*, sometimes synonymous with *inmo*, 'such' or 'thus').[55] In Zen, a person is regarded as 'enlightened' insofar as they see or experience reality *as it is* (thusness); a person is 'deluded' insofar as they *fail to see* reality *as it is*, or see reality *as it is not*. Accordingly, to be 'enlightened' is to be 'normal' (i.e. healthy, in accord, to see accurately), to be 'deluded' is to be 'abnormal' (i.e. ill, off the mark, to see inaccurately).

Now, because in Zen/Buddhist literature the *majority* of beings are treated as being deluded, 'delusion' is often discussed in Zen expressions as synonymous with 'common,' 'average,' 'ordinary,' 'everyday,' etc. Therefore, and this is the important point, Zen *usually* uses the terms 'ordinary,' 'everyday,' etc. as designations for *'delusion'* or *'deluded'* beings and *rarely*, if ever, as references for *'normality'* or *'normal* beings' (i.e. enlightened beings). Zen regards delusion as unhealthy, inaccurate, or out of whack – definitely *not* 'normal.' Therefore, translations that render 'normality' (and its related terms) as 'common,' 'ordinary,' 'everyday,' and the like can be and often are seriously misleading.

Fundamental Propositions

[To research] this truth of moment-by-moment utter entrustment, we must research the mind. In the mountain-still state of such research, we discern and understand that ten thousand efforts are [each] the mind being evident, and the triple world is just that which is greatly removed from the mind. This discernment and understanding, while also of the myriad real dharmas, activate the homeland of the self. They make immediate and concrete the vigorous state of the human being in question.
Shobogenzo, Gyobutsu-yuigi[56]

To Dogen, mind was at once knowledge and reality, at once the knowing subject and the known object, yet it transcended them both at the same time. In this nondual conception of mind, what one knew was what one was—and ontology, epistemology, and soteriology were inseparably united. This was also his interpretation of the Hua-yen tenet "The triple world is mind-only." From this vantage point, Dogen guarded himself against the inherent weaknesses of the two strands of Buddhist idealism: the advocacy of the functions of mind (*shinso*) by the school of consciousness-only and the advocacy of the essence of mind (*shinsho*) by the school of *tathagata-garbha*—both of which were vulnerable to a dualism between phenomena and essence. Thus, philosophically speaking, Dogen maneuvered between monistic pantheism and reductionistic phenomenalism.
Hee-Jin Kim[57]

Here I present the basic outline of Zen cosmology by way of setting out its most fundamental propositions. Independent of the discussion following this section, these proposals are incomplete, therefore largely unintelligible. My task throughout the remainder of this study is to demonstrate the significance and interdependence of these proposals in a way that presents a comprehensive cosmology that is both accessible and convincing. The success of this task is understood as being dependent on demonstrating the truth of these propositions to be self-evident; not necessarily *obvious*, but *experientially verifiable*.

1. The Verifiability of Knowledge Concerning the Nature of Reality

1. Accurate knowledge of the true nature of reality (i.e. self/world, the universe) is accessible and experientially verifiable.[58]

2. Nonduality

1. 'Nonduality' is a universal quality of reality.
2. 'Nonduality' and 'duality' are *coessential* foci; nonduality and duality are nondual, interdependent; each presupposes the other.[59]
3. 'Duality' is the foci of nonduality (nonduality/duality) experienced as, hence existent as, the *differentiation* of reality.
4. 'Nonduality' is the foci of nonduality experienced/existent as the *unity* of reality.
5. Both (all) foci of any nondual pair (multiple) are *equal* in actuality, significance, and value.

3. The Nonduality of Enlightenment and Delusion[60]

1. Enlightenment and delusion are nondual, thus equal in actuality, significance, and value.
2. Enlightenment is only and always realized *within* and *through* delusion; delusion is only and always realized *within* and *through* enlightenment.

4. The Nature and Dynamics of Enlightenment and Delusion

1. Enlightenment is the experiential verification of reality, the normal sentient capacity that is *genjokoan* ('the actualization of the universe').
2. Delusion is the experientially verifiable existential quality of reality that enables experiential verification (i.e. *genjokoan*).
3. With the experiential verification of reality (enlightenment) sentient beings see (experience, know) their true nature (their unborn/imperishable identity in/as the universe).
4. In seeing their identity in/as the universe, sentient beings see enlightenment/delusion is infinite and eternal.

5. The Doctrine and the Experiential Verification of Emptiness

1. The Buddhist doctrine of emptiness (*sunyata*) is multifaceted; the significance of *any one* facet is *dependent on* its context within *every* facet.[61]

2. The *experiential verification* of emptiness – the *reality* treated and presented by the *doctrine* of emptiness – is also multifaceted; the authentic experiential verification of *any one* facet is *dependent on* the experiential verification of *every* facet.

6. Dharmas: The Fundamental Constituents of Reality

1. Dharmas are the fundamental constituents of reality, the ultimate/primordial fabric (ontology) of existence-time (*uji*), the essence *and* form of self *and* not-self.[62]
2. The experiential verification of reality (enlightenment) is the experiential verification of dharmas.
3. Apart from dharmas nothing exists and nothing is experienced.
4. The myriad dharmas (i.e. all dharmas) constitute the totality of reality.
5. A dharma is a *particular* instance of reality.
6. A dharma is a phenomenon in and of existence-time (*uji*); all dharmas possess/display spatial-temporal (phenomenal) form.
7. The *appearance* of a dharma (i.e. the form in which it is experienced) and the *reality* of a dharma (its existential essence, or true nature) are nondual.[63]
8. Dharmas are the content (ontology) *and* the means of experience (epistemology); dharmas are 'what' are experienced, and dharmas are 'how' experience occurs.[64]
9. Dharmas are autochthonous; dharmas originate/inhabit (appear/exist) at/as the location-time (*uji*) they are experienced; dharmas are identical to the location-time (dharma-position) of their appearance (in/as experience).
10. Dharmas are empty (*sunya*); void of independent existence; the helpful formula is: dharmas are empty (*sunya*), emptiness (*sunyata*) is dharmas, *therefore*, dharmas are dharmas, emptiness is emptiness.
11. Dharmas are interdependent;[65] *each* dharma and *all* dharmas exist at/as *each* location-time and *all* location-times.

7. The Universal Normality of Dharmas[66]

1. That each and all dharmas are 'reality as it is' demonstrates the universal normality of dharmas.[67]

2. The recognition of the universal normality of dharmas is the basis of Zen's affirmation of the universal accessibility to enlightenment (i.e. the intrinsic Buddhahood of all sentient beings).
3. The recognition of the universal normality of dharmas is the basis of Zen's affirmation of language (specifically, mythopoeism[68]) – as the vehicle of Dharma-transmission.[69]

8. Dharmas: The Constituents of Existence and Experience

1. Existence (existence-time, ontology) is dharmas.[70]
2. Experience (experienced/experiencer, epistemology) is dharmas.[71]
3. Existence and experience are nondual.
4. It is futile, meaningless, and ultimately irrational to affirm, deny, or otherwise speculate about the existence or non-existence of realities independent of or transcendent to sentient experience.[72]

9. Consciousness is Dharmas[73]

1. The true nature (ontology) of consciousness (epistemology) is dharmas.[74]
2. The true nature of dharmas is consciousness.[75]
3. The totality of existence-time (i.e. the myriad dharmas/the one universe) is manifest as/of consciousness/dharmas.

10. Zen Practice-Enlightenment

1. Zen *Practice* (*shu*) and *enlightenment* (*sho*), or practice-enlightenment (*shusho*), are nondual (coessential foci of *realization; genjo*).
2. Zen doctrine and methodology are nondual (coessential foci of practice-enlightenment; *shusho*).
3. Zen doctrine/methodology is intrinsic to (i.e. *essential to* and *coextensive with*) Zen practice-enlightenment.
4. The praxis (active practical application) of Zen practice-enlightenment consists of the actualization of normality (reality as it is) by individual human beings.
5. The reason (*dori*; function, significance, essence) of Zen practice-enlightenment is the actualization of *annuttara-samyak-sambodhi* (universal liberation and fulfillment, the normality of reality).

11. Language, Thinking, and Reason

1. Language, thinking, and reason are interdependent.
2. Zen practice-enlightenment is *grounded in* and *dependent on* the accurate understanding and skillful use of language (hence thinking and reason).
3. Language is the (only) means whereby communication to/from self/other is realized; language exhausts all things and activities (i.e. dharmas) whereby sentient beings transmit/receive knowledge (epistemology).
4. The language of Zen expression is mythopoeic.[76]

12. The Zen of Words and Letters

1. Normal (enlightened) human beings (Buddhas) see and use language as it is; dharmas communicating dharmas with dharmas or Buddha alone together with Buddha.[77]
2. The single most significant contribution Zen has to offer contemporary civilization is insight and knowledge concerning the soteriological potential of language.[78]
3. The single greatest barrier to Zen wisdom is the widely accepted fallacies of Zen's nominalist, instrumentalist, or antithetical view of language.[79]

13. Self is the root metaphor of Zen expression[80]

1. Self is the root metaphor of Zen expression.[81]
2. The self of an individual sentient being and the self of all sentient beings (the universal self; Buddha) are nondual.[82]

14. Self-Expressions

1. All expressions are self-expressions; expressions from, of, and to the self.[83]
2. As self-expressions dharmas are the normal language of the self.[84]
3. The self is polycentric.[85]

15. The Normality of Buddhas and Ordinary Beings

1. Ordinary beings are deluded about enlightenment – to be deluded about enlightenment is, as it is, to be an ordinary being.
2. Buddhas are enlightened about delusion – to be enlightened about delusion is, as it is, to be a Buddha.
3. To see (experience, know; epistemology) dharmas is to see *dharmas as they are*.
4. To be 'enlightened about delusion' (Buddha) is to see 'dharmas as they are' *as they are*; to 'clearly see' or 'see normally.'
5. To be 'deluded about enlightenment' (an ordinary being) is to see 'dharmas as they are' *as they are not*; to 'distortedly see' or 'see abnormally.'
6. To see true nature (*kensho)* is to see Buddha (*kenbutsu*) *is* dharmas as they are.
7. To see true nature (or Buddha) is to see *seeing* is dharmas as they are; to see dharmas *are* 'what' is seen *and* dharmas *are* 'the means' of seeing.
8. Normal seeing (*kensho, kenbutsu*) is the self/Buddha seeing reality actualized (transmitted) as/of expressions of Buddha; dharmas seeing dharmas as self-expressions.
9. Normal seeing (*kensho, kenbutsu*) possesses the intrinsic quality of evoking or begetting (inherently) novel *expressions* of recognition (more accurately a 'self-cognition' – a 'novel' expression does not technically qualify as a *re*-cognition).
10. In accord with the reason (*dori*) of language, each novel expression of recognition instantaneously increases the capacity to beget novel expressions ad infinitum.
11. The products of evaluation, assessment, critical analysis, or reason (e.g. judgments, critiques, conclusions, etc.) beget in/as normal seeing are *integral* elements/qualities of the dharmas that beget them, thus *revelatory of* the normality (thusness, 'as isness') of those dharmas.
12. The failure to see/heed the products of reason, etc. beget in/as normal seeing is a failure to realize dharmas as they are. While such a failure amounts to 'nondoing' rather than 'doing,' because it fails to actualize (thus fails to increase) what could be actualized, it has a *restraining* or *hindering* effect; in *not* 'increasing the life of Buddha' it effectively 'decreases the life of Buddha' – this is the closest thing to 'evil' recognized by Zen cosmology.[86]

16. Self and Spirit

1. Idolatry, worship or attachment to an image, idea, doctrine, or method, is an impenetrable obstacle to seeing true nature (*kensho*, *kenbutsu*, enlightenment, etc.).[87]

17. Iconoclasm

1. Iconoclasm (apocalypse/revelation) is an intrinsic quality of the universe; being a ceaseless advance into novelty (*genjokoan*), the whole universe arises-and-perishes in/as each place-time.
2. Thus iconoclasm is a natural quality of all aspects of Zen (i.e. iconoclasm is not confined to apparent instances of eccentric, deviant, or sacrilegious words or deeds).

18. The Nobility of Suffering[88]

1. The 'truth of suffering' (*dukkha*), as presented by Buddhism's 'Four Noble Truths,' resolves the question/problem of suffering by revealing suffering *as it is*; to see suffering *as it is*, is to see the way to liberation from suffering as it is.[89]

Clarifications

In fact, the truth cannot be communicated until it is perceived.
Percy Bysshe Shelley[90]

Concerning Dharmas

The description of dharmas as the fundamental constituents of reality is meant *unconditionally*; it does not leave open any possibility for the existence of a 'force,' 'essence,' or 'nature' *more fundamental* than dharmas. Because dharmas are always *particularities*, they are usually discussed in terms of 'elements,' 'constituents,' or 'units,' rather than 'natures,' 'forces,' or 'essences.' Thus, the actual significance of the expressions could be lost or confused by giving too much weight to the technical or literal definition of specific terms. Briefly, that dharmas are 'the most fundamental reality' should be understood as meaning that dharmas are not *constituted of* anything *more fundamental* than themselves – dharmas neither 'come down to' nor are 'made up of' *more basic* elements *or subtler* essences. If an essence exists, for example, it *only exists as* a dharma. In sum, reality is fundamentally dharmas as they are, and dharmas are dharmas through and through.

Recognizing every phenomenon (i.e. every sight, sound, smell, taste, feeling, and thought) as a dharma and every dharma as a phenomenon, an *actual* and *particular* instance *of* reality, has many crucial implications, three of which include:

- It makes it incumbent to see all dharmas as *equal in status* concerning their actuality (existent nature), significance (*dori*; meaning, reason) and value (worthiness); the import being a total absence of superiority and inferiority among dharmas in regard to their true nature, reason (*dori*), or merit.
- It eliminates any obligation to account for an evolutionary, hierarchical, or developmental *progression* of dharmas. Being ever and always 'as they are,' dharmas do not undergo any transformation, entropic or evolutionary. Thus, dharmas are impervious to elemental analysis.

- It renders irrelevant any debate involving speculative or hypothetical notions concerning unverifiable (*imperceptible, unknowable,* etc.) realities; if something exists, it is a dharma – an *experientially verifiable* reality, an *observable, intelligible* phenomenon.

To recognize the truth of the *autochthonous* (i.e. originating in/at the location they are encountered) nature of dharmas is to recognize the *fallacy* of nominalism;[91] no dharma can be a mere *representative*, *symbol*, or *signifier* of a reality *independent of* itself. All dharmas, including words, names, ideas, perceptions, signs, mental images, and anything else that can be experienced, described, pointed to, or particularly singled out in any way is – as it is – an essential element of the universe, an integral instance of (total) existence-time (in Zen 'an expression of Buddha'). Being *autochthonous* by nature means dharmas are *their own* cause and effect, *their own* meaning and reason. Further, as the *essential*, and *only*, *constituents of the universe*, each and all dharmas are of intrinsically universal significance and value. The universal significance and value of dharmas is discerned by seeing them through the normal (i.e. enlightened) eye (in Zen, seeing them through 'the eye to read scriptures' or 'the True Dharma-Eye').

In light of *Shobogenzo's* (hence Zen's) vision of existence-time (*uji*), existence (ontology; being) and time are not-two (nondual); dharmas are not simply existents *in* time, they are existents *of* time, and (all) time is *in* and *of* existents (i.e. dharmas). In short, dharmas do not exist independent of time, and time does not exist independent of dharmas.

On a corollary note, since (all) existence demonstrates the quality of 'impermanence,' time too is impermanent. In Zen the nonduality of impermanence and time is treated in terms of 'ceaseless advance' or 'ever passing' – 'ceaseless' and 'ever' connoting 'permanence' or 'eternity,' 'advance' and 'passing' indicating 'impermanence' or 'temporal' (temporary). Accordingly, 'impermanence' is 'permanent' and 'change' is 'changeless' – existence-time ever-always (eternally) advances (changes).[92] Dogen's vision of reality exploits the significance of this to the utmost, unfolding its most profound implications with his notion of 'the self-obstruction of a single dharma' or 'the total exertion of a single dharma' (*ippo gujin*). This notion reveals a number of important implications concerning the nature of existence-time; two of which are:

- Each and all dharmas reveal, disclose, or present the whole universe (the totality of existence-time).
- Each and all dharmas are inherently infinite and eternal.

Great Delusion and Great Enlightenment

Insofar as the terms 'delusion' and 'enlightenment' are used to designate the nondual foci 'enlightenment' and 'delusion' (enlightenment/delusion), delusion is 'great delusion' (*daimei*) and enlightenment is 'great enlightenment' (*daigo*). The point here is that, while the term 'delusion' is commonly used to designate 'wrong' or 'distorted' views, and the term 'enlightenment' to designate 'right' or 'accurate' views, the terms are not limited to those meanings.

For example, Dogen says that 'Buddhas are enlightened about delusion' (*Shobogenzo, Genjokoan*) which means, for one thing, that Buddhas do not exist *independent* of delusion – delusion and enlightenment are *nondual*, hence, coessential and coextensive. The recognition of delusion as 'great delusion' is one of the key insights informing Zen expressions on the unlimited potential for the expansion or advancement of realization (practice-enlightenment). It is also an insight that resolves an *apparent* paradox; that of the capacity of dharmas to simultaneously 'expand' and 'contract.'

To clarify, the significance of 'great delusion' can be generally understood in light of the truth of *how* dharmas are experienced. The (only) way dharmas are experienced is by *distinguishing* them *from* what they are not – this *dharma* is *this* dharma *by virtue of the fact* that *it is not* anything else in the universe. Thus, the *reality* (existence/experience) of any dharma always *consists of* 'what *is* that particular dharma' *and* 'what *is not* that particular dharma.' To think of, speak about, or act upon any dharma *requires* (is dependent on) distinguishing *what is* that dharma from *what is not* that dharma – requires *the existence of what is* and *the existence of what is not* that dharma. The reason (*dori*) of 'great delusion' can thus be seen as inherent to the reason of experience/existence itself; experiencing *some*thing (i.e. a dharma) intrinsically-involves *not* experiencing *every*thing. In sum, 'great delusion' designates the truth that *seeing* anything *depends on* (thus is inclusive of) *not-seeing* everything – in short, seeing (enlightenment) *is* blindness (delusion).

The wisdom (true knowledge) disclosed by the recognition of 'great delusion' is that eternal omnipresence and infinite complexity is *inherent* to each and all dharmas. If, as we just saw, the existence

(existence/experience) of a dharma *depends on* the existence of *not* that dharma, then experiencing a dharma is (also) experiencing the 'presence' of 'a lack' (everything that is *not* that dharma). As experience *is* existence, and the reality of a dharma is inclusive of what *is* and what *is not* that dharma, the existence of *any* dharma is the existence of *every* dharma. To say the same thing from the other perspective, the whole of existence-time *is* each particular instance of existence-time.

Moreover, due to the quality of *passage* inherent to the nature of dharmas, their 'arrival' and 'departure' are *unceasing* – as *Shobogenzo* says, 'Before donkey business is finished, horse business begins.' With this we get a sense of what it means to say dharmas are infinitely complex as well as eternally omnipresent. The recognition of dharmas as infinitely complex is the reason informing the refrain in Zen records urging us to strive on; to continuously apply ourselves, to diligently refine our skill, and to sustain our effort. Eternal omnipresence and infinite complexity means delusion is ever-present and unlimited (i.e. 'great') – just as enlightenment is ever-present and unlimited.

Finally, delusion is inherent to reality whether beings are aware of it or not. At the same time, the distinction between *being aware* of it and *not being aware* of it is of the utmost significance in Zen; it is the distinction between 'Buddhas' and 'ordinary beings.' In the *Genjokoan* fascicle of *Shobogenzo*, Dogen underscores this distinction by asserting that to see dharmas *as they are* is to 'sense something is lacking.' To '*sense something is* lacking' is to *experience* 'the presence' of 'a lack.' The 'presence of this lack' is most comprehensively treated by the Buddhist doctrine of emptiness which we explore later. For now it suffices to notice that *being aware* of this 'presence' in/as (all) dharmas is being Buddha 'enlightened about delusion,' which also means being 'enlightened about enlightenment' – *being unaware* of this 'presence' is being an ordinary being 'deluded about enlightenment,' which, of course, also means being 'deluded about delusion.'

Authentic Zen, Authentic Culture

Authentic Zen practice-enlightenment ultimately amounts to authentic human *culture*. Here 'culture' is meant in its fullest sense; civilization, humankind, refinement, wisdom, creativity, ethos, mythos, growth, ingenuity, enhancement, fulfillment, sacrament, enjoyment, ornament, art, etc. For authentic culture is the form and essence of Zen practice-enlightenment, the very reason (*dori*) of Zen. Zen 'practice' is the way or activity of culture, Zen 'enlightenment' is the expression or realm of culture. This practice-enlightenment is an ever-enhancing universal process of liberation and fulfillment. The place-and-time of this way and realm is the here-and-now of the individual sentient being; its richest fields for cultivation are the expressions of awakened hearts and minds that ring out through space and time in the ceaseless actualization of the universe into novelty.

Authentic Zen can be accurately discerned by its intrinsic quality of establishing, engaging, and refining the normal human capacity of 'nonthinking' – authentic practice-enlightenment. Nonthinking (thinking not-thinking) is the human capacity of seeing true nature (*kensho*) or seeing Buddha (*kenbutsu*).

To see true nature is to see dharmas *as they are*, rather than through the 'dark glass' of systematic theories, generalizations, literal definitions, or fixed formulas. The true nature of the self and the world simply cannot be discerned from a perspective grounded on speculative assumptions, fixed doctrines, codes, schools, or established institutions. Of the various species identified as 'Zen,' all that conform to orthodox views, literal definitions, unverifiable claims, exclusive memberships, or objective standards of any kind are not authentic Zen or authentic culture. They are, therefore, of no relevance to this study except where their influence might obscure the vision of authentic Zen, thus call for refutation and rectification.

The Normality of Dharmas

I want to notice also the reason Zen expressions are not concerned with the existence or non-existence or the superiority or inferiority of dharmas; all such issues are clearly verified as irrelevant by the genuine Zen practitioner. Zen practice-enlightenment involves – thus can *only begin with* – discerning the true nature (thus, actual significance) of reality. One thing this entails is the experiential verification of the *ceaseless becoming* of reality, that is, seeing that each and all the particular dharmas ever-advancing here-now in a continuous stream of ever-novel experience constitutes the very fabric of existence-time. This is, in *Shobogenzo's* terms, 'actualizing the universe' (*genjokoan*). The process, pattern, or arrangement whereby this actualization is performed is recognized in Zen cosmology as the *normal* activity of the self (individual being/universal Buddha), and therefore as *exemplifying* the *normal* configurations, dynamics, and reason (*dori*) of existence.

Zen doctrine and methodology therefore consciously directs its expression to the self as its 'audience,' which is also consciously recognized as its 'source.' According to Zen cosmology the self is *at once* the myriad particular subjects of all individual beings and the one universal subject that is the universe – these 'two' can and do differ, but they cannot and do not conflict with (interfere, or obstruct) one another. The truth of each individual subject is the *normality* of the one universal subject, the truth of the one universal subject is the *normality* of the individual subject. The significant implication of our present concern is that what is produced by the interaction of an individual being with dharmas far transcend the effect they have on that individual alone. The *response* by an individual evoked through the interplay of the individual and a dharma needs to be recognized as being *as intrinsic to the dharma* as it is to the individual; the response should not mistakenly be attributed to the individual being alone.

Two Modes of Self-Actualization (Soul-Making); Genjokoan

Zen's vision of reality as an ever-ongoing self-actualization of the universe (*becoming* Buddha) is presented by *Shobogenzo* as a dynamic process involving the mutual cooperation and nonobstruction of all things, beings, and events throughout existence-time. Each dharma and all dharmas are thus regarded as *equally essential* elements to each and all others. This essential equality applies to all beings, regardless of whether or not they are aware of it. Those beings that are aware of this (i.e. Buddhas) can and do *intentionally* participate in the actualization of the universe, while those beings that are unaware of it (i.e. ordinary beings) are *passively* actualized *by* the universe. The distinction between *actualizing* and *being actualized* is a distinction of perspective, not attributes. This distinction is often treated by *Shobogenzo* in terms of 'turning the wheel' or 'twirling the flower' (of the Buddha-Dharma); intentionally *actualizing* as *turning*, passively *being actualized* as *being* turned.

Part 2 Zen and Contemporary Thought
Science and Zen in Light of Dogen and Shobogenzo

Contemporary Cosmology and its Flaw

Epistemology

By the 1950s, when institutional science had reached an unprecedented level of power and prestige, the historian of science George Sarton approvingly described the situation in a way that sounds like the Roman Catholic Church before the Reformation:

> Truth can be determined by the judgment of experts... Everything is decided by very small groups of men, in fact, by single experts whose results are carefully checked, however, by a few others. The people have nothing to say but simply to accept the decisions handed out to them. Scientific activities are controlled by universities, academies and scientific societies, but such control is as far removed from popular control as it possibly could be. [Sarton, G. (1955), Introductory essay, in J. Needham, ed., *Science, Religion and Reality*, Braziller, New York.]

Bacon's vision of a scientific priesthood has now been realized on a global scale. But his confidence that man's power over nature would be guided by 'sound reason and true religion' was misplaced.
Biologist Rupert Sheldrake[93]

In its most general sense, epistemology is the study or understanding of knowledge. Our epistemology defines our understanding of the nature and dynamics of what we *can* know, what we *do* know, and *how* we know it. In other words, our fundamental beliefs about what knowledge is, as well as its reliability (or unreliability), is our epistemology. Accordingly, our epistemology functions as the *primary organ* for our acquirement, processing, and application of knowledge. As such, it largely determines how we think, speak, and act in relation to *objects of* knowledge (i.e. the known) *as well as* to ourselves as *subjects of* knowledge (i.e. the knower). For example, if our epistemology regards objects of knowledge as existing *independent of* ourselves, we will think, speak, and act in relation to everything we know as if it exists distinct and separate from ourselves, *and* we will think, speak, and act in relation to ourselves as if we exist distinct and separate from everything we know. If, on the other hand, our epistemology holds that the known exists *interdependently with* the knower, we will think, speak, and act in relation to everything we know as if it exists as an intrinsic element of ourselves, *and* think, speak, and act in relation to ourselves as if we are intrinsic elements of everything we know.

Obviously, the more accurate our *view* of knowledge is, the greater our ability to acquire, process, and use knowledge will be. Less obvious, but just as true, the more our epistemology ascribes the *reliability* of knowledge to our personal capacities, the greater our confidence in our knowledge and abilities to apply it will be. For example, if our epistemology holds that the *only* reliable knowledge is knowledge that has been personally verified, we will be confident in whatever knowledge we confirm and will not hesitate to utilize our capacities for verifying the validity of any view, teaching, or proposition we encounter. Conversely, if our view regards the reliability of knowledge as being dependent on any authority *independent of* ourselves, we will inevitably be vulnerable to deception, thus to dangerous delusions like the belief that comet-transport through asphyxiation is a good idea. While this example is extreme, the consequences of accepting the fallacy based 'representational theory of knowledge', the prevailing epistemology in science as well as the world generally, are just as devastating, if not as sensational.

The Representative Nature of Dharmas in the Prevailing Cosmology

Living a human life is a philosophical endeavor. Every thought we have, every decision we make, and every act we perform is based on philosophical assumptions so numerous we couldn't possibly list them all. We go around armed with a host of presuppositions about what is real, what counts as knowledge, how the mind works, who we are, and how we should act. Such questions, which arise out of our daily concerns, form the basic subject matter of philosophy: metaphysics, epistemology, philosophy of mind, ethics, and so on…

Though we are only occasionally aware of it, we are all metaphysicians—not in some ivory tower sense but as part of our everyday capacity to make sense of our experience. It is through our conceptual systems that we are able to make sense of everyday life, and our everyday metaphysics is embodied in those conceptual systems.
George Lakoff and Mark Johnson[94]

Clarity of perception and thought evidently requires that we be generally aware of how our experience is shaped by the insight (clear or confused) provided by the theories that are implicit or explicit in our general ways of thinking. To this end, it is useful to emphasize that experience and knowledge are one process, rather than to think that our knowledge is about some sort of separate experience. We can refer to this one process as experience-knowledge (the hyphen indicating that these are two inseparable aspects of one whole movement).
Physicist David Bohm[95]

Physicist and author N. Lee Swanson observes:

> Some of the things science asks us to believe, with little or no proof, are more fantastic to a reasoning person than anything religion has put forward.
> N. Lee Swanson[96]

If most of us did not actually *concede* 'to believe, with little or no proof' a large number of 'fantastic' things 'science asks us to,' Dr. Swanson's statement might simply be an interesting point. In light of the facts, however, it qualifies as an understatement. For example, one such belief that is widely accepted is that 'an objective reality exists independently of subjective reality.' This proposition not only lacks any empirical evidence to support it, it is *contrary to* the evidence we do have; even more significantly, it is *inherently unverifiable*.

Further, to accept this belief *requires us* to accept it as *the most fundamental* element of our understanding of the world and our self – thus the basis of *all* our thoughts, words, and deeds. For the belief that an objective reality exists independent of us inherently determines *what* we *can* think, speak, or do about *anything*. In short, to ascribe to this belief is to make dualism *the basis* of our understanding and conduct – all our thoughts, words, and deeds will necessarily *begin with* this presupposition. As we shall see, accepting this belief comes with other obligations also, like the obligation to regard our experiential capacities as inherently unreliable. For now I want to notice Dr. Swanson's statement that immediately follows the passage above:

> And some of the really interesting data that scientists have uncovered is not believed by scientists themselves.
> N. Lee Swanson[97]

The reasoning here harmonizes with what I said about the 'determining' force inherent to accepting the belief in independent realities. The 'data that scientists have uncovered', like the nonduality of 'the observer' and 'the observed' is 'not believed by scientists themselves' *because* they have accepted the belief that independent realities exist. Nonduality and dualism are simply incompatible – objective reality is either independent of subjective reality or it is not. Scientists cannot accept the nondual nature of reality uncovered by their own experiments because of their inability to relinquish their belief in dualism.

Clearly, then, dualism is a tenacious weed. Not only was it fiercely clung to and fervently defended for centuries despite an absence of proof or even the possibility for verification, it continues to prevail despite the overwhelming amount of scientific evidence demonstrating that the knower and the known constitute a *unified whole*.

Now, if Zen's view of the nondual nature of reality is true – as the scientific evidence indicates – then it is clear that by accepting dualism as a first principle, contemporary epistemology begins by stepping away from the truth and with each succeeding step, advances further into confusion. In short, to see the 'known' as *independent* of the 'knower' is to see them *as they are not*.

To clarify, in accepting dualism, contemporary epistemology obliges itself to account for how one independent reality – a knower – could be aware of the existence of a separate independent reality – a known. Since it would be *impossible* for an independent reality to experience *another* independent reality – for such would deny the 'independent' quality of both – the *only* epistemology that *can* be constructed on a basis of dualism is one grounded on an *unverifiable speculation*.

Now, the particular *unverifiable speculation* that presently serves as the foundation of scientific cosmology and the prevailing worldview generally is known as the 'representational theory of knowledge.' According to the representational theory, *everything* we *experience as* things, beings, and events, are not the *real* things, beings, and events themselves but *representations* (re-presentations) *of* real things, beings, and events. This *unverifiable assumption* is perhaps most apparent in the common, instrumentalist or nominal view of language. According to this theory, words, names, teachings, stories, etc. are merely signs, symbols, or indicators that *represent, refer to, stand for,* or *point to* 'realities.' That is, words, letters, utterances, sentences, gestures, and all other elements of language are simply *provisional devices independent of* and *inessential to* the 'realities' they indicate.

While it may not be as obvious in other facets of the contemporary worldview, the same 'representational' reasoning is presupposed and applied to every aspect of human knowledge. For example, as language is viewed as *instrumental* for *representing* real things, beings, or events, so too sensation, perception, conception, emotion, and consciousness are all viewed as *instrumental*. In other words, *the reality we experience as* a sensation, perception, conception, emotion, or consciousness – everything apparent to a conscious subject – is not *the reality itself*, but a mere *representative* or *reconstruction of* the reality itself. The common/scientific view of 'perception,' for example, is described in New World Encyclopedia thus:

> Our perception of the external world begins with the senses, which lead us to generate empirical concepts representing the world around us, within a mental framework relating new concepts to preexisting ones. Perception takes place in the brain. Using sensory information as raw material, the brain creates perceptual experiences that go beyond what is sensed directly.[98]

Such conclusions are inevitable to any cosmology or worldview grounded on dualism. The dualism explicitly demonstrated by the 'representational theory of knowledge' is presupposed in nearly every sphere of our civilization, including science. The standard science of visual perception, for example, contends that *the flower we see* is not *the real flower* but, at best a *representation of* the real flower. This representation is supposed to be constructed by the mind (typically equated with the brain) from impressions produced by stimulation of the eye by physical particles and waves produced by the interaction of light with the real ('objective') flower, and the brain's capacity to 'fill in gaps' resulting from inherent physical limitations of the eye (e.g. limited peripheral and color ranges, physical blind spots, etc.). This same basic process is also supposed by science to explain hearing, smelling, tasting, and feeling (tactile sensation).

Since, according to this theory, the *subject* for whom the mind/brain fashions its 'representation' is the mind/brain *itself*, it begs the question as to why the mind/brain bothers with 'filling in gaps.' If it is 'smart enough' to fill in the gaps, why isn't it smart enough to 'get the picture' in the first place?

In any case, the fact that this speculative theory of knowledge is often held up as a quintessential example of the extraordinary capacity of human reason might go a long way in explaining the severe intellectual, emotional, and spiritual poverty demonstrated by contemporary civilization. Further, when such an unreasonable epistemology is coupled with common views about the nature of thought (or cognition), the reasonableness of human reason appears to be open to debate.

Briefly, thoughts are commonly regarded to be unlike any other kind of object in human experience. Not only are thoughts a class of object unique unto themselves, they are considered to be *less real* than most other kinds of objects experienced. If a perception is the 'appearance in and of the mind' representing an *objective reality*, a thought is an 'appearance in and of the mind' of a *subjective fabrication*. Thus, not only are they 'not real' *in themselves*, thoughts do not even *represent* realities. In actual practice, thoughts are commonly treated as *inherently unreliable,* even *misleading* as evinced by the tendency to regard 'subjective knowledge' as equivalent to 'dubious knowledge.'

In sum, then, according to contemporary epistemology, the products of language are merely *instrumental*, perceptions merely *representative*, and thoughts merely *fanciful*. In short, *all* forms of human knowledge/experience consist of *subjective constructs that exist independent of objective reality*. The implication is obvious; we are inexorably obstructed from ever arriving at certain knowledge concerning the true nature of reality (whether of our self or the world). For no human being has ever encountered anything other than language, perception, or thought.

Irrational Rationality

Broadly speaking, our concern has to do with reason and rationality in Dogen's soteriology, which has been grossly neglected in Dogen studies. We may ask why we should bother with the subject in the first place when the issue is in such disrepute in this day and age of postmodernism? ...whatever the merits and demerits of postmodernism may be, I am deeply convinced more than ever that no age in human history calls for the genuine understanding and re-vision of reason more urgently than ours.
Hee-Jin Kim[99]

Here we meet the *intrinsic irrationality* of contemporary epistemology, the *prevailing* view of human experience/knowledge. If language, perception, and thought are inherently unreliable then the representational theory – *a product of* language, perception, and thought – asserting the unreliability of language, perception, and thought is, *by its own definition*, unreliable – even if the theory *could* somehow be verified, it would, *thereby*, be confirmed unreliable!

Despite a general acknowledgement of its *logical inconsistency*, the representational theory of knowledge continues to function as a first principle in nearly every system of contemporary thought. This means, for example, that hundreds of millions of children are presently being systematically indoctrinated in the fallacy that all things, beings, and events are ultimately fabrications of their own minds (or brains). Further, this means that the conduct of the vast majority of the civilized world is governed by fallacious, even dangerous assumptions.

In light of its presupposition of the existence of an objective reality *independent* of, and generally impervious to, subjective experience, contemporary epistemology is clearly seen as unequivocally grounded in dualism. Further, in its particulars concerning the nature and dynamics of experience/existence, this epistemology inherently presupposes humankind to be forever barred from certain knowledge of any kind. Therefore, the contemporary worldview, according to its own methodology, asserts humans intrinsically lack the capacity to know reality as it is; that all our experience consists of subjective constructs that may or may not represent real objects of an external world. Finally, our knowledge of reality ultimately amounts to speculations *about* a self and a world that is, at best, *inferred* through the analysis of subjective constructs fashioned by the brain's capacity to 'represent' the 'real' (non-mental) world from after-effects of the world's influence on the sense organs and the mind's capacity to 'fill in the gaps.'

The Nature of Subjectivity in Contemporary Cosmology

The systematic recognition that the exclusive source of meaning and purpose in the world is the human mind, and that it is a fundamental fallacy to project what is human onto the nonhuman, is one of the most basic presuppositions—perhaps *the* basic presupposition—of modern scientific method. Modern science seeks with obsessive rigor to 'de-anthropomorphize' cognition. *Facts* are out there, *meanings* come from in here. The factual is regarded as plain, stark, objective, unembellished by the human and subjective, undistorted by values and aspirations... If the object is to be properly understood, the subject must observe and analyze that object with the utmost care taken to inhibit the naïve human tendency to invest the object with characteristics that are properly attributable

only to the human subject. For genuine and valid cognition to occur, the objective world—nature, the cosmos—must be viewed as something fundamentally lacking in all those qualities that are subjectively, inwardly most present to the human mind as constituting its own being: consciousness and intelligence, sense of purpose and intention, capacity for meaning and communication, moral and spiritual imagination. To perceive these qualities as existing intrinsically in the world is to 'contaminate' the act of knowing with what are in fact human projections.
Richard Tarnas[100]

[Our modern world view] ...confines the idea of subjectivity to human persons. Only they are permitted to be subjects, to be agents and doers, to have consciousness and soul. The Christian idea of person as the true focus of the divine and the only carrier of soul is basic to this world view. The Christian concentrated focus on actual living persons has also come to mean that the psyche is too narrowly identified with the ego personality. Also basic to this modern view of persons is the psychology of Descartes; it imagines a universe divided into living subjects and dead objects. There is no space for anything intermediate, ambiguous, and metaphorical.
James Hillman[101]

If we belittle tiles as being lumps of clay, we will also belittle people as being lumps of clay. If people have a Heart, then tiles too will have a Heart.
Shobogenzo, Kokyo[102]

Now I want to single out one of the significant paradoxes from the many intrinsic to the contemporary worldview. Despite its view that the 'objective' world is *realer* than the 'subjective' world, the common view attributes subjectivity with a unique *sovereignty* and *intrinsic value* that merit a *quality of respect* denied to objectivity. This unique, intrinsically valuable subjectivity is commonly attributed only to humans, sometimes to gods corollary with devils, demons, and angels, rarely to animals or plants, and almost never to elements (e.g. water, fire, air, etc.), minerals (e.g. ore, gold, granite, etc.), or other objects of experience (e.g. clouds, mountains, words, works of art, products of imagination, etc.). Briefly, 'objective' things or events are assumed to *lack* subjectivity, and therefore to *lack intrinsic value*; effects on them by the actions of subjective agents are considered to be experientially inconsequential to them.

The basic nature and dynamics of this fundamental dualism between objectivity and subjectivity are eloquently outlined in these words from Richard Tarnas:

> The world outside the human being lacks conscious intelligence, it lacks interiority, and it lacks intrinsic meaning and purpose. For these are human realities, and the modern mind believes that to project what is human onto the nonhuman is a basic epistemological fallacy. The world is devoid of any meaning that does not derive ultimately from human consciousness. From the modern perspective, the primal person conflates and confuses inner and outer and thus lives in a state of continuous magical delusion, in an anthropomorphically distorted world, a world speciously filled with the human psyche's own subjective meaning. For the modern mind, the only source of meaning in the universe is human consciousness.
> Richard Tarnas[103]

The contemporary view of subjectivity is elaborated by the archetypal psychologist James Hillman in his *Re-visioning Psychology*. In the following passage Hillman expands on the nature of this view by providing some context of its origin and highlighting a number of its significant implications, and limitations:

> This is a restrictive view and it has led us to believe that entities, other than human beings, taking on interior subjective qualities are merely 'anthropomorphized' or 'personified' objects, not really persons in the accepted meaning of that word. If we find persons elsewhere than in living human bodies, we conclude that these persons have been transferred from 'in here' to 'out there.' We believe we have unconsciously put our experiences into them; they are merely fictional or imaginary... We do not believe that imaginary persons could possibly be as they present themselves, as valid psychological subjects with wills and feelings like ours but not reducible to ours. Such thinking we say is legitimate only for animistic primitive people, or children, or the insane.
>
> This view moreover believes that each individual body can contain no more than one psychic person; as we have one body so we are one soul. To find other persons within oneself, to be divided into several souls, a field of multiple personalities—although this notion has often been maintained even in our Western culture—is an 'aberration' called personified thinking. Persons appearing either in the world or in myself other than my ego-subjectivity are called

personifications, their livingness is said to be resultant of mine, their animation derived from my breath.
James Hillman[104]

Now if our experience of fellow humans is not qualitatively different from our experience of sunsets, pillars, trucks, dream butterflies, or flowers why do we ascribe subjectivity to humans while denying it to forests, bicycles, ponds, and houses? Clouds appear to us of their own accord; they move, act, expand, and decrease independent of our intentions – yet, the view that clouds lack subjectivity is presupposed by contemporary cosmology, considered self-evident. Further, the child or aborigine, the poet, and the contemporary adult that does regard a cloud as a sentient being is judged naïve, eccentric, or insane, respectively. Does the fact that other humans look and act like us verify their subjectivity? Does the fact that a cloud doesn't look and act like us verify the absence of subjectivity in it?

Setting aside questions about the merits of the common view for the moment, imagine how it might be to live in a world where humans were not the only 'people,' a world in which all things, beings, and events were seen, experienced, and treated as *persons*. While we moderns might find intellectual reassurance in the advanced 'rationality' of our understanding; certain primal peoples *experience* life as a realm teeming with an infinite variety of persons whose thoughts, words, and deeds are of intrinsic significance and value. Where we see a cloud as an objective atmospheric condition, they might encounter an ancestor or a goddess. We are both endowed with the same experiential capacities. What makes the actual experience of the cloud so different is the perspective from which it is experienced, that is the individual's cosmology. A 'primal' person brought up in a society ascribing to 'contemporary' cosmology experiences clouds as atmospheric conditions. A 'contemporary' person raised in a society ascribing to a 'primal' cosmology experiences clouds as sentient beings.

The point I want to get at is that the *actual experience* of a person is largely *determined by* their particular viewpoint, their cosmology. The implication is obvious; if the epistemology of a particular cosmology is grounded on a fallacy, the individual that ascribes to it will inevitably *experience* reality *as it is not*. The *only* difference between experiencing a stone as an 'inanimate object' and experiencing it as a 'sentient being' is an individual's particular viewpoint (i.e. their cosmology). To say the same thing from the opposing angle, to *actually experience* a stone as a sentient being only requires us to view it from the appropriate perspective.

But, someone may protest, scientific facts are *scientific facts*; clouds and stones *are* insentient things, *not* persons. I am not denying the validity of this; I am simply pointing out that this 'validity' *depends on* the perspective from which it is viewed – that is, what Dr. N. Lee Swanson calls the 'frameworks' of our 'Core Beliefs':

> The framework of those of us that were born in the 20th century Western world is largely the result of science and the scientific revolution. There are some residual religious beliefs, but the primary concept that we have about **how the world is** comes to us from science.
> N. Lee Swanson[105]

I do not want to belabor the point, but I would strongly suggest that it is of utmost importance to come to a clear understanding as to what 'scientific facts' actually are. Clearly, if we are going to allow scientific facts to influence our understanding (hence our conduct), we would be well advised to develop a solid grasp of the process of 'scientific method' – the systematic process involving, among other things, empirical observations, measurements, repeatable experiments, and accurate predictions by which 'scientific facts' are produced.

One important thing about scientific method that we should be clear about is the fact that science itself recognizes 'scientific facts' to be no more than 'hypotheses' – possibilities not certainties. Another important thing to keep in mind is that the 'first principles' of scientific method are theoretical presuppositions – agreed upon standards, consensually accepted conjectural assumptions. As the etymology of the word indicates, a 'presupposition' is a notion 'supposed prior to' or 'in the absence of' verified experiential knowledge.[106]

My purpose here is not to disparage science or dispute the virtues of scientific method. Clearly science has achieved much and possesses vast potential for enhancing civilization. As the biologist Rupert Sheldrake rightly points out:

> Since the late nineteenth century, science has dominated and transformed the earth. It has touched everyone's lives through technology and modern medicine. Its intellectual prestige is almost

unchallenged. Its influence is greater than that of any other system of thought in all of human history.
Rupert Sheldrake[107]

Here I am simply attempting to point out the importance of recognizing that science possesses real limitations as well as real potential. The principles of science should not be applied outside its inherent boundaries – as it is, for instance in the case of 'scientism' and 'pseudo-skepticism' – for the same reason that the principles of boxing should not be applied outside its particular field; the probability of unnecessary injury.

The Fundamental Flaw of the Representational Theory of Knowledge

Because [real existence] is only this exact moment, all moments of existence-time are the whole of time, and all existent things and all existent phenomena are time.
Shobogenzo, Uji[108]

The main problem with the dualism of contemporary cosmology is its inherent inability to account for the experiential absence of an independently objective world. This problem comes in the form of a dilemma brought into relief when the question is raised as to the ascertainment of knowledge of or about the existence of 'independent objects' (the external world). For an independent reality is, by definition, inherently unverifiable, thus acquiring reliable knowledge concerning it is impossible. For it is self-evident that no independently existing object has ever been or ever could be encountered – any and all possible encounters are defacto *subjective* experiences. Faced with this undeniable truth, honest advocates of the representational theory are compelled to acknowledge that there is no way to verify what 'independent objects' are *or even whether they exist*. Yet, even while *theoretically* acknowledging the inability to know what's true or not true, those operating in accordance with this view *practically* conduct themselves as if it were an absolute truth – even to the point of medically suppressing those that fail to go along with the consensus.

> From the modern perspective, if I see the world as if it were communicating humanly relevant meaning to me in some purposeful, intelligent way, as if it were laden with meaning-rich symbols—a sacred text as it were, to be interpreted—then I am

> projecting human realities onto the nonhuman world. Such an attitude toward the world is regarded by the modern mind as reflecting an epistemological naïve state of awareness: intellectually undeveloped, undifferentiated, childish, wishfully self-indulgent, something to be outgrown and corrected through the development of a mature critical reason. Or worse, it is a sign of mental illness, of primitive magical thinking with delusions of self-reference, a condition to be suppressed and treated with appropriate medication. Richard Tarnas[109]

Again, I want to be clear, this is the case in spite of the fact that the so-called 'objective reality' of the representational theory, *according to its own advocates*, consists of a notion, concept, or idea *constructed by the human mind alone*. Further; according to the theory itself, not only has its proposed 'objective reality' *never been* experienced, it *cannot be* experienced – it is *inherently* unverifiable. This means that *every* assertion, discovery, scientific fact, and observation made from the perspective of the common (dualistic) worldview – not only those of the scientific community – *are not*, and can *never be* more than *hypothetical* notions based on, thus *dependent* on, the *hypothetical* notion that an *unverifiable* reality *exists*. From this it follows that *if* the *hypothetical* 'objective reality' does *not* exist, *every* assertion, discovery, idea, and observation *based on it* is wrong.

Despite some persistent difficulties, the fact that the notion of an independent objective reality is a conceptual speculation rather than an empirical observation was given little critical attention and even less practical consideration for a long, long time. After all, hypothetical or not, unverifiable or not, this notion proved to be of extremely effective pragmatic use in numerous ways in many various spheres of human interest. While it was long recognized as being far from perfect, the evident practicality of the dualistic presupposition at the core of the scientific worldview seemed to suggest it was at least in the right ball park. The fact it *was* so practically successful for so long and in so many spheres is undoubtedly the reason it continues to stand *despite* having lost its legs – not to mention its liver, heart, and brain – decades ago.

While the scientific worldview, and the dualism informing it, was losing its appeal before Einstein established his theories of relativity (1905, 1919), $E = mc^2$ instantly revived its reputation, if not its validity. Did not the success of relativity virtually (if not *actually*) *verify* the accuracy of the representational theory which presupposes it? So it must have seemed, even after the official birth of quantum mechanics shortly thereafter. It may be pointless to wonder what might have happened if quantum mechanics – and its evidence of the nondual nature of reality – had arrived first. Nevertheless, it does not seem far-fetched to imagine the revolutionary potential of the 'new physics' might have been significantly greater had it not stood in the shadow of, and apparent opposition to the theories of relativity. For, if quantum mechanics was right, the representational theory was false.

Like the vision of reality proclaimed by sages in all times and places, the vision of reality presented by the findings of quantum mechanics indicated that if any independent objective realm did exist, it had no influence in or on the universe we inhabit. According to the new physics, nothing in our universe – not atoms, sub-atomic particles, mass, energy, things, beings, events, not even space or time – existed independent of subjective experience (consciousness, sentience). In short, either quantum mechanics was wrong or objective reality did not exist independently. The Zen master Eihei Dogen was right:

> The whole universe is utterly without objective molecules: here and now there is no second person at all.
> *Shobogenzo, Bussho*[110]

Coming to light so close on the heels of General Relativity's official confirmation in 1919, this revelation of quantum mechanics was largely ignored or dismissed as erroneous. Nevertheless, the evidence was indisputable – not even Einstein refuted that. He did, however, believe there must be a flaw in it somewhere and suggested the evidence might be 'incomplete' in some way. The notion that objective reality did not exist independent of subjects was simply not something he could swallow. And while Einstein spent much of the rest of his life attempting to disprove what the evidence showed; his efforts not only failed, some of it actually increased support for the validity of quantum mechanics.

Once, putting his consternation into plain English, as he was reportedly apt to do, Einstein quipped:

> Do you really believe that the moon is not there unless we are looking at it?
> Albert Einstein[111]

As Einstein himself clearly recognized, the evidence of quantum mechanics was no mere snag or hiccup; it was a death knell, not just for General Relativity and the representational theory of knowledge, but for dualism itself — the very foundation of the scientific worldview and almost every other realm of higher learning. If dualism was untenable, as quantum mechanics indicated, then the continued acceptance of the representational theory by scientific cosmology could only be understood as a deliberate and unnecessary obstruction to an accurate vision of reality.

Everyone agrees that thinking, speaking, and acting on the basis of fallacious assumptions is unwise, even dangerous. Nevertheless, the majority of persons with the greatest influence on the course of human civilization are thinking, speaking, and acting on the basis of fallacious assumptions.

Today, nearly a century later, the evidence of nonduality revealed by quantum mechanics has not only been repeatedly verified, it has been vastly corroborated by verified evidence from many other realms of science. The evidence of nonduality from these diverse realms has been accepted to various degrees in specific fields and, thereby, the fallacy of dualism *technically* acknowledged. Why, then, does dualism continue to be *practically* applied even within most of those fields?

While the significance of the evidence is easy enough to grasp intellectually, its implications make it difficult to accept, despite a solid intellectual grasp — as evinced, for example, in the case of Einstein. As I have suggested, at least part of the problem, perhaps the bulk of it, has less to do with the reluctance to admit our present cosmology is fallacious, and more to do with the inability to envision an adequate alternative. As those raised on the notion of a flat Earth must have discovered when its roundness was proven, intellectually understanding a truth is something altogether different than *realizing* that truth to the marrow of one's bones.

At the same time, I would contend that if our present, apparently unreliable, 'scientific knowledge' could be comprehensively reevaluated from a *nondual* perspective it would confirm many of the assertions proclaimed by visionaries down through the ages. For example, that neither *the moon* nor *we* exist 'there' or 'then' regardless of when we look or don't look; all things, beings, and events exist only and always here-now. From the nondual perspective the question is not about when we look or don't look, or whether the moon is there or not there, the question is about *who* looks or doesn't look, and *what moon* is there or not there here-now.

From the nondual perspective, Einstein would not have been compelled to reach the conclusion he did. For no quandary would have arisen in the first place. From the nondual perspective *all things* are recognized as *interdependent*. That is *neither* objects *nor* subjects (or any other species of reality) exist as separate, independent entities. The question provoking Einstein's conclusion would not arise because from the nondual perspective the true nature of the moon as well as the one looking or not looking is self-evident. From the nondual perspective, it is obvious that we can only speak meaningfully of 'the moon' and 'somebody' *because of* their nondual existence – that is, because of the actual normality or 'as it is' *reality of* the moon-and-somebody.

In reality, subjects and objects are never actually experienced apart from each other. The simplest explanation, and the one supported by quantum mechanics and other scientific evidence, is that this is because they do not manifest or inhabit *separate* realities. While a subject is always and distinctly experienced as a subject, and an object is always and distinctly experienced as an object, subjects and objects constitute a single unified reality – just exactly as they are always experienced to do. To insist on the 'independent existence' of one or both of these is to inject an unverifiable factor into the equation which violates Ockham's razor by introducing an unnecessary complication.

As experienced from the nondual perspective, the moon is *really the moon* and the self is *really the self*; the moon is *nondual* (object/subject), and the self is *nondual*. When – the place/time – 'somebody is looking,' the moon and the self are *fully existent as* 'looking,' when 'somebody is not looking,' the moon and the self are *fully existent as* 'not looking.'

Science and Contemporary Cosmology

When I was first taught about Einstein's equation $E=mc2$, it was presented as if mass can be converted into energy and vice-versa. But it is more fundamental than that. Mass *is* energy.
N. Lee Swanson[112]

You need to recognize that the truth of the matter is that mountains are fond of those who are wise, and that they are fond of those who are saintly.
Shobogenzo, Sansuikyo[113]

The evidence revealed by the actual experiments of science itself has long since provided more than enough reason for advancing a serious inquiry into a nondual cosmology. If science is to maintain its integrity as an advocate of truth, such an inquiry is demanded. Yet that minority of scientists who have professed, provided evidence, and convincingly argued for the nondual nature of reality have largely suffered the fate common to visionaries throughout the ages – marginalization. Fortunately, however much it might have muffled the truth, marginalization has not concealed the cracks at the foundations of contemporary cosmology becoming more evident with the continuously increasing failures of science.

The sadly uncreative moves to keep the *Big Bang Theory* alive in recent decades have only underscored the question as to why the theory has not yet been put out of its misery. While it has technically been treated for what it is, a hypothesis, responses to discovered discrepancies in the theory have been less than inspiring. Rather than indicators to seek a more accurate understanding, discrepancies have been treated as injuries requiring emergency amputations or grafts. For example, an inconsistency between predictions and actual observations concerning the inflation of the universe was 'cured' by supplementing the theory with an unverifiable 'fluctuation' *exactly countering* the flaw. Similar moves followed discoveries that *most* of the matter and energy of the universe predicted was *absent*. The missing *bulk* (about 96% of the universe) was corrected by the 'discovery' of a quantity of 'dark matter' and 'dark energy' that – surprise – *exactly compensated* the amount predicted.

Notice that 'dark,' in dark matter and dark energy, basically means 'undetected.' Sure it's possible, but would such 'reasoning' be as readily accepted from any realm other than science? 'I didn't eat 'em Mommy; you just can't see 'em 'cause they're *dark* cookies.' 'Oh, okay Johnny, my mistake.'

On a related note, major announcements from the realms of quantum mechanics and theoretical physics have dwindled to a trickle in recent decades. Repeatedly finding themselves back where they started, physicists are decidedly more somber today than a few years back when it seemed almost daily someone was hailing the imminent discovery of a GUT (grand unified theory) or TOE (theory of everything). The truth of the matter (pun intended) is that, while quantum mechanics continues to be richly productive in advancing technologies, such advances are almost entirely based on exploiting knowledge that was already evident in its earliest years – the actual range and scope of the knowledge itself has remained largely unchanged for nearly a century. Similar brick walls and viscous circles describe progress in mainstream biology, neurology, linguistics, and psychology, particularly in areas dependent on contemporary (i.e. dualistic) notions of 'consciousness,' a problem area also in fields of animal research, agriculture, robotics, and artificial intelligence, to name only a few.

Because quantum mechanics insists that 'objects' are inherently entangled with 'subjects,' scientists have been perplexed by the 'bizarre' behavior of physical reality for nearly 100 years – for all scientists *know* 'objects' are unequivocally *independent of* 'subjects.' Even a third-grader knows that to be a scientist is first and foremost to be 'objective' – not only to abide by the tenets of dualism, but to avoid, eliminate, and eradicate any and all traces of subjectivity from their methodology. Because objective reality is definitely *not* influenced by, much less *dependent on*, subjective reality, the multitude of experimental observations repeated by multitudes of physicists for the last century *must* be flawed. One thing these experiments have definitely proven is that the presuppositions of science are as tenacious as any religious dogma or article of faith has ever been. As a community, no vassals have been as loyal to their Lord as scientists since the Samurai at the pinnacle of the warrior age in Japan. And, just as the Samurai's ultimate demonstration of loyalty was to sacrifice their essential attribute – their 'courage' or 'guts' (ritually enacted by self-disembowelment) – the contemporary scientist's demonstration of loyalty is to sacrifice their individual capacity for reason.

From the perspective of Zen the behavior of physical reality – the fact that sub-atomic particles are entwined with conscious observers – is in perfect harmony with our actual experience. The 'bizarre' appearance of reality encountered by science is entirely due to the fallacious viewpoint from which it is analyzed. If the presupposition that 'conscious subject' (physicist) and 'physical object' (particle) are *independent* realities was not an infallible truth (as science insists), there would be no need for the fantastic, convoluted theories about how and why physical objects 'act like' conscious subjects are somehow involved with their behavior – physical objects *act like* that because they *are like that*. From the Zen worldview, it would be bizarre if physical objects *did not* appear to be involved with conscious subjects.

Summary: Contemporary Cosmology is Fundamentally Flawed

You are one of the rare people who can separate your observation from your preconception. You see what is, where most people see what they expect.
John Steinbeck[114]

Science is as much a religion as any religion has ever been. The scientific priesthood bestows their thoughts and ideas upon the peasantry as if they were just bringing it down off the mountain. And woe to one who dares question! Scientists themselves hesitate to openly question for fear of retribution [not getting their papers published or their proposals funded]. It's a conspiracy and a fraud. I had to quit my job as a professional scientist in order to think.
Physicist N. Lee Swanson[115]

The first principles of cosmologies, like all systems of thought, are necessarily grounded on fundamental presuppositions; unspoken elemental assumptions. The viability of a system of thought is dependent *first* on possessing first principles grounded on fundamental presuppositions that truly harmonize with reality *as it is*. If first principles are based on presuppositions that harmonize with reality the system *may* or *may not* be viable, if they are not in harmony with reality the system *cannot* be viable. The point; any cosmology incorporating a fallacious first principle is not a viable cosmology.

A fallacious first principle is a false view. False views do not constitute an *absence* of knowledge (ignorance) but the *presence* of distorted knowledge (delusion). Unlike an absence of information, false views are *tangible obstacles* to truth. In the past, for example, false views that the Earth was flat served as obstacles to the truth that the Earth was round.

Just as the *false view* of the world's form was an *obstacle* to the *truth* of the world's form, so the *false view* of the world's *essential nature* is an *obstacle* to the *truth* of the world's essential nature. The point; holding the false view that reality is *dualistic* is an obstacle to the truth that reality is *nondual*.

In sum; the first principles of contemporary cosmology are grounded on a fallacy (dualism), thus contemporary cosmology fails to qualify as a viable system, is inherently unreliable, and ultimately a danger – perhaps *the greatest* danger – to humankind itself. At the very least, the prevailing worldview is an obstacle to discerning the appropriate conduct needed to meet the challenges presently threatening the global population.

Despite the general acknowledgement of some long recognized flaws of dualism, nearly every realm of contemporary civilization (East as well as West) continues to be firmly grounded in it. The representational theory's basis in dualism is clearly demonstrated by its presupposition that the 'real world' and the 'perceived world' are two *independent* realities. To accept this theory as accurate is to see and understand our own experience of reality as intrinsically unreliable. For if all our experience of the world is indirect (not 'presented' to us, but only 'represented'), we never encounter the *actual world* and therefore, are incontrovertibly prohibited from ever confirming even if an objective world exists, much less verifying the accuracy of our knowledge about the world.

The unwillingness or inability to acknowledge the flaw of dualism is, in my view, the single greatest threat to human civilization. All forms of dualism presuppose that reality is actually divided, that we and our world constitute distinct independent entities. Because dualism posits the existence of an objective reality 'independent' of subjective experience (thus inherently unverifiable), dualism (hence the common worldview) invalidates itself by violating the very standards it proclaims; scientific method. Obviously, a systematic theory that *begins* from a false presupposition cannot *end* in truth; likewise, a worldview grounded in dualism is fallacious through and through.

While the dualistic presupposition upon which the common and scientific worldviews are grounded is certainly flawed, this flaw is not irrevocable. It is not as if this flaw, having once been committed, must ever-after be accepted and accounted for – it is merely a *wrong view*, nothing more. The 'way around it' is simple: *see it as it is*, and thereby, *see through it* to the truth. The very evidence that is continuously eroding and undermining every shred of support for the dualistic contentions of the majority, is simultaneously contributing great support to the growing minority that has long been insisting that the only real hope for progressing toward truth requires a full and honest inquiry into a nondual vision of reality. It goes without saying that to qualify as 'honest' such an inquiry must proceed from a viewpoint that is as genuinely free from the conceit of scientific infallibility as it is from the smug sanctimoniousness of religious fanaticism and arrogant sectarian dogmatism.

Part 3 Zen Form, Zen Reason
The Appearance of Reality and the Reality of Appearance

Clear Seeing and Emptiness

The question is not what you look at, but what you see.
Henry David Thoreau[116]

If there is one teaching that is peculiar to Buddhism alone among all the world's religions, I would say it is the principle of sunyata (Voidness or Emptiness). If I were to choose one doctrine among others that best represents the core of Buddhism, I would also choose the principle of sunyata. If someone were to further ask me what is the Buddhist doctrine that is most difficult to explain and comprehend, most misunderstood and misrepresented, I would again say it is the principle of sunyata.
Garma C.C. Chang[117]

"Form is emptiness, emptiness is form." That is, form is form, emptiness is emptiness.
Shobogenzo, Maka-hannya-haramitsu[118]

The vast significance and central importance of emptiness in Zen can be seen in two of its often repeated axioms, 'All things are essentially empty' and 'Emptiness is the true nature of all things.' 'All things are essentially empty' means all things are empty *of selfhood*, all dharmas *lack independent existence*. 'Emptiness is the true nature of all things' means emptiness is the *reality* or *essential nature* (ontology) of all the *various* things, beings, and events (i.e. the myriad dharmas).

Contrary to widespread notions, to be empty does *not* mean to be *unreal*, *nonexistent*, or *provisional*, nor does it mean that variety, plurality, and uniqueness are *delusory* or *illusory*, as if the myriad dharmas were 'made up of' or 'reducible to' one *uniform* or *homogenous* essence or substance. I stress this point because prospective Zen interpreters have historically demonstrated a tendency for presenting distorted notions about emptiness. Such distortions usually amount to a privileging of emptiness (essence, reality) over form (appearance, manifestation). Such privileging is caused and perpetuated by false views consistent with dualism. Briefly, the form (appearance) and emptiness (reality) of dharmas are *conceived* and *treated* as *independent realities*. When form and emptiness are conceived of as separate, distinct realities, they naturally become subject to comparisons of superiority and inferiority. Naturally, emptiness, being envisioned as uniform, universal, and pure is seen and treated as superior to form, which is envisioned as variable, particular, and disparate. Such fallacies concerning emptiness and form spawn teachings and practices that foster quietism and detachment, many of which can be seen thriving in the present day.

From at least as early as its Sixth Ancestor, Huineng (638-713 C E), Zen has been closely associated with the *prajna-paramita sutras* – the most comprehensive treatment of emptiness (*sunyata*) in the Buddhist literature. According to Zen lore, Huineng realized enlightenment simply upon *hearing* a *prajna-paramita* scripture, the *Diamond Sutra*, recited in the street. Huineng's record, the *Platform Sutra*, proclaims the supreme vision of the *Diamond Sutra*, promising enlightenment not only to those that practice its teachings, but even to those that simply *memorize* it.[119]

Numerous subsequent Zen records, including *Shobogenzo*, make frequent use of the *Diamond Sutra's* methodology to present the wisdom of emptiness, that is, insight into the nondual nature of reality. The gist of the *Diamond Sutra's* methodology can be expressed by the formula A is not-A, *therefore* A is A; not-A is A, *therefore* not-A is not-A. In other words, form is emptiness (i.e. not-form), *therefore* form is form; emptiness is form (i.e. not-emptiness), *therefore* emptiness is emptiness.

The basic reasoning of this can be understood by envisioning 'A' as a particular dharma, and 'not-A' as everything else in the universe. With this it can be seen that thinking, speaking, or acting in relation to 'A' *requires* one to distinguish what *is* 'A' from what *is* 'not-A' – thus it is seen that the *existence of* 'A' presupposes (i.e. is *dependent on*) the *existence of* 'not-A.' By the same reasoning, the *existence of* 'not-A' is seen to presuppose the *existence of* 'A.'

To clarify, and emphasize the crucial point, since the existence of 'A' can *only* be discerned by its *contrast with* the existence of 'not-A', the existence of 'A' is *dependent on* the existence of 'not-A' – therefore, the existence of 'A' *is inclusive of* the existence of 'not-A' and vice versa. In other words, the whole of existence-time that is not *explicit* in/as 'A' is and must be *implicit* in/as 'A' – hence, the *reality of* 'A' is constituted of *both* what *is* 'A' and what *is* 'not A.' Therefore, 'A' (and by extension, any particular dharma) is a manifestation *of* the whole universe, total existence-time. This vision of dharmas – as particular forms of the totality of space-and-time – is explicitly asserted and graphically presented by Dogen's teachings on the 'self-obstruction' or 'total exertion' of 'a particular dharma' (*ippo gujin*), which we shall return to shortly.

The Zen practitioner that focuses their attention on dharmas in accordance with the *Diamond Sutra's* methodology is enlightened to (i.e. sees, knows, experiences) the truth that *dharmas* are *dharmas* by virtue of their being *particularities* – that is, by their existing as *some*-thing differentiated from *every*-thing. Experiencing the world through the perspective presented by the *Diamond Sutra*, the practitioner is made intimately aware of the fact that reality only and always consists of *particular* instances of *total* existence-time – apart from specific manifest phenomena (i.e. dharmas) there is no existence or time.

Thus, it is accurate to say that, to experience (epistemology) existence (ontology) is to distinguish *some*thing from *every*thing; if something is not distinguished from everything, *no*thing can be experienced. By applying ourselves to the *Diamond Sutra's* methodology we first come to discern that the existence of a particular dharma is *dependent on* the existence of *everything* 'other than' *that* dharma. Next, we come to discern that the existence of *everything* 'other than' *that* dharma is *dependent on* the existence of *that* dharma. Proceeding along these lines, we come to discern how each dharma inherently presupposes (contains, includes) *every* 'other dharma' and *all* 'other dharmas.' Thus, it is also accurate to say that, to experience existence is to distinguish *every*thing from *some*thing. Now, the first and second 'accurate ways to say' are mutually inclusive; the first way illumines the *form* of dharmas and eclipses the *emptiness* of dharmas, the second way illumines the *emptiness* of dharmas and eclipses the *form* of dharmas. The actuality of dharmas (form/emptiness, illumined/eclipsed) is the same in either 'way of saying it,' and because Zen recognizes this as self-evident, Zen expressions – whether of the first or second 'way of saying it' – presuppose *both* perspectives (i.e. Zen expressions that distinguish dharmas *from* everything *tacitly* recognize dharmas *as* everything, Zen expressions recognizing dharmas *as* everything *tacitly* distinguish dharmas *from* everything).

In sum, the *Diamond Sutra* presents (makes present) the dynamic interdependence of form and emptiness by demonstrating that 'form' is *essential to*, therefore *inclusive of* 'emptiness' (and vice versa). In the terms of *Shobogenzo*:

"Form is emptiness, emptiness is form." That is, form is form, emptiness is emptiness.
Shobogenzo, Maka-hannya-haramitsu[120]

Emptiness

While the *Diamond Sutra* continues to be highly revered in Zen, which remains deeply steeped in its methodology, the concise *Heart Sutra* (*prajna-paramita-hrdaya-sutra*) came to be regarded as the definitive statement on emptiness in Zen, as in other Mahayana traditions. The *Heart Sutra*, as the title suggests, expresses the heart (the essential core) of Buddhism's insight into emptiness. The key phrase, 'form is emptiness, emptiness is form,' is the *Heart Sutra's* crystallization of this insight.

In *Maka-hannya-haramitsu,* the earliest fascicle composed specifically for *Shobogenzo,* Dogen innovatively utilizes the *Heart Sutra* to undermine misleading fallacies about emptiness, while at the same time revealing the true, liberating potential of emptiness.

The *Heart Sutra* was familiar enough in Dogen's time that citing only its first line was enough to identify it as the perspective of his commentary. The fact that he *altered* that first line by adding a single word is significant. The very succinctness and popularity of the *Heart Sutra* makes Dogen's *slight* alteration *starkly* apparent. The additional word initially jumps out as if misspoken; as its implication dawns, however, its purposeful intent becomes obvious. The actual first line of the *Heart Sutra* is:

> Avalokiteshvara Bodhisattva, practicing deep Prajna Paramita, clearly saw that all five skandhas are empty, transforming anguish and distress.[121]

The word Dogen adds is, '*konshin*,' which translates, 'whole-body-mind' or 'his/her whole-body-mind.' Although only one word, the significance of this addition is profound. To get this across in English, translators are compelled to get a bit creative. For example, here are the results of two attempts to translate Dogen's altered citation of the line:

> When Bodhisattva Avalokitesvara practices the profound *prajna - paramita,* the whole body reflects that the five aggregates are totally empty.
> *Shobogenzo, Maka-hannya-haramitsu*[122]

> When Avalokitesvara Bodhisattva practices the perfection of profound wisdom, his whole body is the five skandhas, all luminously seen as empty.
> Shobogenzo, Maka-hannya-haramitsu[123]

To clarify, 'Avalokitesvara' is an 'enlightened being' (*bodhisattva*) of Buddhist mythology, in this case the hero of the *Heart Sutra*. 'Five skandhas' (or five aggregates) is a traditional Buddhist term for the elements that constitute the whole body-mind of an individual human being.[124] To 'reflect' or 'luminously see' means to 'clearly see the truth of something,' to *experientially verify*. The meaning of '*prajna*' varies widely depending on its context, generally connoting 'wisdom,' 'intuitive insight,' 'consciousness,' etc.; as '*prajna-paramita*,' however, the wisdom or insight of *prajna* is 'perfect wisdom' (i.e. the wisdom of emptiness). The last phrase, 'transforming anguish and distress' (unstated in Dogen's citation) means, 'realizing the (soteriological) goal of Buddhism.'

Paraphrases cannot convey the essential meaning of the *Heart Sutra* or *Shobogenzo*, but as long as we keep that in mind, paraphrases *can* help to illumine certain obscurities and thus clear the *way to* that meaning. To that end, consider this paraphrase of the (unaltered) opening line of the *Heart Sutra*:

> Actualizing the Buddhist teaching for liberation (practicing deep *prajna paramita*), Avalokitesvara experientially verified (clearly saw) that his/her whole body-mind (all five *skandhas*) is empty (thereby realizing the Buddhist goal).

Now consider how this paraphrase could be expressed in light of *Shobogenzo's* alteration:

> Actualizing the Buddhist teaching for liberation, the whole *body-mind of* Avalokitesvara experientially verified that his/her whole body-mind is empty (thereby realizing the Buddhist goal).

In his commentary in *Shobogenzo, Maka-hannya-haramitsu*, Dogen immediately follows his (altered) citation of the first line of the *Heart Sutra* with a succinct expression presenting the reasoning (*dori*) of the *Heart Sutra* (hence, the rationale of emptiness):

> The five skandhas are form, feeling, conception, volition, and consciousness, which are the five modes of wisdom. The luminous seeing is itself wisdom.
> *Shobogenzo, Maka-hannya-haramitsu*[125]

'The luminous seeing *is itself* wisdom' – the actual, particular manifest form or activity (i.e. *dharma*; thing, being, or event) of 'luminous seeing' is *prajna* itself, the reality of perfect wisdom. Hee-Jin Kim clearly articulates the implications of Dogen's assertion thus:

> Avalokitesvara and wisdom are not the observer and the observed, but one reality. The luminous vision then is the working of Avalokitesvara/wisdom. Avalokitesvara sees Avalokitesvara; wisdom enacts wisdom. This reflexive mode of thinking comes from "practicing the perfection of profound wisdom."
> Hee-Jin Kim[126]

It goes without saying that when Dogen says, 'clear seeing' he means *right-understanding* and *right-views* as well as *accurate perception*. Shobogenzo, in harmony with all the great Zen classics, frequently urges its audience to remain mindful of the fact that actualizing Buddhist liberation requires more than simply hearing, or even accurately understanding the authentic teachings. The 'clear *seeing*' of Zen practice-enlightenment is a *process* not a product, an *activity* not a resolution. Of course the authentic teachings have to be deeply and carefully studied, learned, and accurately understood, but accurate understanding is ineffectual in the absence of experiential verification (assimilation and application). Avalokitesvara '*practices prajna-paramita*' by actively engaging in the ever-advancing process of 'practicing prajna-paramita' – liberation is not a fixed-form or static-state, but a flowing-form or continuous-activity of study, practice, and verification. Anyone can come to accurately understand authentic teachings, but only experiential verification can actualize authentic liberation.

By now most readers should be able to see the basic reasoning thus far presented: When Avalokitesvara clearly sees his/her own form is emptiness, Avalokitesvara clearly sees he/she is emptiness itself – 'form is emptiness.' When Avalokitesvara clearly sees he/she is emptiness itself, Avalokitesvara clearly sees emptiness is his/her form itself – 'emptiness is form.'

Now, Zen practitioners that go on to verify this teaching in actual practice come to realize the ultimate implication of this key expression of the *Heart Sutra*, 'Form is emptiness, emptiness is form.' For those of us that might not have realized this yet, Dogen elucidates the point:

> When this meaning is propounded in concrete expression, it is said: "Form is emptiness, emptiness is form." That is, form is form, emptiness is emptiness. [This principle applies to] all things and all phenomena.
> *Shobogenzo, Maka-hannya-haramitsu*[127]

As we see here, then, Dogen points out that the *Heart Sutra's* expression, "Form is emptiness, emptiness is form," ultimately leads to the same conclusion arrived at by the methodology of the *Diamond Sutra*, namely, that 'form is form, emptiness is emptiness' and that this applies to *all* the myriad dharmas.

Here it may be worth noticing an obvious truth: to experience (epistemology) one's form (ontology) as empty necessarily requires one to have a form. Hence, it is inevitable that any and every actual experience of emptiness is and must also be an actual experience of form. To clearly see, one must have a form with the capacity to clearly see – form must be *real* form. Likewise, clearly seeing the emptiness of one's form is only possible if one's form is truly empty – emptiness must be *real* emptiness. This is the ultimate point of the *Heart Sutra*'s expression, 'Form is emptiness; emptiness is form.' The import being the *interdependence* of emptiness and form; the reality of form is only possible *because* of the reality of emptiness and the reality of emptiness is only possible *because* of the reality of form. Form *is experienced* as/by emptiness *not-experienced*; emptiness *is experienced* as/by form *not-experienced*. When/where form *is*, emptiness *is*-not; when/where emptiness *is*, form *is*-not. As Dr. Kim puts it:

> When form is verified, emptiness is "shadowed," and there is nothing but form: "form is form." The same holds true of emptiness: "emptiness is emptiness."
> Hee-Jin Kim[128]

This means the *reality* of form is *inclusive of* the *presence* of emptiness (as 'shadowed'); if not for the ('shadowed') *presence* of emptiness, form could not appear. Likewise, the *reality* of emptiness is *inclusive of* the *presence* of form.

This explains the constant emphasis of Zen expressions on the *universal* quality of emptiness (e.g. all things are essentially empty; emptiness is the true nature of all things, etc.). For only by being clearly aware of, and accounting for, this universal quality of reality can we accurately discern and adequately treat *any* particular dharma. To think, speak, or act on a particular dharma without discerning, thus being able to account for, the ('shadowed') 'presence' of emptiness upon which it depends – thus *demonstrates* – is to think, speak, or act on a biased (i.e. one-sided; deluded) view. Any thought, word, or deed that fails to account for the *emptiness* of form not only demonstrates delusion about emptiness, but also delusion about form. The same reasoning applies to the failure to account for the *form* of emptiness.

To clarify, all 'forms' indicated in Zen expressions assume the audience's recognition of the 'presence' of their (the form's) emptiness, and expressions indicative of 'emptiness' suppose the recognition of the 'presence' of form. For example, the Zen expression, 'Drawing water, carrying firewood, these are my marvelous abilities,' assume the audience recognizes the presence herein of, among other things, '*not*-drawing,' '*no*-water,' '*non*-carrying,' and '*not*-firewood.' Any understanding that fails to account for the *presence* of 'not-drawing,' 'no-water,' etc. is inevitably a *misunderstanding*. Likewise, an understanding of emptiness that fails to account for its nondual unity with form is a misunderstanding.

After emphasizing that the ultimate principle of the doctrine of emptiness is that form *is* form, and emptiness *is* emptiness, the *Maka-hannya-haramitsu* fascicle underscores that this principle applies to *all* the myriad dharmas by explicitly identifying a large array of particular aspects and elements of reality as 'instances' of '*prajna-paramita*' or '*prajna itself.*'

> They are hundreds of things, and myriad phenomena. Twelve instances of *prajnaparamita* are the twelve entrances [of sense perception]. There are also eighteen instances of *prajna*. They are eyes, ears, nose, tongue, body, and mind; sights, sounds, smells, tastes, sensations, and properties; plus the consciousnesses of eyes, ears, nose, tongue, body, and mind. There are a further four instances of *prajna*. They are suffering, accumulation, cessation, and the Way. There are a further six instances of *prajna*. They are giving, pure [observance of] precepts, patience, diligence, meditation, and

> *prajna* [itself]. One further instance of *prajnaparamita* is realized as the present moment. It is the state of *anuttara samyaksaṃbodhi.* There are three further instances of *prajnaparamita.* They are past, present, and future. There are six further instances of *prajna.* They are earth, water, fire, wind, space, and consciousness. And there are a further four instances of *prajna* that are constantly practiced in everyday life: they are walking, standing, sitting, and lying down.
> Shobogenzo, Maka-hannya-haramitsu[129]

This intentional dwelling on various and particular instances of reality not only emphasizes the universal nature of this principle, it also stresses the importance of understanding that form and emptiness are nondual, *not* identical. Nonduality denotes unity, *not* uniformity; emptiness and form are interdependent *not* interchangeable. Emptiness is the real emptiness of (all) form, form is the real form of (all) emptiness; to raise one is to raise *both*; to eliminate one is to eliminate *both*. The term 'both' is the key here; emptiness cannot reciprocate, collaborate, coordinate, or work together with emptiness; form cannot cooperate, correspond, concur, or harmonize with form. 'Both' means that the reality of form is *contingent* on the reality of emptiness; the reality of emptiness is *dependent* on the reality of form. To 'clearly see' this and therefore to enact it in our everyday conduct is '*prajna* itself.'

The doctrine of emptiness is often distorted or misunderstood as meaning that emptiness *amounts to* form or that form is *reducible to* emptiness. Ascribing to this fallacy obstructs us from the truth. Because dharmas – form/emptiness units – are 'what' we clearly see as well as 'the means' whereby we clearly see, dharmas are 'clear seeing' itself, in Dogen's words, '*prajna* itself.' One's actual body-mind is identical to the actual dharmas one experiences, and all dharmas one actually experiences are one's body-mind, this principle applies to *all* dharmas. Thus, the 'form' (hence, form/emptiness) of each and all the myriad dharmas are you seeing prajna, prajna seeing you, prajna seeing prajna, you seeing you, seeing seeing seeing, prajna prajna-ing prajna, you you-ing you.

By now we should be able to see that, whatever else it accomplishes, *Shobogenzo's* utilization of the *Heart Sutra* forcefully draws attention to the actively dynamic, energetically animated nature of emptiness.

With this, then, I want to pause to summarize what should be fairly clear concerning the significance of Avalokitesvara's experience in light of *Shobogenzo's* presentation:

The whole of Avalokitesvara clearly sees the whole of Avalokitesvara is emptiness. Avalokitesvara's 'clear seeing,' being facilitated by the five *skandhas,* is emptiness, and clear seeing is *prajna* itself – hence, Avalokitesvara, clear seeing, emptiness, and prajna are four facets of a single multifaceted process or activity. The *reality* of *prajna* is the wisdom of emptiness; the *reality* of *emptiness* is form/emptiness, the *reality* of *form* is form/emptiness, each particular instance of which is an instance of *prajna*. Accordingly, emptiness can clearly see, and emptiness can be clearly seen. Thus we can clearly see that, whatever else it might be, 'practicing *prajna-paramita*' is emptiness clearly seeing emptiness.

Further, we should now be able to see that, whatever else might be true of emptiness, *Shobogenzo* attributes it with at least these *positive* characteristics:

Emptiness is present in/as existence-time
Emptiness is differentiated
Emptiness is active
Emptiness is sentient
Emptiness is intelligible
Emptiness is communicable

Even after this short foray into Dogen's treatment of emptiness, it is clear that his vision cannot be understood or described in negative or apophatic terms. This point merits emphasis; the meticulous attention to, and detailed refutations of negativistic views of emptiness in *Shobogenzo* testifies to the pervasiveness of such distortions in Dogen's own era. The distorting power of negativistic views of emptiness can, has, and does obstruct practitioners from *clearly seeing* any aspect of Zen/Buddhism, not to mention practicing it and actualizing its wisdom.

The Sentient Nature of Reality

I meet with a human being, a human being meets with a human being, I meet with myself, and manifestation meets with manifestation.
Shobogenzo, Uji[130]

> What has been described like this is that life is the self, and the self is life.
> Shobogenzo, Zenki[131]

Dogen's (altered) citation of the *Heart Sutra* followed by the series of affirmative expressions on the nature of the self, the world, and the myriad dharmas presents (makes present) a glimpse into the grand vision of *Shobogenzo*. Right here, in the very first fascicle explicitly composed for *Shobogenzo*, the common thread that binds together and runs throughout the whole of Dogen's masterpiece is prominently evident. That thread is the reason (*dori*) of the nonduality of duality, and the duality of nonduality. In short, experience, existence, and liberation (epistemology, ontology, and soteriology) are nondual; the *experience* of clear seeing, the *existence* of *prajna,* and the actualization of *liberation* are three, but are not three different things. The nature and dynamics of the actualization of the universe (*genjokoan*) advanced by the nonduality of experience, existence, and liberation is creatively brought into relief in numerous ways and from a great variety of perspectives throughout *Shobogenzo*.

To clearly *see* (i.e. know, experience, encounter) is to *be* (i.e. appear, exist, manifest), thus to clearly see liberation (Buddhahood, enlightenment, deliverance) is to be liberation. More precisely, the continuous activity of seeing Buddha (*kenbutsu*) is the continuous activity of becoming Buddha (*gyobutsu*). Your life (sentient *existence*) is what you clearly see (sentient *experience*), what you clearly see is your life.

> So life is what I am making it, and I am what life is making me.
> Shobogenzo, Zenki[132]

With this we come to a point where we can appreciate the full significance of the passage that serves as the pivot of Dogen's *Maka-hannya-haramitsu*:

> In the order of Sakyamuni Tathagata there is a *bhiksu* who secretly thinks, "I shall bow in veneration of the profound *prajnaparamita*. Although in this state there is no appearance and disappearance of real *dharma*s, there are still understandable explanations of all precepts, all balanced states, all kinds of wisdom, all kinds of liberation, and all views. There are also understandable explanations of the fruit of one who has entered the stream, the fruit of [being subject to] one return, the fruit of [not being subject to] returning,

and the fruit of the arhat. There are also understandable explanations of [people of] independent awakening, and [people of] *bodhi*. There are also understandable explanations of the supreme right and balanced state of *bodhi*. There are also understandable explanations of the treasures of Buddha, Dharma, and Sangha. There are also understandable explanations of turning the wonderful Dharma wheel to save sentient beings." The Buddha, knowing the *bhiksu*'s mind, tells him, "This is how it is. This is how it is. The profound *prajnaparamita* is too subtle and fine to fathom."
Shobogenzo, Maka-hannya-haramitsu[133]

The thoughts of this monk (*bhiksu*) go to the heart of the reason of emptiness demonstrated by the vision of *Shobogenzo*; because there *is* no self and there *is* no other in the true multitudinous-oneness of emptiness, true, effective, *understandable* teachings *exist*. Unlike those enamored by and attached to the sublime power of the 'deconstructive' capacity of emptiness (i.e. 'form is emptiness'), this monk strives on, advancing to see *through* to the 'reconstructive' capacity of emptiness (i.e. 'form is form'). Thus, the Buddha says; 'This is how it is. This is how it is.'

There are understandable explanations. *There are* understandable explanations of precepts, balanced states, wisdom, and liberation. The no-self of emptiness does not mean that things are *not real*, that distinctions are *illusory*, or that the *reality* of things is *other than* the *appearance* of things. If such were the case, there would be no reason for Buddha, Dogen, or anyone else to waste time teaching or writing. Zen doctrine and methodology *exists* and *is* effective *because* particular Zen ancestors learned, understood, verified, and actualized *understandable explanations* of reality. Commenting on the monk's thought that, 'Although in this state there is no appearance and disappearance of real *dharmas, there are* still understandable explanations,' Dogen says:

> The *bhiksu*'s "secretly working concrete mind" at this moment is, in the state of bowing in veneration of real *dharmas, prajna* itself—whether or not [real *dharmas*] are without appearance and disappearance—and this is a "venerative bow" itself. Just at this moment of bowing in veneration, *prajna* is realized as explanations that can be understood: [explanations] from "precepts, balance, and wisdom," to "saving sentient beings," and so on. This state is described as being without. Explanations of the state of "being

> without" can thus be understood. Such is the profound, subtle, unfathomable *prajna paramita.*
> Shobogenzo, Maka-hannya-haramitsu[134]

The very act of this monk's 'bowing in veneration' is a manifestation of *prajna* made real (realized) *by* and *as* 'explanations that can be understood.' At the very moment a Zen practitioner encounters an explanation (say, by reading *Shobogenzo*) and thereby comes to an accurate understanding (i.e. is enlightened to a truth), an instance (i.e. a dharma) of *prajna* is actualized (made actual). This newborn dharma (an understanding) is empty – the 'explanation' (Dogen's writing), the 'encounter' (the practitioner's reading), the 'understanding' (the practitioner's insight), its 'particular significance' (the dharma's truth), its 'influence' (on the practitioner's conduct), and its 'effect' (on the world through the practitioner's conduct) are not its 'self', nor are they 'other than itself.' Thus prajna is realized (made real). 'This state' – in/of prajna being realized – is described as 'being without' (i.e. *mu*; emptiness).

Following the illumination of this monks 'secretly working concrete mind' Dogen goes on to underscore how actual, concrete instances of prajna are realized in the everyday world through the body-mind of sentient beings. To do so, Dogen makes creative use of a traditional story from Buddhist mythology. In this story, one of the gods (Indra) asks the Buddha's wisest disciple (Subhuti) how the profound doctrine of emptiness (*prajna-paramita*) should be studied and learned. The disciple responds by saying it should be studied as 'emptiness' (*koku*; space). At this point Dogen states:

> So studying *prajna* is space itself. Space is the study of *prajna.*
> Shobogenzo, Maka-hannya-haramitsu[135]

Apparently still not totally confident in his understanding of this, the god asks:

> "World-honored One! When good sons and daughters receive and retain, read and recite, think reasonably about, and expound to others this profound *prajnaparamita* that you have preached, how should I guard it? My only desire, World-honored One, is that you will show me compassion and teach me."
>   Then the venerable monk Subhūti says to the god Indra, "Kausika! Do you see something that you must guard, or not?"

> The god Indra says, "No, Virtuous One, I do not see anything here that I must guard."
> Subhūti says, "Kausika! When good sons and daughters abide in the profound *prajnaparamita* as thus preached, they are just guarding it. When good sons and daughters abide in the profound *prajnaparamita* as thus preached, they never stray. Remember, even if all human and nonhuman beings were looking for an opportunity to harm them, in the end it would be impossible. Kausika! If you want to guard the bodhisattvas who abide in the profound *prajnaparamita* as thus preached, it is no different from wanting to guard space."
> *Shobogenzo, Maka-hannya-haramitsu*[136]

Dogen goes on to emphasize the significance of this exchange by summarizing and clarifying the main points:

> Remember, to receive and retain, to read and recite, and to think reasonably about [*prajna*] are just to guard *prajna*. And to want to guard it is to receive and retain it, to read and recite it, and so on.
> *Shobogenzo, Maka-hannya-haramitsu*[137]

To conclude our survey of Dogen's treatment of emptiness in *Maka-hannya-haramitsu*, I turn to Hee-Jin Kim's translation and concluding notes of Dogen's final passage, the first line of which Kim translates:

> Therefore is Buddha the Holy One perfect wisdom.
> *Shobogenzo, Maka-hannya-haramitsu*[138]

Dr. Kim points out in a note on this line:

> In this paragraph Dogen expounds the nonduality of the Buddha and wisdom, of the personal and impersonal. He even boldly admonishes his disciples to honor and revere perfect wisdom.
> *Shobogenzo, Maka-hannya-haramitsu*[139]

The translation of the rest of the final passage runs:

> Perfect wisdom is all dharmas. These dharmas are empty in their form – no arising or perishing, no impurity or purity, no increasing or decreasing. The realization of this perfect wisdom is the realization of Buddha the Holy One. Inquire and practice: To honor and revere

[perfect wisdom] is indeed to respectfully meet and serve Buddha the Holy One; to meet and serve him is none other than to be Buddha the Holy One.
Shobogenzo, Maka-hannya-haramitsu[140]

Dr. Kim's note on this final passage reads:

The very act of respectfully meeting and serving is the buddha. This is in accordance with the notion of the enactment-buddha (*gyobutsu*), wherein enactment and buddha are one.
Hee-Jin Kim[141]

The Emptiness of the Self is the Emptiness of Other Than Self

It now is me, I now am not It.
Tung-Shan[142]

Because form is empty of *self* it is empty of *other than* self; having no self, form has no other. The same reasoning applies to emptiness; being empty of *self* it is empty of *other*. In accordance with the reason (*dori*) of the doctrine of emptiness, self is not-self, other is not-other, *therefore* self is self, other is other.

This flower is not-this flower, not-this flower is this flower, therefore this flower is this flower, not-this flower is not-this flower. This flower *is* 'no other than' emptiness (i.e. not-this flower); having no *self*, this flower can have no *other*. This flower is totally this flower *as it is*; this flower is empty, *therefore* (i.e. because it lacks a self) this flower is not-other than this flower (i.e. *there is nothing other than* this flower). To *clearly see* this flower is to clearly see the whole of space and time; practicing deep prajna-paramita we clearly see the whole of this particular flower is empty (i.e. is the totality of 'what' *is* 'this flower' and 'what' *is* 'not-this flower'). Thus we clearly see this flower (and by extension, each and all dharmas) includes and is included by each and all the myriad dharmas.

This is the reason (*dori*) of emptiness – the true nature of all things, beings, and events. All dharmas are empty, thus no dharma has/is an independent 'self,' therefore no dharma ever encounters anything 'other than' its self. This flower, that bird, and this thought are empty, thus there is nothing *other than* this flower, that bird, and this thought.

In the *Shobogenzo, Genjokoan* fascicle's elucidation of the nature and dynamics of Zen practice-enlightenment, Dogen brings our attention to the fact that when we *clearly see* dharmas *as they are* we 'sense something is lacking.' Significantly, *Shobogenzo, Genjokoan* does not state 'we sense something is *illusory,*' '*nonexistent,*' or '*unreal.*' To '*sense something is* lacking' is to *experience* (sense; epistemology) the *presence* (existence; ontology) of a 'real' something (i.e. a lack). It is the 'presence' of this 'lack' that is treated by the Buddhist doctrine of emptiness. To be aware of this presence in/as all dharmas is, in the words of the *Genjokoan* fascicle, to be 'enlightened about delusion' – to be unaware of this presence is to be 'deluded about enlightenment.'

Interdependence: The Duality of Nonduality

Deep down the consciousness of mankind is one. This is a virtual certainty because even in the vacuum matter is one; and if we don't see this, it's because we are blinding ourselves to it.
David Bohm[143]

Consciousness cannot be accounted for in physical terms. For consciousness is absolutely fundamental. It cannot be accounted for in terms of anything else.
Erwin Schrödinger[144]

With this, the groundwork is in place to further expand on the significance of nonduality by considering it in light of the Buddhist vision of interdependence. Until now we have only touched on the question as to how each particular dharma is total existence-time (i.e. the myriad dharmas) and total existence-time is each particular dharma. On this point it has been frequently observed that the existence of any particular dharma is *dependent on*, thus *inclusive of* all the myriad dharmas; this is the central principle of the Buddhist teaching of *interdependence*. Here we will consider more precisely the nature and the reason (*dori*) of the 'dependence' in question.

A dharma is an actual instance of total existence-time. Because all dharmas are *interdependent*, each particular dharma, for example, *this* book here-now, is the whole universe and every particular thing in it. To clearly see *this particular* book is to see total existence-time, fully inclusive of such particular aspects, for instance, as the planet Venus (as well as the sculpture), the apple of yesterday's lunch, and George Washington's teeth six minutes prior to his crossing of the Delaware. In other words, according to the principles of interdependence, to clearly see this particular book *is* to clearly see *that* planet, *that* apple, and *those* teeth as they are, and to clearly see total existence-time *as it is*.

To get a handle on how interdependence actually works, we can begin by envisioning a sheet of paper evenly divided into three sections, left, right, and middle, by two parallel lines. Notice that the middle section exists 'as it is' (i.e. as *the middle* section) *only* because *the left* and *the right* sections exist *as they are*:

	M I D D L E	

Without the right section, the middle section loses its particular quality of being; it would not be the 'middle,' but rather the 'right':

	M Now I R D I D G L H E T

The same reasoning applies in the absence of the left section:

	M Now I L D E D F L T E	

In the absence of both the right and left sections the middle would be the whole:

```
M  Now
I  The
D  W
D  H
L  O
E  L
   E
```

Thus, it is evident that the middle section is *only* actually and distinctly present *as it is* – the 'middle' – by virtue of the right and left sections being actually and distinctly present as they are – the 'right' and 'left.' In other words, the reality/appearance (existence/experience) of the middle section is only actualized (made actual) by the reality/appearance of the left and right sections. In terms of the *Diamond Sutra's* methodology; middle is left/right (not-middle), *therefore* middle is middle.

In sum, the existence of the particular form/essence unity 'middle,' *depends on* the existence of the particular form/essence unities 'left' and 'right.' The same reasoning applies to the existence of the particular form/essence unity 'right,' and the particular form/essence unity 'left.' Hence the existence of the 'middle,' 'left,' and 'right' are *interdependent*. In terms of the Buddhist notion of 'dharma-positions,' the *middle* 'abides in its dharma-position' *as* 'the middle' – it possesses a 'left' and a 'right' and, *at the same time,* it is distinct (or 'cut off') from 'left' and 'right.' The same reasoning (*dori*) applies to the left and right sections. This, then, is the basic reason of the connection/separation – the *interdependence* – of each dharma to/from the myriad dharmas and each dharma to/from each other dharma in/of total existence-time.

Accordingly, Venus, yesterday's apple, and Washington's teeth are integral to *this* book's reality (existence-time) *as it is* – if any of those dharmas were absent or even slightly altered from being 'as they are,' this book would not be *as it is* – the same goes for the planet, the apple, and the teeth. As a particular instance of total existence-time, *this* book appears *at* and *as* a specific, unique location-moment of existence-time. That is, each dharma abides *at* and *as* its *dharma-position*. As mentioned earlier, in *Shobogenzo*, the reason (*dori*) of each particular dharma being an expression of the whole universe is elucidated by Dogen's vision of 'the total exertion of a single dharma' (*ippo gujin*) which asserts and illustrates the nature and dynamics of the 'self-obstruction' or 'nonobstruction' of dharmas.

To illustrate this point and bring some important implications into relief, let's consider another dharma; the clinking sound of ice against glass from a pitcher of lemonade heard by Norma Jean at 2:27 July 17, 1879. That particular dharma *is* (i.e. exists as) *that* particular clinking sound *as it is*.

As a dharma, that particular clinking sound abides in, at, and as its dharma-position; it cannot be replaced or displaced by any other manifestation of existence-time, nor can it be transformed into something 'other than' it is, nor can it cease to exist as it is. That particular form of existence-time does not 'obstruct' any other particular form (i.e. it does not replace, usurp, or alter any other dharma) nor can it be 'obstructed' by any other – it is 'self-obstructive.' To go to that particular place-time is to go to that particular clinking sound. That particular clinking sound is identical to the place-time of its actualization – to be replaced, transformed, or annihilated would be to be 'obstructed' by another dharma or no-dharma, in which case total existence-time would not be *as it is*. The exact place and precise moment (Norma Jean's consciousness/2:27 July 17, 1879) of that dharma's actualization *is* exactly that place-time of total existence-time.

Another particular dharma, say, the little dog with the crooked leg that appears in Joe's dream September 9, 2012 is, as it is, the whole universe. That little dog 'totally exerts' the whole of existence-time. To clearly see that dog *as it is*, is to see total existence-time *as it is*. As a dharma, *that* particular form/essence unit of consciousness constitutes the whole universe as it is experienced/exists in/as that particular 'dharma-position' (Joe's consciousness/September 9, 2012) in/of total existence-time.

To fully discern the total reality of that particular dharma would be to discern the totality of *this* universe *as it is* – *that* particular dharma as it is 'totally exerts' the whole universe *as it is*. The place-time of the little dog is an expression of the myriad dharmas (total existence-time), including the clinking sound experienced by Norma Jean. To clearly see the little dog as it is, is to see the clinking sound as it is – the dog is the whole universe at/as that dharma-position, the whole universe at/as that dharma-position is the dog. The existence of the dog includes the existence of the clinking sound – the sound is *a particular* spatial-temporal aspect *of* the dog's form/essence as it is (i.e. the sound constitutes an actual place-time of the dog's existent past). The dog constitutes a particular place-time of the clinking sound (i.e. the dog is a real place-time *of* the sound's actual future).

All 'past' dharmas exist *as* the actual form/essence of a present dharma's past; all 'future' dharmas exist as the actual form/essence of a present dharma's future. Each and all particular dharmas are form/essence units constituted by/of all dharmas *forming* that dharma's past, all dharmas *forming* that dharma's future, and all dharmas *forming* that dharma's present. Likewise, dharmas are form/essence units constituted by/of the locations/places/spaces of all 'distant' dharmas *forming* that dharma's position. Thus, the appearance/reality of a particular dharma *consists of* a 'body' that is all-inclusive of space and time.

The reasoning (*dori*) of this principle applies to each and all the myriad dharmas. The place-time of Shakyamuni Buddha's enlightenment is the whole universe totally exerted at/as a particular place-time. The place-time of Shakyamuni's birth is total existence-time expressed at/as that specific location-time. Each is a particular instance of total existence-time, each contains and is contained by the other, neither obstructs nor is obstructed by the other – this is 'the total exertion of a single dharma' (*ippo gujin*).

Total existence-time at/as the place-time of Shakyamuni's enlightenment *exerts* and is *exerted by* the place-time of Shakyamuni's birth. Shakyamuni's birth *exerts* Shakyamuni's enlightenment *as* 140 miles *west* and 28 years *after*. The form/essence of Shakyamuni's enlightenment that exists *as* 140 miles east and 28 years prior, is Shakyamuni's birth. Likewise, total existence-time manifest in/as 'holding the door for an old man this afternoon in Albuquerque' is actualized in/as 'Shakyamuni's birth' – 'holding the door' exists *as the* 2500 years *after*, 8000 miles east *of* 'Shakyamuni's birth.'

Summary

In this section I have attempted to provide a reliable perspective of the reason (*dori*) of nonduality in light of the Buddhist teachings of emptiness and interdependence. To this end I tried to show how the reason (*dori*) of the 'nonduality of duality' and the 'duality of nonduality' exhaustively inform Zen doctrine and methodology, which can be seen as crystallized in the statement:

> "Form is emptiness, emptiness is form." That is, form is form, emptiness is emptiness.
> *Shobogenzo, Maka-hannya-haramitsu*[145]

During the course of this discussion we saw how Dogen's assertions that 'There are understandable explanations' both undermine distorted views of emptiness, and emphasize his view that effective teachings are intrinsic aspects of reality itself. Not only is emptiness *not* a denial of the reality of diversity (i.e. plurality of forms, e.g. *understandable explanations*), emptiness is the *reality of* diversity itself.

In our exploration we discussed how Zen's view of emptiness not only affirms the *reality* and *diversity* of the myriad dharmas, it affirms their *sentient nature*. If something exists, it is experienced (sentient), if it is not experienced it does not exist.

We also discussed Dogen's notion of 'the total exertion (or nonobstruction) of a single dharma' (*ippo gujin*) – the place-time (i.e. dharma-position) of a dharma is the whole of existence-time exerted at/as that particular place-time. Each particular dharma is an *actual*, *intrinsic*, and *essential* element of *this* universe *as it is*. In other words, each dharma presents (makes present) the whole universe, and the whole universe is presented (made present) by/as each dharma. In light of this reasoning (*dori*) *each* dharma, *all* dharmas, and *the whole universe* are not three different things – to see any one of these is to see all three, failing to see one of these is failing to see any of the three. The following passage helps clarify this reasoning, and suggests some of the profundity of its implications:

> He who knows but a single mote of dust knows the whole world: he who fully comprehends one thing comprehends all the myriad things that comprise the universe. He who fails to comprehend all the myriad things will not comprehend even one of them. When someone has fully trained himself in this principle of comprehending and has reached full comprehension, he will not only see the myriad things that comprise the universe but will also see each one of them. This is why the person who studies one mote of dust will undoubtedly be studying the whole universe.
> *Shobogenzo, Shoaku Makusa*[146]

This Sutra: Zen Expressions, Expressions of Zen

A bigoted believer in nihilism blasphemes against the sutras on the ground that literature [i.e., the Buddhist scriptures] is unnecessary [for the study of Buddhism]. If that were so, then neither would it be right for us to speak, since speech forms the substance of literature. He would also argue that in the direct method [literally, the straight path] literature is discarded. But does he appreciate that the two words 'is discarded' are also literature? Upon hearing others recite the sutras such a man would criticize the speakers as 'addicted to scriptural authority'. It is bad enough for him to confine this mistaken notion to himself, but in addition, he blasphemes against the Buddhist scriptures. You men should know that it is a serious offence to speak ill of the sutras, for the consequence is grave indeed!
Huineng[147]

When students are beginners, whether they have the mind of the Way or not, they should carefully read and study the Sagely Teachings of the sutras and shastras.
Eihei Dogen[148]

How sad is the aridity of contemporary Zen schools! They laud unintelligent ignorance as transcendental direct-pointing Zen. Considering unsurpassed spiritual treasures like Focusing the Precious Mirror and the Five Ranks to be worn-out utensils of an antiquated house, they pay no attention to them. They are like blind people throwing away their canes, saying they are useless, then getting themselves stuck in the mud of the view of elementary realization, never able to get out all their lives.
Hakuin Ekaku[149]

In order to understand Zen teachings we need to understand Zen's own view about the nature and role of teachings. First, Zen sees teachings *as* teachings – expressions that communicate knowledge. Accordingly *Zen* teachings are expressions that communicate the knowledge or wisdom of Zen. Second, Zen recognizes teachings are dharmas – particular forms of reality. Thus, in harmony with the principles of nonduality, the subjective and objective qualities of a Zen teaching constitute a unique unified instance of existence-time. The *appearance* and the *reality* of a Zen teaching are nondual – its *form* and its *essential nature,* constitute a *unified* reality. The significance of this is brought into relief by this passage from Huang Po:

> The preaching of the Tathagata is identical with the Dharma he taught, for there is no distinction between the preaching and the thing preached; just as there is none between such varied phenomena as the Glorified and Revealed Bodies of a Buddha, the Bodhisattvas, the Sravakas, the world-systems with their mountains and rivers, or water, birds, trees, forests and the rest. The preaching of the Dharma is at one and the same time both vocal and silent.
> Huang Po[150]

Dogen makes the same point more succinctly:

> Again, when we consider the concrete situation of the words of buddha, there is no case of them being preached separately from the voice.
> *Himitsu-shobogenzo, Butsu-kojo-no-ji*[151]

'The preaching of the Tathagata' or 'the words of Buddha' – the *form* of a Zen teaching – 'is identical with the Dharma he taught' or not separate 'from the voice' – the *essence* of a Zen teaching. In other words, a Zen teaching is an instance *of* Zen itself – a *form* of Zen that communicates the *reality* of Zen. Accordingly, a Zen *teaching*, whether it is a scripture, sermon, record, saying, gesture, symbol, ritual, or any other *form* is an instance of Zen *itself*.

Like other wisdom traditions, Zen/Buddhism refers to teachings with various terms and names, e.g. Dharma (teaching, law), Sutra (scripture), Sermon, etc. In *Shobogenzo, Shoho Jisso,* teachings are referred to as 'this sutra.' The commentary of this fascicle is based on a teaching from Buddhist scripture[152] concerning the 'nature of dharmas,' the main point of which is expressed, 'all dharmas are real form.' *Shobogenzo, Shoho Jisso* centers on a passage of the scripture wherein Shakyamuni Buddha asserts that the 'supreme enlightenment (*anuttara samyaksambodhi*) of all bodhisattvas' *belongs to* 'this sutra' and proclaims:

> This sutra opens the gate of expedient methods and reveals true real form.
> *Shobogenzo, Shoho Jisso*[153]

Dogen begins his comments by clarifying that 'bodhisattva' is synonymous with 'Buddha' asserting such are 'without differences in maturity' or 'excellence.' He then proceeds to underscore that this *expression itself* is 'in every case' *no other than* 'this sutra.' This move emphasizes the radical nonduality of *a Buddhist expression about* complete enlightenment and *complete enlightenment itself*. Dogen affirms this understanding of the passage by highlighting a significant implication; *the experience of* (i.e. subjective encounter with) 'this sutra' and *what is experienced* (i.e. objectively encountered) *as* 'this sutra' are *coessential elements of* 'this sutra' itself – the subject and object *of* this 'sutra' *are* 'this sutra':

> The subject of "belonging" and the object of "belonging" are both "this sutra."
> *Shobogenzo, Shoho Jisso*[154]

While Dogen's expression is perfectly clear, what it says is so alien to the common worldview it might fail to register without close attention. For example, since the common view presupposes objective reality to exist independently of subjective reality, it might be easy to overlook that Dogen's contention – that *both* the subject *and* object of 'this sutra' *are* 'this sutra' – means *the one* experiencing 'this sutra' and *what* is experienced *as* 'this sutra' are *not two* different realities. According to Dogen's reasoning (*dori*) here, *existent* Zen teachings ('this sutra') *experience* Zen teachings. From the perspective of a cosmology grounded in dualism this is nonsensical; from the perspective of a nondual cosmology it is self-evident. Indeed, in a nondual cosmology not only is the unity of *expresser* and *expressed* obvious, the interdependent nature of *all* aspects of subjective and objective reality is explicitly established. If so, when *you* experience 'this sutra,' *this sutra* experiences 'you.' As Dogen puts it:

> At this very moment, 'this sutra' really experiences 'all bodhisattvas.'
> *Shobogenzo, Shoho Jisso*[155]

This makes it obvious why it is not possible to arrive at an accurate appreciation of Zen from the perspective of the prevailing cosmology (or any view grounded in dualism). Zen teachings about reality cannot be understood from a perspective of dualism because reality is nondual. *Any understanding of Zen that is arrived at from such a perspective will inevitably be a wrong understanding.* Attempting to understand nondual teachings from a perspective grounded on dualism would be like, in Zen terms, attempting to go South by heading toward the North Star.

Dogen's elucidation on the nature of Zen expressions includes this observation:

> The sutra is not sentient, the sutra is not insentient, the sutra is not the product of doing and the sutra is not the product of nondoing.
> *Shobogenzo, Shoho Jisso*[156]

This statement can be seen as accounting for the fact that Zen expressions (this sutra), like all dharmas, need to be understood in light of the reason (*dori*) of nonduality. Briefly, 'this sutra', being *empty* (like all dharmas), is not sentient *or* insentient, not a product of doing *or* nondoing. Sentient and insentient are two *foci* of a *unified* (nondual) reality; they are interdependent, *coessential* and *coextensive*. The way up and the way down are not to be thought of in terms of either/or, but in terms of and/also. The way up *is* the way down, sentient *is* insentient, doing *is* nondoing. 'Sentient' is meaningless without 'insentient,' any actual 'product of doing' is and must be *equally* 'a product of nondoing.' The point is that 'this sutra' (and by extension, any actual Zen teaching) is not 'made up of' these or those *attributes*, and cannot be 'reduced to' this or that *quality*; this sutra is, *as it is*, this sutra.

It should be noted that while Dogen's expression is structured in negative terms – *not* this, *not* that – it is not apophatic (i.e. Dogen is not denying the experiential, communicable, or intelligible nature of 'this sutra'). In a moment we will see that Dogen does not confine himself to asserting what 'this sutra' is *not*, but also offers assertions as to what it *is*. First, however, I want to notice how simply recognizing 'this sutra' is a dharma tells us a number of other things 'this sutra' is *not*. For instance, this sutra is *not* 'confined to a special realm, state, or condition,' is *not* 'indescribable,' is *not* 'incommunicable,' is *not* 'transcendent to language,' and is *not* 'inaccessible to normal human experience and understanding.'

With this, then, we are ready to notice that the principles of nonduality *impose* whatever 'is not' expressed upon whatever 'is' expressed. In short, a Zen expression that *explicitly* asserts something 'is not' *implicitly* asserts *that same* something 'is.' For example, to *explicitly* assert 'this sutra *is not* sentient, *is not* insentient' is to *implicitly* assert 'this sutra *is* sentient, *is* insentient.' Accordingly, Zen teachings are clearly not confined to merely expressing what 'Zen,' 'enlightenment,' 'Buddha,' 'true nature,' or anything else is *not*, as suggested by many contemporary works on Zen. With this, then, let's see how Dogen's instruction not only asserts what 'this sutra' *is not* or *does not* do, but also asserts what 'this sutra' *is* and *does*:

> Even so, when it experiences *bodhi,* experiences people, experiences real form, and experiences "this sutra," it "opens the gate of expedient methods." "The gate of expedient methods" is the supreme virtue of the Buddha's ultimate state, it is "the Dharma abiding in the Dharma's place," and it is "the form of the world abiding in constancy." The gate of expedient methods is not a temporary artifice; it is the learning in practice of the whole universe in ten directions, and it is learning in practice that exploits the real form of all *dharma*s.
> *Shobogenzo, Shoho Jisso*[157]

Now we are ready to consider the important notion of 'expedient methods' (*upaya*), more commonly translated as 'expedient means' or 'skillful means.' From the nondual perspective, the expedient methods of Zen are seen as the *phenomenal form* or *forms* of Zen. For *each* and *all* the elements that make Zen accessible to human beings are Zen's expedient means. In other words, besides its expedient means there is no method, teaching, or other reality at any place or time that could be actualized, much less described as 'Zen.' In fewer words, Zen's 'expedient means' is 'Zen as it is.'

In the most general sense 'expedient means' include the entire range of Zen/Buddhist doctrine and methodology. In a less general sense, 'expedient means' emphasize specific skills and techniques particular to Zen/Buddhism. Also, like the 'expedient means' of law or of medicine, for example, the term 'expedient means' in Zen tends to underscore the fact that all *actual manifestations* of Zen are only realized in and as the *active* engagement of Zen practice-enlightenment. In other words, just as law or medicine is only realized (made real) in and as the *active application* of the *means* specific to law or medicine, Zen is only realized in and as the *active application* of the *means* specific to Zen. In sum, Zen's 'expedient means' need to be understood in light of the fact that the only *actual manifestation of* Zen is *realized* Zen, and the only realized Zen is that *actually performed* in and as its expedient means – the *ends* and *means* of Zen are nondual.

Like those of law or medicine, the skillful means of Zen consist of many and various particular elements. Each particular 'skillful means' can be accurately identified as 'Zen' but Zen cannot be identified as any particular 'skillful means.'

To clarify, in law, for example, entering a plea, presenting evidence, and making a closing argument *all* constitute 'skillful means.' At the same time, each is a *particular* aspect with *unique* characteristics. Accordingly, presenting evidence, entering a plea, or making a closing argument *can* be accurately identified as 'law,' but to identify law as presenting evidence, entering a plea, or making a closing argument would be to *reduce* the true nature of law to one *abstract element* of law. Likewise, writing a treatise, sitting in meditation, or providing instruction can each be accurately identified as 'Zen,' but to identify Zen as writing a treatise, sitting in meditation, or providing instruction would be to *reduce* the reality of Zen to an *abstract element* of Zen. Therefore, *any* view that identifies the 'skillful means' of Zen as one or more *particular elements of* Zen, demonstrates a distorted view of *both* 'skillful means' and 'Zen.'

I stress this point because I see the widespread misunderstanding of Zen's expedient means as a major factor in the perpetuation of many distorted notions about Zen. Contemporary accounts of the skillful means of Zen tend to skew their true significance by focusing almost exclusively on 'provisional' or 'temporary' elements of skillful means. The fact that some classic Zen records, when read from a dualistic perspective, can also appear to emphasize provisional aspects of skillful means does little to clarify the issue. In any case, the concentration on provisional qualities, combined with a near absence of attention to non-provisional qualities has resulted in widespread views of skillful means as little more than non-essential *supplements* to 'real' Zen, mere 'temporary devices' useful only for guiding beginners or dull minded students.

Contemporary works frequently explain expedient means in terms of a traditional Buddhist analogy that liken 'skillful means' to 'a raft used to reach the other shore.' A raft, it is explained, serves as the *means* to an *end*; reaching the other shore – as *a raft* is discarded upon *reaching the other shore*, the *skillful means* of Buddhism are discarded upon *reaching enlightenment*. Another favorite is the traditional Zen analogy of a 'finger pointing to the moon' and 'the perception of the moon' – the pointing finger, we are told, has no *intrinsic value* but is merely an *instrumental means* to a *real end*; the perception of the moon; likewise, the *skillful means* of Zen have *no intrinsic value* but are *merely instrumental* for directing us to enlightenment.

The emphasis in contemporary accounts along with the unquestionable effectiveness demonstrated by certain provisional and temporary devices make it too easy to overlook the fact that there is much, much more to Buddhism's skillful means. As Dogen's comment above asserts, skillful means is 'not a temporary artifice.' Despite dualistic interpretations to the contrary, the 'non-provisional' 'non-temporary' qualities of skillful means is in fact consistently emphasized in the classic Zen records. For example:

> There is originally no word for truth, but the way to it is revealed by words. The way originally has no explanation, but reality is made by explanation.
> Shih-shuang[158]

> There are four kinds of people who study. The highest are those with practice, with understanding, and with realization. Next are those with understanding, and with realization but without practice. Next are those with practice and understanding but without realization. Lowest are those with practice, but without understanding or realization.
> *Zen Dawn*[159]

> There is another type of Zen teacher who tells people not to make logical assessments, that they lose contact the minute they speak, and should recognize the primordial. This kind of 'teacher' has no explanation at all. This is like sitting on a balloon—where is there any comfort in it? It is also like the croaking of a bullfrog. If you entertain such a view, it is like being trapped in a black fog.
> Foyan[160]

> I have observed that people of the present time who are cultivating their minds do not depend on the guidance of the written teachings, but straightaway assume that the successive transmission of the esoteric idea [of Son] is the path. They then sit around dozing with their presence of mind in agitation and confusion during their practice of meditation. For these reasons, I feel you should follow words and teachings which were expounded in accordance with reality in order to determine the proper procedure in regard to

awakening and cultivation. Once you mirror your own minds, you may contemplate with insight at all times, without wasting any of your efforts.
Chinul[161]

If the true significance of skillful means is frequently muddled in modern accounts on the subject, *Shobogenzo* is adamant and unequivocally clear; provisional or temporary expedients may be used as skillful means in Zen, but skillful means are absolutely *not* provisional or temporary aspects of Zen. Nevertheless, the intrinsic, enduring aspect of skillful means that Dogen calls the 'supreme virtue of Buddhas ultimate state,' the 'form of the world abiding in constancy,' and '*not* a temporary artifice,' continues to be widely neglected.

Fortunately some contemporary scholars have consistently underscored the folly of notions that 'real' Zen is something that somehow exists independently of Zen doctrine and methodology. The works of Hee-Jin Kim, for example, clearly demonstrate how Dogen's Zen is utterly beyond the capacity of anyone that ascribes to such superficial notions of expedient means. *Shobogenzo's* vision of Zen radically rejects the slightest hint of dualism, thus utterly denies any and all possible notions of Zen/Buddhism as dualistically divided into 'means' and 'ends.' From the Zen perspective, the notion that 'using a raft' and 'reaching the other shore' could possibly exist independently of each other not only diverges from the truth of nonduality, it subverts it.

The *means* of Zen and the *ends* of Zen are not two different realities of Zen. The skin, flesh, bones, or marrow *independent* of a whole body-mind are dead, useless, and meaningless; and a whole body-mind *independent* of skin, flesh, bones, or marrow is dead, useless, and meaningless – for skin, flesh, bones, and marrow are *interdependent* constituents of a whole body-mind; and a whole body-mind consists of the *interdependence* of skin, flesh, bones, and marrow. Likewise, each of the various *skillful means* of Zen is the whole body-mind of Zen. The whole depends on the particulars, the particulars depend on the whole, and each particular depends on each and all particulars.

To sum up: as total existence-time is the myriad dharmas and the myriad dharmas are total existence-time, so Zen is the many skillful means and the many skillful means are Zen. Zen is not sentient, Zen is not insentient, Zen is not a product of action, Zen is not a product of nonaction; Zen *is* the means/ends, the using-a-raft/reaching-the-other-shore, that is the actualization of the universe (*genjokoan*).

Zen Cosmology

All events are coordinated... All things depend on each other; as has been said, 'Everything breathes together.'
Plotinus[162]

Because [real existence] is only this exact moment, all moments of existence-time are the whole of time, and all existent things and all existent phenomena are time. The whole of existence, the whole universe, exists in individual moments of time. Let us pause to reflect whether or not any of the whole of existence or any of the whole universe has leaked away from the present moment of time.
Shobogenzo, Uji[163]

Zen Master Banzan Hoshaku says:

Mind-moon, alone and round.
Light swallows myriad phenomena.
Light does not illuminate objects,
Neither do objects exist.
Light and objects both vanish,
This is what?

What has now been expressed is that the Buddhist patriarchs and the Buddha's disciples always have the state of 'mind-moon.' Because we see the moon as the mind, it is not the mind unless it is the moon, and there is no moon which is not the mind. 'Alone and round' means lacking nothing. That which is beyond two and three is called 'myriad phenomena.' 'Myriad phenomena,' being moonlight itself, are beyond 'myriad phenomena'; therefore 'light swallows myriad phenomena.'
Shobogenzo, Tsuki[164]

Clearly, the recognition that the 'known world' and the 'knowing subject' are nondual not only *invalidates* the prevailing worldview, it *diametrically contradicts* it. According to the common view, 'knowledge *of* reality' exists *independently* of 'reality *itself.*' For example, your 'knowledge of a tree' is regarded as a *product of your mind* (or brain) while 'a tree itself' is regarded as a *product of the external world*, and each of these 'products' are regarded as existing *independently* of the other. Knowledge of a tree is *one reality*, and a tree itself is *another, different reality*. Obviously, this view is directly opposed by the view that 'known' and 'knower' are nondual.

Our worldview *determines* how we think, speak, and act in the world. If reality is nondual, then ascribing to the prevailing worldview (or any view grounded in dualism) *compels* us to think, speak, and act in a way that diverges from how the world actually is.

How long it might take the scientific world, much less the general community, to accept the evidence for nonduality and adapt itself accordingly is anyone's guess. Efforts by groups and individuals within the sciences and other realms of civilization continue to progress, but contemporary advances remain far short of what is needed; a comprehensive nondual worldview. Fortunately Zen, having continuously developed and refined its understanding of nonduality for centuries, has a wealth of knowledge and wisdom to contribute to these efforts. It is my conviction that when contemporary discoveries and insights are seen in light of Zen's recognition of the nondual nature of 'knowledge' or 'experience' (epistemology) and 'being' or 'existence' (ontology), much that is wanting in current attempts to establish a reliable worldview will be brought into relief.

The Mental Nature of Reality – The Real Nature of Mentality

To Dogen, mind was at once knowledge and reality, at once the knowing subject and the known object, yet it transcended them both at the same time. In this nondual conception of mind, what one knew was what one was—and ontology, epistemology, and soteriology were inseparably united. This was also his interpretation of the Hua-yen tenet 'The triple world is mind-only.' From this vantage point, Dogen guarded himself against the inherent weaknesses of the two strands of Buddhist idealism: the advocacy of the functions of mind (*shinso*) by the school of consciousness-only and the advocacy of the essence of mind (*shinsho*) by the school of *tathagata-garbha*—both of which were vulnerable to a dualism between phenomena and essence. Thus, philosophically speaking, Dogen maneuvered between monistic pantheism and reductionistic phenomenalism. Hee-Jin Kim[165]

From its very beginning Buddhism has emphasized the mental nature of reality. The first verse of the *Dhammapada*, one of the earliest and most revered expressions of Buddhism, reads:

> We are what we think.
> All that we are arises with our thoughts.
> With our thoughts we make the world.
> *Dhammapada*[166]

'What we know' and 'what we are' are not two different realities. In a general sense, then, the epistemology of Buddhism can be understood to be a form of 'idealism.' And, while Buddhist idealism differs from western forms, its key notion, most commonly expressed in terms of Berkeley's, *esse est percipi*; 'to be is to be perceived,' is in full agreement, granted the Buddhist understanding of 'being' and 'perception' are accounted for. In short, like most western forms of idealism, Zen recognizes reality as essentially *mental* in nature. 'To be is to be perceived,' or 'to exist is to be experienced' – *the existence* of something is *dependent on* its *being experienced*.

The logic of this reason, being unfettered by dependence on unverifiable assumptions, is more comprehensive than the logic of the reason informing the prevailing epistemology, but the fact that this reason appeals not to external authority, but to direct personal experience is what truly makes it warrant serious consideration.

The reasoning of the nonduality of 'knower' and 'known' in Zen is clearly presented in an early fascicle of *Shobogenzo* titled, *Soku Shin Ze Butsu*; This Mind is Buddha. 'Buddha' is 'Butsu,' 'this mind' is 'soku shin'; 'shin' means 'mind' and 'soku' means 'here-now' or 'this.' '*Soku Shin Ze Butsu*' is translated by Gudo Nishijima & Mike Cross as, 'mind here and now is buddha.' In this fascicle Dogen assures us:

> What every buddha and every patriarch has maintained and relied upon, without exception, is just 'mind here and now is buddha.'
> *Shobogenzo, Soku-shin-ze-butsu*[167]

This fundamental principle – This Mind is Buddha – is presupposed throughout the classic literature of Zen. Comprehensive, multifaceted Buddhist teachings on the nature and dynamics of 'this mind' constitute many of Buddhism's most profound expressions, and some of its most often misunderstood and misrepresented expressions. Dogen and other

Zen masters before and after dedicated much time and energy clarifying what it actually means to assert, 'We are what we think' or 'mind here and now is Buddha.' For instance, Dogen went to lengths to carefully explain that 'this mind' (that 'is Buddha') is all-inclusive; the 'one totality' – whatever is, *is* this mind, all that is, *is* Buddha.

Dogen was also persistent in stressing that when the Zen masters identify the 'one mind' *as* the 'myriad dharmas' they are not speaking generally or arbitrarily. 'The many' is not *reducible to* 'the 'one,' 'the one' is not *made-up of* 'the many' – 'the one' is *identical to* 'the many' and vice versa. Just as 'one family' is constituted of and by 'all its particular members,' the 'one universe' is constituted of and by 'all its particular times-and-places.' In short, as 'all its members' *is* 'a family,' 'the myriad dharmas' *is* 'the universe.' Dogen clarifies:

> 'The mind that has been authentically transmitted' means one mind as all *dharma*s, and all *dharma*s as one mind.
> *Shobogenzo, Soku-shin-ze-butsu*[168]

'Buddha' and 'one mind' are not different things – 'this mind *is* Buddha,' and 'Buddha' *is* 'all dharmas.' If 'all dharmas' *is* 'one mind,' then each and every '*particular* dharma' – being an *essential* element of '*all* dharmas' – is mind (or Buddha). Thus Buddha (or mind) is *all* dharmas, therefore is *each* and *every* particular dharma.

> Clearly, 'mind' is mountains, rivers, and the earth, the sun, the moon, and the stars.
> *Shobogenzo, Soku-shin-ze-butsu*[169]

Buddha – mind – *is* (*not*, 'is like') mountains, rivers, and the earth, the sun, moon, and stars. Mind *is* houses and streets, animals, guns, plants, thoughts, bombs, corpses, laughter, and cancers. Mind *is* all particular dharmas *as they are*; *particular* dharmas. All particular dharmas *are* this mind *as it is; this* mind. This tree *is* the mind *as it is*, the mind *as it is*, is all dharmas, hence *is* this tree. That this tree is mind 'as it is,' means mind only exists *as mind* by virtue of this tree existing *as this tree*. Because this tree *is* mind 'as it is,' it actually goes too far to say 'is mind,' and is more accurate to simply say 'this tree.' As Dogen puts it:

> Mind as mountains, rivers, and the earth is nothing other than mountains, rivers, and the earth. There are no additional waves or

> surf, no wind or smoke. Mind as the sun, the moon, and the stars is nothing other than the sun, the moon, and the stars.
> Shobogenzo, Soku-shin-ze-butsu[170]

The point to get is that, in Zen, it is not dharmas *in general* but *particular* dharmas that are recognized as the fundamental elements, or better *activity*, of the universe *as it is*. The universe spoken of by *Shobogenzo* as 'this mind,' 'Buddha,' 'one mind,' or 'all dharmas' is not merely *the sum* of all things or *the totality* of everything throughout space and time; it is *the very things* and *events* you are experiencing right here-now (*soku*), it is the very *you right here-now* experiencing things and events. The very things, events, and you that right here-now is 'this mind' are not arbitrary miscellany or various generalities; but the actual mountains, rivers, and earth *you see* here-now, *the* sun, *the* moon, *the* stars here-now.

If, as Zen contends, 'to exist is to be experienced,' then it is also accurate to say 'to be experienced is to exist.' Thus dharmas are not only *what* we experience, but also the *means whereby* we experience. The sun, for example, is *what* we see and feel as the sun, and the sun is *how* we see and feel the sun. Likewise, Zen teachings are *what* we read/hear/understand as Zen teachings, and Zen teachings are *how* we read/hear/understand Zen teachings.

Existence is Experience

> Consciousness is never experienced in the plural, only in the singular. Not only has none of us ever experienced more than one consciousness, but there is also no trace of circumstantial evidence of this ever happening anywhere in the world. If I say that there cannot be more than one consciousness in the same mind, this seems a blunt tautology — we are quite unable to imagine the contrary...
> Erwin Schrödinger[171]

> Enlightenment by oneself without a teacher (*mushi dokugo*).
> Zen axiom (Zen's standard for 'authenticity')

> Do not add legs to a snake.
> Zen Proverb (Zen's version of Ockham's Razor[172])

The classic literature of Zen bristles with assertions insisting that 'enlightenment' – the capacity to see the true nature of reality (i.e. dharmas) – is not something that exists 'objectively,' like a teaching to learn or discover, or something that exists 'subjectively,' like a potential capacity to activate or attain. Enlightenment, the Zen masters assure us, is our birthright; it is and always has been immediately active and accessible here-now (*soku*) and nowhere else. The refrain in the classic records is so constant as to be nearly continuous; the true nature of dharmas is precisely what is manifesting before your very eyes here-now. 'Look, look,' the masters assert, 'To see is to see true nature; seeing *is* true nature, true nature *is* seeing.' To be (ontology; existence) is to be experienced (epistemology; knowledge), our *existence* is *exactly* our *experience* here-now; our *experience* is *exactly* our *existence* here-now – this (here-now; *soku*) mind *is* Buddha.

To hold that a reality exists above, beyond, or otherwise *independent of* one's experience or knowledge of reality, is to *supplement* one's view of knowledge (epistemology) with an abstract concept. Moreover, because the concept in this case not only lacks any basis in experience but contradicts it, to truly hold such a view is to bestow more trust in *a hypothetical notion* than in *one's actual experience*. In short, an epistemology that presupposes a reality that exists *independent of* one's knowledge not only presupposes the *unreliability of* one's own experiential capacities, it does so *irrationally*. To supplement a view with an unfounded and *unnecessary* conjecture is to *add complexity* to it *for no reason* – in Zen this is called 'adding legs to a snake,' in science it is known as 'Ockham's Razor.'

To be (exist) is to be experienced (conscious, known; epistemology), to be experienced is to be. To see is to believe (realize; make real); to believe is to see.

Believing a reality *exists* in the absence of *experience of* that reality is idolatry; reifying a *purely abstract concept* (i.e. a hypothetical assumption). Idolatry entails accepting as 'true' or 'real' something one has not experienced, hence something that is in direct contrast to one's actual knowledge. Idolatry, then, not only involves granting 'truth' to a mere conjecture, but granting *more* trust to an external authority (e.g. orthodoxy, dogma, consensus, etc.) than to the evidence of one's own actual experience.

Contemporary cosmology qualifies as idolatry in the above sense in that it *begins* by accepting *as true* the mere hypothesis, 'reality is *not* what it *appears* to be' (i.e. what we *experience as* reality, is *not* reality itself). In contrast, Zen cosmology begins by *recognizing* the truism, 'what we *experience as* reality is *the only* reality we will ever experience' (i.e. that 'reality *is* what is experienced' is self-evident). Thus, Zen not only refuses to accept notions *about* reality that are contrary to our *actual experience of* reality, it denigrates the practice of purely speculative conceptualization, which it recognizes as not merely futile, but harmful.[173] Again, where the common worldview asserts the inherent unreliability of subjective reality (i.e. the realm of experience or knowledge), Zen recognizes subjective reality as the *only* realm wherein things, beings, and events are encountered and ever could be encountered. Further, where the common view sees 'imperfection' or 'unreliability' as the epitome (hence 'normality') of the human condition (e.g. to err is human, *only* human, etc.), Zen recognizes 'Buddhahood' as human normality, and the normal subjective capacities of human beings as the 'mystical powers and wondrous functions' of Buddha. In *Shobogenzo, Jinzū*, for example, Dogen appeals to the famous Zen expression of Layman Pang to elucidate the point:

> The mystical power and wondrous function,
> Carrying water and lugging firewood.
>
> We must investigate this truth thoroughly. 'Carrying water' means loading water and fetching it. There being our own work and self-motivation, and there being the work of others and the motivation of others, water is caused to be carried. This is just the state of mystically powerful buddha.
> *Shobogenzo, Jinzū*[174]

The true nature of normal human experience/existence is the 'mystical power and wondrous function' also called 'the six mystical powers' of 'Buddha alone together with Buddha.' To emphasize that Layman Pang's expression identifying these 'powers' is not some kind of esoteric message but means exactly what it says, Dogen points out that 'carrying water' means 'loading water and fetching it.' To make it absolutely clear that the 'mystical power and wondrous function' of Buddha is not anything other than 'normal human capacities,' Dogen goes on in the same fascicle to clearly identify the 'six mystical powers' as the 'six senses' of normal human subjectivity (i.e. seeing, hearing, smelling, tasting, feeling, and thinking).[175]

From the nondual perspective, our subjective capacities for knowledge or experience, and the objective elements that are known or experienced are a single unified reality. This mind (or Buddha) that sees, hears, smells, tastes, feels, and thinks, *is* the myriad dharmas that are seen, heard, smelled, tasted, felt, and thought. This mind/the myriad dharmas is not, as the common view supposes, something to be wary of; our mind is not out to mug us.

Of course Zen recognizes there are valid reasons to doubt sensation, perception, conception, etc. (e.g. illness, injury, wrong views, etc.), but it does insist on acknowledging the fact that there is no valid reason for accepting the purely hypothetical notion that reality is 'other than' it appears to be. It is intrinsically irrational to posit the existence of a reality we cannot experience; if such a reality existed it would, by definition, be *inherently unverifiable*. Recognizing unverifiable notions *as they are – unverifiable* – Zen recognizes them as not simply irrelevant but, in that they can only *add unnecessary complications* to our understanding, in the spirit of Ockham's Razor, are contrary to sound reason.

Where the common view finds 'inherent fallibility' in the 'all too' human condition, Zen sees the 'inherent fallibility' of any 'reason' that asserts the inferiority of subjective knowledge or the superiority of objective knowledge. The Zen axiom 'Enlightenment by oneself without a teacher' (*mushi dokugo*) is not a doctrine, precept, or revelation to be discovered, learned, accepted, or acquired through any external authority (e.g. system of thought, consensus, code, religion, etc.); it is a truth to make self-evident through personal experiential verification.

In direct observation we do not find our normal capacities for experiencing or knowing reality to be unreliable. Just the opposite, we find the reliability of our experiential capacities to be self-evident; our direct personal observation confirms that reality is *exactly as it appears* to be, it is *precisely as we experience*. We don't think twice about negotiating a staircase or diving into a pool, our hand finds the cup exactly where our eyes tell us it is, the snake on our path is duly noticed, though we are not on the lookout for snakes. Seeing, verification, knowing, existing; these are not different things.

The aspiration for enlightenment (*bodhicitta*), according to Zen, is an inherent quality of the human condition. Indeed, when we directly observe our own knowledge/experience our desire to know ourself is self-evident. And just as water is naturally available for the fulfillment of our inherent desire to slake our thirst, the myriad dharmas are naturally available for the fulfillment of our inherent desire for self-knowledge. We know we *can* slake our thirst (i.e. water exists) from the fact that we *want* to slake our thirst. We know we can realize enlightenment from the fact that we want to realize enlightenment.

> We know that we are "people who are it" just from the fact that we want to attain "the matter that is it." Already we possess the real features of a "person who is it"; we should not worry about the already present "matter that is it." Even worry itself is just "the matter that is it," and so it is beyond worry. Again, we should not be surprised that "the matter that is it" is present in such a state. Even if "it" is the object of surprise and wonderment, it is still just "it." And there is "it" about which we should not be surprised.
> *Shobogenzo, Inmo*[176]

Now, any attempt to fulfill our inherent desire to know ourself that begins from the assumption that our 'self' is something that is not experienced (hence does not exist) will be as futile, and as detrimental, as attempting slake our thirst by beginning from the assumption that what does not exist is water. Whether we know it or not, water *as it is* exists and can fulfill our desire to slake our thirst. Likewise, whether we know or do not know ourselves, our 'self' is total existence-time, not one dharma of the myriad dharmas is other than ourself.

> To seek to know ourself is the inevitable will of the living. But those with Eyes that see themselves are few: buddhas alone know this state. Others, non-Buddhists and the like, vainly consider only what does not exist to be their self. What buddhas call themselves is just the whole earth. In sum, in all instances, whether we know or do not know ourselves, there is no whole earth that is other than ourself.
> *Shobogenzo, Yui-butsu-yo-butsu*[177]

Zen is concerned only with the truth or 'the great matter of life-and-death,' thus is interested only in what *can be* known, what *can be* experienced. Therefore, Zen's interest in dualism is limited to revealing its inherent perniciousness, that it can *only* obscure one's vision. Accordingly, Zen expressions about the nondual nature of reality are more affirmations of truth, than they are refutations of fallacies. For seeing reality as nondual is not only seeing reality *as it is*, it is seeing it exactly *as it appears to be*. In short, to see reality as nondual requires nothing more than abstaining from attributing it with an unexperienced and unapparent 'something' (e.g. independent objectivity, an unseen force, a hidden essence, etc.).

In contrast, ascribing to dualism requires one to affirm that, contrary to our actual experience, reality is *not as it appears*, even that reality is *as it cannot appear.* While the human capacities for speculation and imagination are certainly capable of concocting bizarre and unverifiable notions, only the human capacities for vanity and folly are capable of granting them greater credence than actual experience.

For centuries proponents of dualism have made countless attempts to account for the 'real' distinction between the *known* or *experienced* world and the *actual* world; none have succeeded. Nevertheless, nearly all those regarded as the 'great minds of western civilization' have uncritically accepted the 'truth' that 'the world we *know*' is *not* 'the *real* world' – thus billions of us are informed by an *unquestioning conviction* that the 'real world' is both 'other' and 'more fundamental' than the world we see and know.

It seems incredible that so many could be so convinced in the unreliability of their own eyes by ungrounded assertions about the existence of an *undetected, unverifiable* reality. Yet the common view continues to be *the common* view; reality is not what *we see*, but what *others say*. Nevermind that the *actual experience* of such proponents is *exactly the same* as that of the three year-old child not yet 'enlightened to the fact' that the world *she sees* is not the *real* world but merely a representation inside her skull.

Here it is worth noticing that what makes an independent reality *unverifiable* – verification would disqualify it *as* 'independent' – also makes it *irrefutable* (i.e. it cannot be disproved). There is no way to falsify something that *cannot be known*. This fact has not gone unnoticed by abstract speculators – or charlatans. In truth, it has served as a talisman of ultimate *immunity from reason* for both species by providing an ever-available escape; *ineffability*, the magic cloak of cultic obscurity, esotericism, and mystical mumbo-jumbo of all kinds.

This brings us to another point. Despite popular stereotypes, the classic Zen records scorn esotericism, innuendo, irrationality, anti-intellectualism, and every other camouflaged form of escape from obligations to clearly and comprehensively elucidate Zen doctrine and methodology. Zen expressions are designed to enlighten, not confuse. In light of this, if Zen expressions *appear* cryptic, bizarre, or non-responsive, we would do well to reconsider our perspective. For authentic Zen expressions are *never* cryptic, bizarre, or non-responsive, but *always* direct, appropriate, and demonstrative. On a related note, the fact that Zen expressions are often succinct, and commonly use abbreviations to allude to classic sources, does not mean Zen teachings are not comprehensive or explanatory. For example, Zen does not simply assert that dualism is futile, obstructive, and perniciousness, it comprehensively elucidates the fallacious nature of its reason and directly demonstrates its irrelevance by pointing out, for instance, that if our *knowledge of* reality truly was distinct from the *true nature of* reality, we could *never know it*.

Objects of Consciousness

To verify the truth of Zen's view that existence (ontology) and experience (epistemology) are nondual is to recognize that whatever is true concerning *existence* must also be true of *experience* (and vice versa). To clarify the significance of this and bring some important implications to light, I want to turn to the traditional Buddhist device of considering consciousness as divided into 'six modes.'

Briefly, this traditional Buddhist system recognizes consciousness as functioning in six distinct modes, each of which is constituted of a sense organ, a sense field, and a sense capacity.[178] The six sense organs, together with the six sense fields, and the six sense capacities constitute the elements or realms of the human sensorium[179], which Buddhism calls the 'eighteen *dhatus*' (realms). From the Zen/Buddhist perspective the sensorium constitutes the totality of existence-time. As Dan Lusthaus observes:

> These eighteen *dhatus* constitute the sensorium, and according to Buddhism the sensorium is all-inclusive. Buddha forcefully makes that point in the Sabba sutta (sutra) of the Samyutta Nikaya (4.15). When asked 'What is everything?' (sabba), i.e. describe what is the case exhaustively and inclusively, Buddha replies as follows:
>
> > At Savatthi... the Exalted One said: –
> > 'Brethren, I will teach you 'the all' [*sabba*]. Do listen to it.
> > And what, brethren, is the all? It is the eye and visible, ear and sound, nose and scent, tongue and savor, body and tangible things, mind and mental-states. That, brethren, is called "the all."
> > Whoso, brethren, should say: 'Rejecting this all, I will proclaim another all, – it would be mere talk [*vaca-vatthu*, lit. "a linguistic matter," i.e. having only words, not things as a referent] on his part, and when questioned he could not make good his boast, and further would come to an ill pass. Why so? Because, brethren, it would be beyond his scope to do so.'[180]

In the commentary following his citation of this passage, Lusthaus highlights several crucial points often overlooked in contemporary works, and almost entirely neglected by the traditional community of contemporary Zen. For example:

> When the eye comes into contact with a visible object, visual consciousness arises. In the absence of those precipitating conditions (the sense organ, the sense object and their contact), no consciousness arises. It is as if Buddha intentionally omits the six consciousnesses precisely because consciousness is frequently associated by claimants to "another all" with that all beyond sensation. These fields, viz. the sensorium, are everything (*sabba*). The cognitive sensorium is all-inclusive. Nothing whatsoever exists outside the eighteen *dhatus*. This should be kept in mind by scholars who try to impose some 'ineffable' extrasensory or non-sensory 'reality' into Buddhist thought.
>
> Note also the consequences Buddha assigns to holding or promoting an erroneous view. (1) That view will be unsupportable, indefensible in the face of a critical challenge… (2.) … not only does it entail holding to a position one is incapable of defending, but it would require making claims about what lies entirely outside one's experience and knowledge. (3) Most importantly, it leads to disadvantageous karmic consequences… Holding false views, then, is not a neutral or harmless affair. Rather, such views harbor dire consequences.
> Dan Lusthaus[181]

Now, the six modes of consciousness are eye-consciousness, ear-consciousness, nose-consciousness, tongue-consciousness, body-consciousness, and mind-consciousness. Each of these consciousnesses is recognized as an inherent capacity to discern – thus *actualize* (i.e. make actualize)[182] – the 'type' or 'kind' of phenomena (i.e. dharmas) belonging to its particular mode. For example, dharmas that are discerned/actualized visually are 'objects of eye-consciousness,' dharmas that are experienced/appear audibly are 'objects of ear-consciousness,' and so on. In this manner each and all the myriad dharmas are experienced/appear in/as one or more of six types of phenomena; sights, sounds, smells, tastes, tactile sensations, and thoughts. Thus each and all dharmas are recognized and treated as 'objects of consciousness.' In other words, 'the myriad dharmas' is *everything* known or experienced and 'everything experienced' is the myriad dharmas – existence only and always consists of *particular* sights, sounds, smells, tastes, tactile sensations, and thoughts that are seen, heard, smelled, tasted, felt, and thought by particular sentient beings in/as existence-time.

Notice that if something 'other than' or 'independent of' objects of consciousness *did* exist, sentient beings would not only be *utterly unable to verify its existence* (it could not be seen, heard, smelled, tasted, felt, or thought), sentient beings would be *utterly uninfluenced by it* (any influence would, by definition, be detectable – hence an 'object of consciousness'). In short, if anything besides consciousness exists, it is *utterly* and *absolutely irrelevant to* sentient beings.

Thus the traditional Buddhist division of consciousness into six modes clearly and simply reveals how all things, beings, and events are and must be phenomena, spatial-temporal forms of consciousness. And, when dharmas are seen as 'objects of consciousness' dharmas are recognized as inevitably both 'what' sentient beings are *sentient of*, and 'what' *makes* sentient beings *sentient*. Seen as *what makes* sentient beings *sentient*, dharmas are seen to be the very source and fabric of sentience, consciousness itself, *life* itself. Again, then, Zen affirms, to exist is to be experienced; to be experienced is to exist.

By assimilating the truth of this (through learning, practicing, verifying, and actualizing it), sentient beings naturally enhance and refine their capacity for the transmission of wisdom. By clearly seeing that one's self (i.e. one's existence) is one's world (i.e. one's experience), sentient beings recognize the whole universe, the totality of self/other, is an unceasing activity of self-expression – one's self is realized by one's world, and one's world is realized by one's self:

> So life is what I am making it, and I am what life is making me.
> *Shobogenzo, Zenki*[183]

In sum, then, 'what' a sentient being *is* (ontology) is 'what' a sentient being is *sentient of* (epistemology). Sentience is consciousness, consciousness is only and always someone (self) conscious of something (other) – apart from either a self or an other 'consciousness' is meaningless:

> When speaking of consciousness of self and other, there is a self and an other in what is known; there is a self and an other in what is seen.

Shobogenzo, Shoaku Makusa[184]

The traditional western view of 'mental objects' (i.e. thoughts) as being utterly unique among the various kinds of objects is so deeply etched into the contemporary worldview that a few comments are called for before proceeding. The view that the existent nature or reality of thought is uniquely distinct from the reality of other kinds of phenomena is grounded in and perpetuated by dualism. The 'bracketing out' of thought as a separate reality is no minor flaw in the grand scheme of modern cosmology. Indeed, this particular fallacy has far reaching consequences.

Previously I stated that ignorance, amounting to *a lack of* knowledge, is easily amended, but that delusion, amounting to a *presence* of *distorted knowledge*, can be extremely resistant to correction. That the delusion concerning the nature of thought is grounded in dualism is crucial. This dualistic view of thought not only hinders our normal capacity to think, it hinders all our experiential capacities. To view 'thoughts about reality' as distinct from 'reality itself,' is necessarily to view thoughts about reality as *inherently unreliable*. For one that ascribes to a worldview that presupposes thought to be unreliable, it is *natural* to dismiss all other worldviews – constituted of 'thoughts' or 'systems of thought' – as unreliable also. In short, because adherents of the common worldview regard thoughts as inherently unreliable, such adherents are extremely resistant to the only remedy for the delusion from which they suffer – reasonable thinking.

Nevertheless, when adherents of the common view do become truly convinced of its possible fallibility (usually through either inspiration or desperation), the nondual nature of thought is fairly easy to verify. For verification is realized through one's own seeing, hearing, smelling, tasting, feeling, and thinking here-now. One needs only to simply, but sincerely, focus attention on their own experience – their actual experience of a self and a world here-now – to recognize that *all* 'objects of consciousness,' not only *thoughts*, are *mental* in nature.

Sights, sounds, tastes, smells, tactile sensations, *as well as* thoughts are *only* and *always* experienced in, as, and by the mind (i.e. consciousness). Just as no thoughts are experienced/appear independent of your mind, no forms, sounds, flavors, fragrances, or feelings are experienced/appear independent of your mind. In making the effort to sincerely observe this over time, one cannot fail to suddenly or gradually awaken to the truth that the crash of thunder or barking of a dog (objects of ear consciousness) are no more or no less 'objects of consciousness' than are *imagined* train whistles or voices in *dreams* (objects of mind consciousness) – 'you' are not merely 'your thoughts,' you are your sights, sounds, tastes, smells, tactile sensations and your thoughts, and *they* are *you*.

The Consciousness of Dharmas

It is one of the triumphs of the human that he can know a thing and still not believe it.
East of Eden, John Steinbeck

The very act of respectfully meeting and serving is the buddha. This is in accordance with the notion of the enactment-buddha (*gyobutsu*), wherein enactment and buddha are one.
Hee-Jin Kim[185]

Each and every particular dharma is an actual instance *of* the whole universe, a particular expression *of* Buddha, an individual dharma *of* the myriad dharmas that constitute the one mind, total existence-time, reality *as it is* here-now. The *reality* of dharmas (i.e. ontology) and the *appearance* of dharmas (i.e. epistemology) are nondual. That the *reality* and *appearance* of dharmas is nondual means dharmas *are* experience; *sentience, consciousness, subjectivity*.

To clarify I will spell it out; mountains, shoes, walls, bacteria, stars, baseball games, sand, armies, bicycles, penguins, bombs, bar mitzvahs, oceans, bowling pins, soup ladles, and all other particular things, beings, and events in/of total existence-time are *sentient* beings, animated subjects, individual agents, doers, thinkers – *persons*. Accordingly, no dharma is more or less real, more or less significant, or more or less valuable than any other dharma.

Now, according to Zen, enlightenment or Buddhahood – the supreme aim of Zen – is realized by seeing one's true nature (*kensho*) or seeing Buddha (*kenbutsu*). As we saw earlier, the *Heart Sutra* presents this experience in terms of 'clearly seeing one's body-mind is empty.' Above we saw how Dogen, with the help of Layman Pang, emphasized that expressions like 'clear seeing,' 'true nature,' and 'one's body-mind' are not esoteric, ambiguous, or superhuman; 'clear seeing' is dharmas *as we perceive them*, 'true nature' is dharmas *as they are experienced*, 'one's body-mind' is dharmas *one knows as* one's body-mind.

Our 'mystical powers and wondrous functions' are seeing, hearing, smelling, tasting, feeling, and thinking. Seeing is dharmas actualized as visual forms, images; hearing is dharmas as audible forms; smelling is dharmas as fragrant forms; tasting is dharmas as flavor forms, feeling is dharmas as tactile forms; thinking is dharmas as thought forms. 'Seeing one's true nature' is seeing (experiencing, knowing) dharmas as they are – to see dharmas are not-dharmas, therefore dharmas are dharmas – that is 'seeing one's true nature.' Again, 'seeing Buddha' is seeing forms as they are – to see forms are non-forms, therefore forms are forms – that is 'seeing Buddha,' also called 'meeting the Tathagata.'

> Sakyamuni Buddha addresses a great assembly: "If we see [both] the many forms and [their] non-form, we at once meet the Tathagata."

> "To see the many forms" and "to see [their] non-form," as described now, is a liberated bodily experience, and so it is "to meet the Tathagata." Realization in which this eye of meeting the Buddha is already open in experience is called "meeting buddha..."
>
> The effort in pursuit of the truth, and mastery of experience of the [Buddha's] state, which we are performing to the tips of the toes in the present and which we have continued since establishing the mind and taking the first step: all are vivid eyes and vivid bones and marrow running inside meeting buddha. This being so, the whole world of the self and all worlds in other directions, this individual and that individual, are all equally the effort of meeting buddha.
> *Shobogenzo, Kenbutsu*[186]

To 'establish the mind' is to awaken to our own true nature – to 'see Buddha' – to realize the ultimate authority of our own capacity to 'clearly see' – to realize that the normal eye is the 'True Dharma-Eye.' Normal vision is unified vision, vision that sees here-now *as it is*, abnormal vision is di-vision, vision that sees here-now *as it is not*. When seen with the normal eye – the True Dharma-Eye – reality is neither mysterious nor ineffable, neither concealed within nor waiting to be discovered without; its location is evident and its time is conspicuous.

The True Dharma-Eye sees the nondual truth of reality as the reality of nondual truth. If the message of Zen could be crystallized into one succinct phrase it would be, 'the myriad dharmas always around you *is* you – seeing this is seeing Buddha, seeing Buddha is making Buddha, making Buddha is being Buddha.'

From the nondual perspective it is obvious that the true nature of an object experienced and the true nature of the subject experiencing it are not two different things. Thus where the prevailing epistemology sees the sense organs as *keyboards*, *conveyors*, *interpreters* or *translators of* objective reality *to* subjective reality, Zen sees the sense organs as *bridges*, *channels*, or *joints* connecting/separating objective reality to/from subjective reality. The sense organs do not convey signals *from* an alien (independent) realm *to* the mind of an isolated self; the sense organs are integral aspects of the 'actualization of the universe' (*genjokoan*) itself which is experienced/exists *as* the world/self unity a human being calls 'myself.' 'What we experience' – dharmas – is 'what we are.' And since experience is ever active, never static, 'what we are' is an 'activity,' a 'doing.' And this 'doing' that 'we are' is a continuous 'ordering,' 'fashioning,' or 'arranging' of dharmas – the particularities or 'bits and pieces' we experience as 'myself.'

> In a similar manner, we are continually arranging bits and pieces of what we experience in order to fashion them into what we call 'a self', which we treat as 'myself': this is the same as the principle of 'we ourselves are just for a time'.
> *Shobogenzo, Uji*[187]

The point here is that in Zen's view, the *actual existence of* 'objects' is the *actual experience of* 'subjects.' In other words, besides what *appears* in/as consciousness, there is nothing that can or could have any influence on us whatsoever. Further, the accuracy of this point, and its significance, is not only attested to and presupposed throughout Zen doctrine and methodology, it is experientially verifiable – indeed, it is self-evident to anyone willing to make the effort to honestly understand it. As Whitehead accurately observed:

> In fact, self-evidence is understanding.
> Alfred North Whitehead[188]

By 'making the effort to honestly understand it' I mean simply utilizing your normal thinking capacity to give some focused attention to the following points (truisms?) in light of your own actual knowledge and experience:

- It is impossible to experience an 'object' independent of a 'subject' – if it *is experienced* it is experienced *by* a subject, if it *is not experienced* it cannot be called an 'object.'
- Therefore, consciousness is an *inherent quality* of every object – no object has been, or could be encountered apart from consciousness.
- The same applies to subjects; consciousness is an *inherent quality* of every subjective experience – no subject has been, or could be encountered apart from consciousness.
- Every instance of consciousness consists of *both* objective and subjective elements – consciousness, by nature, is *someone* conscious of *something*.
- Therefore, every assertion or belief that something 'exists' *independent of* 'experience,' is false.[189]
- Finally, any claim or view that *anything* independent of experience could be verified *to exist*, or could have any influence on us whatsoever, is false.

The truth of these points should be self-evident – these are obvious facts taken for granted in our everyday life, plain and simple truths that inform (if tacitly) our natural understanding ('self-evidence') of reality. In short this means that the nondual nature of reality, which is presupposed by these points, is already evident for anyone to verify – more, it is not only evident, but functional in the actual conduct of our daily lives.

It is our capacity to think, our 'discriminating mind' or 'thinking mind' that serves as the catalyst for our awakening to the true nature of reality. While the 'thinking mind' is frequently dismissed, ignored, or denigrated by popular 'Zen' books or teachers, the classic records of Zen recognize and emphasize its crucial place in authentic practice-enlightenment.

> In general there are three kinds of mind. "The first, *citta,* is here called thinking mind. The second, *hrdaya,* is here called the mind of grass and trees. The third, *vrddha,* is here called experienced and concentrated mind." Among these, the *bodhi*-mind is inevitably established relying upon thinking mind. *Bodhi* is the sound of an Indian word; here it is called "the truth." *Citta* is the sound of an Indian word; here it is called "thinking mind." Without this thinking mind it is impossible to establish the *bodhi*-mind. That is not to say

that this thinking mind is the *bodhi*-mind itself, but we establish the *bodhi*-mind with this thinking mind.
Shobogenzo Hotsu-bodaishin[190]

I am emphasizing the principles of nonduality to an extent that, proportional to other aspects of Zen cosmology, goes beyond that given them in the classic Zen sources because the extent to which dualism effects contemporary civilization is greater than that of the civilizations of those sources. While dualism was a problem in those eras, the wisdom of nonduality was always present to some degree in the populations addressed by the classic Zen literature. In contrast, the principles of nonduality are strange, if not completely alien to the majority of the present population. Further, of those that are familiar with nonduality, many misunderstand it, even to the point of subversion. Finally, contemporary proponents of dualism are legion, and the systems and methodologies that perpetuate it are far more sophisticated and effective than ever before.

This brings us to the main point I have been attempting to flesh out here. Zen's view of reality is harmonious with *how we actually experience reality*. Therefore, the fact that *not only* Zen's view, but even the scientific evidence of nonduality is almost universally ignored or denied in the contemporary world demonstrates just how pervasive and *tenacious* dualism actually is. Evidently, the common mind is so conditioned by the tenets of dualism that few even bother to seriously question the basic assumptions informing their understanding of reality, much less attempt to verify the accuracy of that understanding.

Whether it is called 'scientific fact,' 'objective truth,' 'enlightened view,' or 'religious revelation,' the fallacy that 'Reality *Is Not* As It Appears' is embraced as a self-evident truth – this 'truth' is encountered at birth and continuously elaborated through old age from and within nearly every sphere of civilization. Therefore, when Zen, science, or one's own experience even hints at the self-evident truth, 'Reality *Is* As It Appears' it is instantly dismissed as an obvious fallacy.

If I belabor the point it is because I need to get through the kind of conditioning that makes it easy, natural even, for most of us to believe *our own experience* is *not* as we experience it to be – even that our own experience is unreliable if not intrinsically misleading.

The truth of nonduality asserted by Zen is not complicated, marvelous, or earth-shattering, much less inexpressible, inconceivable, or esoteric – it is the most common and obvious truth of human experience. Moreover, by recognizing the plain truth that *actual* experience is more reliable than abstract speculations *about* experience, we become equipped with a universally accessible means for achieving and verifying an accurate understanding of even the most far-reaching implications of human existence. Nevertheless, it does require one to sincerely consider the possibility that Zen's view is accurate – thus the possibility that one's present view is erroneous.

Dharma Transmission

The abstract reasoner attempts to give independent reality to the qualities of the things he sees, and in the same way he tries to abstract the quality of his perception. It is to him that we owe the association of the mind and brain. The intellect to him is a special department concerned with reasoning, and other departments should not meddle with it. Emotion is another department, formally ascribed to the heart... Thought, being largely reflection, it is an "inward" activity: those who specialize in "outward" activity are not thinkers, but the practical people who do things. Scientists should be trained to see the sun as a fact; artists to see it emotionally as beautiful...

All this pigeonholing of activity is nonsense to Blake. Thought *is* act, he says... The more a man puts all he has into everything he does the more alive he is.
Northrop Frye[191]

The fundamental concept of understanding was activity in Dogen's thought. Understanding was indispensably associated with our whole being—we understood as we acted and acted as we understood. The activity of the body-mind served not only as the vehicle of understanding, but also as the embodiment of truth. Often in conventional thought, knowledge and truth are ascribed solely to the functions of sensation and reason, while the functions of feeling and intuition are considered merely subjective. Such an artificial compartmentalization of human activity has created some distorted views of the subject. For Dogen, however, the problem of understanding invariably involved the whole being which he called the "body-mind" *(shinjin)*. "Body-mind" was one of Dogen's favorite phrases, and he often used the phrase "mustering the body-mind" *(shinjin o koshite)* to show the human attempt to understand the self and the world.
Hee-Jin Kim[192]

As a tradition, activity, or institution of human civilization, 'Zen' denotes a path, manner, or way of life, rather than a particular structure or form. To revere a 'Zen' that consists of an authorized version, exclusive sect, prescribed method, formal practice, dogmatic code, or any other fixed form is to exalt a lifeless idol. In Zen's vision, reality itself consists of the expression of Dharma, an unceasing advance into novelty, an ongoing creative activity. Zen practice-enlightenment (*shusho*) is *genjokoan*, '*actualizing* the fundamental point' – not the actualiz*ed*, actu*al*, or actual*ize* of past, present, or future, but a ceaseless actualiza*tion* of existence-time here-now which fully includes and transcends past, present, and future. More particularly, practice-enlightenment consists of clearly seeing the true nature of reality and, thereby, actualizing one's thoughts, words, and deeds harmoniously with that truth in and as the self/world here-now.

To clarify, consider Hee-Jin Kim's analysis of the following passage from *Bendowa;* one of Dogen's clearest articulations of his view of practice-enlightenment. In this translation Kim, following the lead of Norman Waddell and Masao Abe[193], renders 'Bendowa' as 'negotiating the Way':

> In the *Shobogenzo*, "Bendowa" (1231), Dogen succinctly enunciates his Zen: The endeavor to negotiate the Way (*bendo*), as I teach now, consists in discerning all things in view of enlightenment, and putting such a unitive awareness (*ichinyo*) into practice in the midst of the revaluated world (*shutsuro*).[194]

Dr. Kim clarifies by bringing the salient points into relief thus:

> This statement clearly sets forth practitioners' soteriological project as negotiating the Way in terms of (1) discerning the nondual unity of all things that are envisioned from the perspective of enlightenment and (2) enacting that unitive vision amid the everyday world of duality now revalorized by enlightenment. Needless to say, these two aspects refer to practice and enlightenment that are nondually one (*shusho itto; shusho ichinyo*).
> Hee-Jin Kim[195]

Authentic Zen practice-enlightenment consists of 'these two aspects' – *discerning* dharmas as they are, and *actualizing* that discernment here-now. It is worth noting that the 'practice-enlightenment' advocated by Dogen (hence Zen) differs significantly from the 'practice-enlightenment' advocated by most contemporary Zen teachers. Many contemporary Zen teachers refrain from even acknowledging the reality of an 'enlightened perspective,' fewer still advocate discerning all dharmas from the enlightened perspective, and even fewer encourage enacting that perspective in the 'world of duality.' Therefore, whatever most contemporary teachers *do* proclaim as 'practice-enlightenment,' it must be different from that expounded by Dogen. Judging from the classic Zen records, this is not unique to our era; authentic practice-enlightenment has evidently always been something engaged by a minority of those in the Zen community. In harmony with those records, then, I do not say *no* contemporary teachers proclaim authentic practice-enlightenment, only that they are few.

It is not necessary to detail exactly what the majority of contemporary Zen teachers *do* advocate as practice-enlightenment except to explain my reason for making the point in negative terms, which may be telling enough. I stated this in terms of what 'is not' advocated rather than 'what is' because there is little consensus among contemporary Zen teachers in regard to what authentic practice-enlightenment actually consists in/of.

In any case, the point here is that Zen is a dynamic activity, not a fixed form. This dynamic activity is presented in the classic literature as a communication of enlightened wisdom '*from* the mind *to* the *mind*' or '*from* Buddha *to* Buddha.' Known formally in Zen as 'Dharma-transmission,' 'mind to mind transmission,' or, Dogen's favorite term, '(the transmission of Dharma) from Buddha alone together with Buddha' (*yui-butsu-yobutsu*). In *Shobogenzo*, Dharma-transmission is portrayed as the ever-ongoing unified activity/expression of the self and all Buddhas past, present, and future in the ceaseless actualization of universal liberation. As 'activity,' Zen is seeing, knowing, experiencing, etc. As 'expression,' Zen is seen, known, experienced, etc. 'Seeing' is true nature, and 'seen' is true nature. If it is 'seeing true nature' it is Zen. If it is not 'seeing true nature' it is not Zen.

> Seeing your nature is Zen. Unless you see your nature, it's not Zen.[196]
> Bodhidharma, Traditional founder of Zen

From the perspective of the individual, Zen practice-enlightenment consists in 'seeing true nature' (*kensho*) or 'seeing Buddha' (*kenbutsu*) and conducting oneself accordingly. When one clearly sees reality as it is – particular dharmas here-now – one is enabled to think, speak, and act appropriately. In other words, to see dharmas as they are is to 'clearly discern' or 'accurately read' reality. Each and all dharmas are 'expressions of reality,' 'expressions of Buddha' – to see dharmas *as they are*, is to *accurately read* (hence *understand*) expressions of reality. As expressions of Buddha, dharmas are scriptures (*sutras*); words of Buddha. To see the true nature of a mountain or ocean is to accurately understand an expression of Buddha, to understand an expression of Buddha is to see Buddha (*kenbutsu*). Accordingly, to see Buddha (*kenbutsu*) is to hear and understand dharmas as 'this sutra.'

> Sakyamuni Buddha addresses Bodhisattva Universal Virtue: "If there is anyone who receives and retains, reads and recites, rightly remembers, practices, and copies this *Sutra of the Flower of Dharma,* we should know that that person is meeting Sakyamuni Buddha, and hearing this sutra as if from the Buddha's mouth."
>
> In general, all the buddhas say that "to meet Sakyamuni Buddha" and to realize the state of Sakyamuni Buddha is to realize the truth and to become buddha. Such behavior of buddhas is originally attained through each of these seven practices. A person who performs the seven practices is "that person" whom "we should know," and is "the very person here and now, as he or she is." Because this is just the state in which we meet Sakyamuni Buddha, it is directly "hearing this sutra as if from the Buddha's mouth." Sakyamuni Buddha, since having met Sakyamuni Buddha, is Sakyamuni Buddha. Thus, the form of his tongue universally enfolds the three-thousandfold [world]: what mountain or ocean could be other than the Buddha's sutras? For this reason, "the very person here and now" who copies is meeting alone with Sakyamuni Buddha. "The Buddha's mouth" is constantly open through the myriad ages: what moment could be other than the sutras? For this reason, the practitioner who receives and retains the sutras is meeting solely with Sakyamuni Buddha. The virtue of not only the eyes and ears but also the nose and so on, may also be like this. The front and the back, the left and the right, taking and leaving, an instant of the present, also, are like this. We have been born to experience "this sutra" of the present: how could we not rejoice to be meeting Sakyamuni Buddha? Life is an encounter with Sakyamuni Buddha.
> *Shobogenzo, Kenbutsu*[197]

Thus, the *nondual unity* of essence and form is the keystone of Zen doctrine and methodology; the profundity of its significance is intimated by Dogen's often repeated, 'Nothing in the universe is concealed.' As the keystone of Zen doctrine, the nondual unity of essence and form is the reason (*dori*) 'there *are* understandable explanations.' As the keystone of

Zen methodology, it is the activity of 'practice-enlightenment,' 'solely seated (meditation),' or 'thinking not-thinking' (or 'nonthinking'). *Because* essence and form *are* nondual, the *essence* of existence is *knowing-dharmas* and the *essence* of *knowing-dharmas* is *existence*. To be more precise, existence *is* knowledge, and knowledge *is* existence.

To clarify, 'essence' means 'reality *as it is*,' '*the true nature of* reality,' or '*thusness*' (i.e. ontology; what is *the actual* material or fabric of existence-time). 'Form' means 'reality *as it appears*,' '*phenomena*,' or '*dharmas*' (i.e. epistemology; what is *known* or *encountered* by sentient beings, i.e. sights, sounds, smells, tastes, tactile sensations, and thoughts). 'Essence and form are nondual' means all reality *is dharmas* and all dharmas *are real*. Therefore, the 'essence of existence' is 'knowing-dharmas' (i.e. seeing, experiencing, or understanding appearances, for example, appearances of 'understandable explanations'). Likewise, 'knowing-dharmas' is the 'essence of existence' (i.e. the true nature, reality, or 'fabric' of appearances, for example, appearances of 'understandable explanations').

In sum, *because* essence and form *are* nondual, the 'enlightened perspective' (i.e. the 'essence' of normal seeing; *kensho, kenbutsu*) *can be* activated by dharmas, for example, 'understandable explanations' of techniques to focus consciousness on dharmas here-now (i.e. Zen's 'skillful means'). For the place-time (reality, essence) dharmas are known is the place-time dharmas exist, and the place-time dharmas exist is the place-time dharmas are known. This place-time being only and always here-now, nothing (i.e. no dhama) in the universe is concealed.

> In the great truth of the Buddha-Dharma, the sutras of the great-thousandfold [world] are present in an atom, and countless buddhas are present in an atom. Each weed and each tree are a body-mind. Because the myriad *dharma*s are beyond appearance, even the undivided mind is beyond appearance. And because all *dharma*s are real form, every atom is real form. Thus, one undivided mind is all *dharma*s, and all *dharma*s are one undivided mind, which is the whole body. If building stupas were artificial, buddhahood, *bodhi*, reality as it is, and the buddha-nature, would also be artificial. Because reality as it is and the buddha-nature are not artificial, building images and erecting stupas are not artificial. They are the natural establishment of the *bodhi*-mind: they are merit achieved without artificiality, without anything superfluous.
> *Shobogenzo, Hotsu-mujoshin*[198]

While it may be contrary to the suggestions of many that claim to represent Zen or Dogen, true nature, according to the classic Zen records (including *Shobogenzo*) is ever and always immediately present, particular, and precise. Notions or assertions suggesting that Zen is somehow mysterious, ineffable, or inexpressible are simply off the mark. The only place such terms can be accurately applied in Zen is to *definite* mysteries, *particular* unknowns, and *specific* inexpressible experiences. Indeed, in Zen, the terms definite, particular, and specific accurately characterize *all dharmas*. Dogen's refrain, 'Nothing in the whole universe is concealed' means exactly what it says; no reality is the least bit obscure or vague. To emphasize this truth, the assertion that 'real form is all dharmas' runs like a mantra throughout *Shobogenzo*, for example:

> The realization of the Buddhist patriarchs is perfectly realized real form. Real form is all dharmas. All dharmas are forms as they are, natures as they are, body as it is, the mind as it is, the world as it is, clouds and rain as they are, walking, standing, sitting, and lying down, as they are; sorrow and joy, movement and stillness, as they are; a staff and a whisk, as they are; a twirling flower and a smiling face, as they are; succession of the Dharma and affirmation, as they are; learning in practice and pursuing the truth, as they are; the constancy of pines and the integrity of bamboos, as they are.
> *Shobogenzo, Shoho-Jisso*[199]

In this Dogen agrees with Blake, 'Anything capable of being believed is an image of truth.'[200] From the Zen perspective 'anything' that is 'capable of being believed' *is* and must *already be* a reality – a dharma, *form* of reality, *object* of consciousness, *image* of truth. To see a mountain is to experience a mountain and to experience a mountain is to see a mountain. The very 'substance' of a mountain is (*exists as*) its *appearance*, image, or form in/as the mind, in/as Buddha. A mountain is a self/world phenomenon.

The notion that our 'self' is something that looks around and encounters 'a world' that exists before, after, or otherwise independent of its being encountered is a false notion, a delusion. 'Things' or 'a world' being encountered *is* 'ourself.' To recognize sights, sounds, tastes, smells, tactile sensations, and thoughts here-now as our 'self' is enlightenment.

If a sentient being (or self) is the actualization of dharmas here-now, dharmas here-now are the actualization of a sentient being. When you see a mountain, a mountain is seen by you. A mountain makes you what you are, you make a mountain what it is – 'you' is mountain-made, 'a mountain' is you-made.

Dogen frequently speaks of 'pictures' or 'paintings' as well as 'fences, walls, tiles, and pebbles' in acknowledging that Buddha exists nowhere else but in the very 'human-made' (experientially realized) dharmas constituting the here-now of every moment of our existence. But while it is true that the myriad dharmas are 'actualized by sentient beings' it is also true that sentient beings are 'actualized by the myriad dharmas' – thus we need to be wary of selfish pride or egocentricity. Mountains, paintings, fences, walls, tiles, and pebbles depend on us, but we also depend on them – from our perspective the myriad dharmas are objects, from their perspective we are objects. We need to learn from them in order to interact normally with them, to ably respond (responsibility) – to learn from them is to recognize them as the very words and deeds of the Buddha-Dharma.

> If we want to inquire into this mind, it is present in visible fences, walls, tiles, and pebbles; and if we want to experience this mind, it is present in the realization of fences, walls, tiles, and pebbles. Now, though these fences, walls, tiles, and pebbles are produced by human beings, at the same time they are words and deeds of Dharma. Who could hold sway over them? When we see them like this, it is evident that "fences, walls, tiles, and pebbles" are beyond substance before our eyes, and that substance before our eyes is not "fences, walls, tiles, and pebbles." In sum, fences, walls, tiles, and pebbles on this side are illuminating us as yonder objects; and we on this side are being illuminated by fences, walls, tiles, and pebbles as yonder objects.
> *Himitsu-shobogenzo, Butsu-kojo-no-ji*[201]

In his best known meditation treatise, *Fukanzazengi*, Dogen cites some of the familiar forms of Buddha frequently mentioned in the classic Zen records as 'words and deeds of Dharma', agents of actualizing Zen practitioners:

> Moreover, the changing of the moment, through the means of a finger, a pole, a needle, or a wooden clapper; and the experience of the state, through the manifestation of a whisk, a fist, a staff, or a shout, can never be understood by thinking and discrimination.

Fukanzazengi[202]

Many Zen students will immediately recognize the 'means of a finger' from the Zen koan wherein Master Gutei 'always raised one finger' in response to questions about Zen, the 'needle' to the story of Kanadeva meeting Master Nagarjuna, the 'staff' in connection with Master Teshan, and the 'shout' with Master Rinzai. The *specific particularity* in which the Buddha is manifest (*a* finger, *a* pole, *a* whisk, etc.) is characteristic of Zen's *universal inclusivity* and nondiscrimination – all dharmas are equal in status, value, and significance, for each is an essential person of Buddha-nature, an integral form of Shakyamuni Buddha, an image of truth. Thus, when encountering Zen masters, Buddha is shown to shine forth as all manner of things no matter how apparently mundane or even profane.

> A monk asked Tozan, 'What is Buddha?'
> Tozan said, 'Three pounds of flax.'
> *Classic Zen Koan*

> Someone asked, 'What is Shakyamuni's Body?'
> The Master said, 'A dry piece of shit.'
> Master Yunmen[203]

Of course, this does not mean Zen is averse to 'sacred' or 'spiritual' objects or activities. Zen practitioners speak of and treat spiritual or religious items (monk's robes, sutras, icons, rosaries, etc.) with as much reverence as those of any religious tradition. The point is not that 'religious' items or activities are insignificant or mundane, but that all items and activities are sacred, are Buddha. This is the true significance of the Zen saying, 'the normal mind is the Tao' (often subverted to mean, 'the Tao is mundane,' 'the Tao is ordinary,' or 'the Tao is nothing special'). In short, Zen does not deny the 'divinity' of Buddha or the 'sacredness' of religious objects and activities; it affirms the 'divinity' or 'sacredness' of every reality, every actual instance of which is a particular experience/existence, of a particular being, at a particular location-time. A monk harboring a view that 'divine light' (of Buddha) was somehow *superior to* or *other than* 'normal light' took it up with the great Zen master Joshu:

> A monk said, 'In the day there is sunlight, at night there is firelight. What is 'divine light'?'

>   The master said, 'Sunlight, firelight.'
>   Joshu[204]

To demonstrate the fact that the only reality in the universe is the reality of *particular things* (*dharmas*), the Zen masters don't only raise fingers, deliver blows, shout, or twirl a flowers, they also study, learn to develop and apply reason, cultivate practice, and verify and refine true teachings – this is what Dogen calls solely-sitting (*shikantaza*), and describes as actualizing the universe (*genjokoan*) through the transmission of the treasure of the true Dharma-eye. Nothing in the whole universe is concealed, for each and all the myriad dharmas are ever-already the thoughts, words, and deeds of Buddha alone together with Buddha – look, look!

The Language of The Self

We speak not only to tell other people what we think, but to tell ourselves what we think. Speech is a part of thought.
Oliver Sacks[205]

The Mythopoeic Nature of Zen Expression

In the language of literal description, paradox indicates a failure of consistent logic or correspondent accuracy. Literal description, then, is the appropriate choice for assembly instructions, driving directions, reference books, and whatever else demands consistent logic and correspondent accuracy. In the language of mythopoeism however, paradox is not only functional, it is necessary.

The very *reason* and *efficacy of* myth and metaphor is its capacity to communicate what, in literal terms, is incommunicable. Indeed, it is only because the meaning and significance of poems, myths, koans, and other figurative or imagistic expressions cannot be conveyed through literal forms of expression, that mythopoeic language exists. If such significance *could be* conveyed literally, mythopoeic expressions could only be seen as intentional attempts to confuse or delude people (which literalists often *do* ascribe to Zen koans). In sum, mythopoeic language is a vehicle with the capacity to convey knowledge that is otherwise incommunicable.

The general or common sense that myth and metaphor are superfluous, misleading, or deceptive – thus pointless if not harmful – has long been rooted in the contemporary worldview. This is to be expected; according to the understanding of 'knowledge' posited by this worldview (the representational theory) there is no need for mythopoeism – certain knowledge is *unattainable*, and what knowledge *is* attainable (i.e. speculative, abstract knowledge) can be *literally* measured and communicated via universal standards of 'objectivity.' From this perspective, the products of myth and metaphor can only be considered ornamental or entertaining at best, or, more often, as remnants of outdated, vulgar, or superstitious beliefs and institutions.

Fortunately, the true potential of mythopoeism as well as the limitations of literalism continues to be disclosed and communicated at an exponential rate, thanks to ongoing efforts in the fields of psychology and comparative mythology, as well as related developments within the spheres to the biological and cognitive sciences, which continue to enjoy a great increase of interest.

Even in the absence of these advances, however, most of us can recognize a clarifying, enlightening capacity is intrinsic to metaphoric language if we simply devote a little time considering the plain facts. For instance, when a friend informs us that sunrise was at 0615 we naturally grasp the *truth* of the expression, even though it is *literally* nonsense; we *know* the sun does not *literally* rise, yet we understand the truth of 'sunrise.' We constantly use similar literal fallacies, contradictions, and paradoxical expressions to accurately communicate in nearly every area of our everyday lives.

It is usually only when we try to verify or refute the products of *abstract* speculation – hence *subtracted* from their actual context – that we get entangled in arguments confined by the limitations of dictionary definitions. The expressions of poetry, koans, and myth are *informed by* wisdom concerning the true nature of reality, thus by wisdom *of* the true potential of language.

The Zen master Shibi once said, 'The whole universe is one bright pearl.'[206] According to dualistic or literal standards, Shibi's assertion is unequivocally false, irrational, meaningless nonsense. In accordance with Zen or nondual standards however, Shibi's statement is not only true, rational, and infused with ultimate meaning, it is charged with liberating potential. The power of such a metaphor is often precisely *due to* its *paradoxical* quality – the fact that *it is* 'literally false.' For instance, upon hearing Shibi's assertion the Zen practitioner immediately grasps the truth that the whole universe *is* and *is not* 'one bright pearl.' Nobody is foolish enough to think Shibi means the whole universe is *literally* one bright pearl, thus the actual truth (real knowledge) communicated by the expression must abide at a deeper level.

If we fail to grasp the truth communicated by the word 'sunrise' the failure does not rest with the *word* or the *person* that expresses it, but with *our ability to discern* its true meaning. The truth that 'the whole universe is one bright pearl' is not rendered false by our failure to grasp it – nor is it rendered true by subjecting it to a literal definition; its actual truth endures *as it is*, and *only* as it is – even if only one being understands it.

Some scholars, by attempting to subject the language of Zen to (dualistic) literal standards, have cited isolated passages from *Shobogenzo* in support of their claims that the work is 'inconsistent.' To charge *Shobogenzo* with inconsistency based on such standards is about as reasonable as charging our friend with lying for saying that sunrise occurred at 0615. We do not need linguistic expertise or a degree in postmodern philosophy to recognize that 'sunrise' is not *its* reality and still recognize the truth actually communicated. As Dogen says:

> This 'One Pearl' is still not Its name, but It can be expressed so, and this has come to be regarded as Its name.
> Shobogenzo, Ikka Myoju[207]

Something That Can Be Metaphoric

Our Highest Ancestor in India, Shakyamuni Buddha, once said, "The snowcapped Himalayas are a metaphor for the great nirvana." You need to know that He is speaking metaphorically about something that can be metaphoric." Something that can be metaphoric" implies that the mountains and nirvana are somehow intimately connected and that they are connected in a straightforward manner. When He uses the term "snow-capped Himalayas", He is using the actual snowcapped Himalayas as a metaphor, just as when He uses the term "great nirvana", He is using the actual great nirvana as a metaphor.
Shobogenzo, Hotsu Mujo Shin[208]

If accurately grasped and assimilated, the point brought to light by Dogen here could eradicate one of the most pernicious plagues on the contemporary Zen community; ignorance and delusion concerning the true nature of language. To '*speak metaphorically* about something' is to speak 'about something that *can be* metaphoric' – something that *can be metaphoric* is something that *actually exists* – to use the *phrase* 'snow-capped Himalayas' is to use the *actual* snow-capped Himalayas. If the snow-capped Himalayas *did not exist* they could *not be spoken of* metaphorically; if they *can be spoken of* metaphorically, they *must exist*; and *if they exist*, they *can be spoken of* metaphorically. Thus, *every* dharma *can be* spoken of metaphorically. Moreover, using *any* dharma metaphorically is using the *actual* dharma.

With this we begin to get a handle on the reason (*dori*) of Zen's insight into the true potential of language. That is, the reason informing Zen's recognition and treatment of the products of language as self-expressions (expressions of self). In light of Zen's nondual vision of reality, the reason Zen recognizes the products of language as self-expressions is obvious.

To clarify, for example, let's consider the nature of language in context of the Zen/Buddhist notion of '*bodhicitta*' (aspiration for enlightenment). In Zen, *bodhicitta* is recognized as a normal (i.e. healthy, inherent) desire to see one's own true nature, to know one's own self.

> The mind of a sentient being is destined to desire to know its own self.
> Shobogenzo, Yuibutsu-yobutsu[209]

As a dharma, an actual instance of *bodhicitta* is a particular form in/of existence-time. Accordingly, a sentient being's 'desire to know its own self' can only be satisfied by an actual occurrence of that being's cognition of itself, an actual manifestation of self-awareness. As Zen sees the true nature of one's own self (hence, self/other) is dharmas, Zen sees *self-awareness* as *awareness of dharmas as self* – thus the self-awareness of dharmas. Therefore, the aspiration of the *self* to know itself (*bodhicitta*) is the aspiration of *dharmas*; enlightenment of the *self* (i.e. satisfaction of the desire to know its own self) is enlightenment of *dharmas* – self-knowledge is dharma's-knowledge.

'Self' is the root metaphor of Zen. By this I mean, first, the expression 'root metaphor' *exemplifies the nature of* the self; to identify the self as 'a metaphor' is to express the self metaphorically – to communicate knowledge about the self by exemplifying (rather than describing or defining) the self. Second, 'root metaphor' *communicates the significance of* the self; as a *root* metaphor 'self' can (and always does) apply to *both* the individual self *and* the universal or world self. The significant implication here is that because *all* expressions are necessarily expressions of *some* self, all expressions must ultimately be recognized (and accordingly treated) *as* metaphors. If the entire reality of the self is dharmas – autochthonous, self-generating forms of existence-time – then all *expressions* must be *forms of the self*. Thus it would be accurate to say; all forms are self-expressions, or; all expressions are figures of the self, or; all the self is expressed forms, that is, the self is figurative expressions – metaphors.

Here I want to emphasize that to recognize expressions *about* the self as forms *of* the self is to recognize the futility of attempting to achieve self-awareness (*kensho*, or *kenbutsu*) through conceptualization alone. To achieve an accurate intellectual understanding of the self would be, at best, to acquaint one's self with a *conceptual* view or image of one's self – a *representation* of the self. *Bodhicitta* is the self's aspiration to see *itself*, not to see a *representation* of itself. This is the reason (*dori*) that informs the many explicit refutations of mere literal, conceptual, or intellectual approaches to enlightenment that are a hallmark of Zen literature.

To see the true nature of the self is to *present* (make present) the self to the self. As the self is activity/expression itself, Zen's method is to prompt the self to *express itself* and thereby *evoke* self-cognition. For example, to 'speak metaphorically about something that can be metaphoric' is an expression *of* the self (in/as Dogen/*Shobogenzo*) that communicates *to* the self (in/as Dogen/*Shobogenzo*'s audience) *about* the self (in/as self/other). Thus the self's desire to know itself is prompted by a confrontation with (an expression of) itself that (if successful) evokes the self to cognize (or 'prehend' in Whitehead's sense[210]) itself. It is significant to note that when such occurrences are actualized, the self's cognition (of itself) naturally *begets* (indeed, *consists of*) a *novel expression* (of cognition) – thus the self ever-begets itself anew.

Since 'self' is 'something that *can be* metaphoric,' using the *term* 'self' is using the *actual* self, hence the term 'self' can never be understood as a *mere instrument* signifying or representing the 'actual' self. Further, since *all* terms are self-expressions (expressions of self), this reasoning (*dori*) applies to all terms (even apparently meaningless or erroneous ones); and since *all* dharmas are real, *every* dharma is 'something that can be metaphoric.' Therefore, nothing (i.e. no dharma) can be accurately understood as *only* an expedient or *merely* a 'finger pointing to the moon.' From the nondual perspective, there is no such thing as a *mere* simile, analogy, or parable – no expression is *only a means to* an end or *merely* 'a raft to reach the other shore.'

This is crucial, thus it is worth attempting to spell out its reasoning in the context of some key points already explored.

- The form (appearance) of dharmas and the essence (reality) of dharmas are nondual; dharmas are form/essence units of reality (existence-time, the universe, Buddha).
- The true nature of the self (self/not-self) is dharmas; the myriad dharmas are the self.

- Expressions are (the myriad) dharmas; hence, 'self,' 'expressions,' and 'dharmas' are synonymous.
- The myriad dharmas are realities (*actual*), thus *all* dharmas *can be* metaphoric – particular forms in/of existence-time possessing particular significance (intelligibility).
- The myriad dharmas are *expressions of* the self, and expressions of the self *are* the myriad dharmas; the myriad dharmas are *self-expressions*.
- 'The self,' 'expressions,' or 'dharmas,' are not fixed forms, but dynamic activities, therefore might be *more truly* (if less literally accurate) called 'express*ing*,' 'self-*ing*,' 'dharma-*ing*.'
- 'Self-ing' is the self *as it is* (thusness, normality), 'expressing' is expressions *as they are*, 'dharma-ing' is dharmas *as they are*; the thusness (normality, as is-ness) *of* reality is Zen.
- Hence 'self' – being dharmas as they are – is the root metaphor of Zen.

In this light, then, we could say dharmas are the normal expression of reality, the language of/as self-and-other. As is characteristic of language, the reason (*dori*) of dharmas must be accurately understood to be effectively utilized. Ordinary knowledge is communicated *to* an individual only when the language (written, verbal, or body-language) used is *clearly understood* (i.e. accurately heard, read, received *as it is*). Likewise, self-knowledge is accurately communicated *to* the self only when dharmas (forms, sounds, smells, tastes, feelings, or thoughts) are seen, heard, smelled, tasted, felt or cognized *as they are*. In Zen, the communication of self-knowledge is called 'mind to mind transmission,' 'transmission from Buddha alone together with Buddha,' etc. The capacity to clearly see dharmas as they are (i.e. accurately understand the language of the self-and-other) is called the 'eye to read scripture,' the 'living eye,' the 'Buddha-eye' – or Dogen's favorite, the 'true dharma-eye,' frequently used in his writings, most notably *Shobogenzo*; the 'True Dharma-Eye Treasury.'

The ordinary (deluded, or abnormal) eye sees dharmas *as they are not*, that is, it sees dharmas partially – in accordance with biased views, thus abstractly, literally, or conceptually e.g. as representations, independent realities, illusory, provisional etc. The Buddha (enlightened, or normal) eye sees dharmas *as they are* – reality as it is, thusness, existence-time here-now e.g. self-expressions, forms/figures of the self-and-other, etc.

The Buddha-eye or true Dharma-Eye sees *seeing* as it is, that is; it sees that seeing is both the 'essence' (i.e. ontology) and the 'knowledge' (i.e. epistemology) of self-and-other. The self-and-other (i.e. dharmas *as they are*) is 'what' the true Dharma-eye sees *and* the self-and-other is 'how' the true Dharma-eye sees. And, in seeing that 'seen' and 'seeing' are nondual, the seer sees that 'seeing,' 'seen,' and (the true Dharma) 'eye' are three *interdependent* aspects of one reality; the true self is the seer/seen/seeing (Buddha) – thus the oneness of Buddha and the self are realized.

> How should we understand this oneness of Buddha and the self? Observe the activities of Buddha for awhile. Buddha's activities take place with the entire great earth and with all sentient beings. If they are not with all existence, they are not yet the activities of Buddha. Hence from arousing the desire for enlightenment to the attainment of enlightenment, Buddha is enlightened and conducts himself always with the whole world and with all sentient beings.
> *Shobogenzo, Yuibutsu-yobutsu*[211]

Seeing its own true nature, the self verifies its eternal enlightenment and its eternal delusion. The experience of eternal enlightenment is the self realizing the universal liberation and fulfillment of all beings by recognizing *its identity with* all beings (i.e. the myriad dharmas), *hence* its beginningless and endless nature; 'all beings' is, has always been, and will ever be what is as it is. The experience of eternal delusion is the self realizing the infinite potential of the self-generating nature of its existence; its very reality constituting a *continuous advance into novelty*. As already noticed, moved by its intrinsic desire to know itself (*bodhicitta*), the self meets itself; meeting itself results in (i.e. is constituted of) a *self-expression* of cognition, a novel *expression* of self. And, as is the normality or reason (*dori*) of language, this novel expression abides at/as its dharma-position in/of total existence-time, thus self/other (Buddha, reality) begets novel expressions ad infinitum.

Enlightenment – seeing the true nature of the self – is an experiential *activity*, not a fixed state or condition. Enlightenment does not bestow Zen mastery or the capacity to teach Zen. Nor does it endow one with supernatural powers, supernormal intelligence, or saintliness, much less remove one from moral obligations, causation, or delusion. Enlightenment amounts to a *normal* perspective, a perspective from which an *accurate* view of reality is accessible in/as the here-now of existence-time.

An accurate view is *not* omniscience, but a view *from which* accurate knowledge can be realized. When one stands on a mountaintop surrounded by clouds, one's view of the world, thus one's place in it, is constricted. When the clouds clear, one's view naturally expands, increasing one's capacity to accurately view the world, and one's place in it – which nevertheless still requires effort and intention. Similarly, by clearing away the clouds of delusion (e.g. false presuppositions, bias, etc.), enlightenment clarifies one's view of the true nature of reality, providing a reliable perspective from which one can confidently venture forth; a perspective consisting of certainty concerning the nature of self-and-other manifest as an unshakable trust in the *normality* of one's own body-mind – an entrustment by the individual self in/to its dharma-position in/of total existence-time (Buddha).

Seeing is Fashioning

For the cosmology of a civilization both reflects and influences all human activity, motivation, and self-understanding that takes place within its parameters. It is the container for everything else.
Richard Tarnas[212]

What has been described like this is that life is the self, and the self is life.
Shobogenzo, Zenki[213]

The Zen tradition of 'Dharma transmission' or 'Buddhas alone together with Buddhas,' presents the reason (*dori*) of the advance of the universe into novelty. This reason harmonizes with the reason of self-generation inherent to the metaphorical nature of reality.

Briefly, the doctrine of transmission presents the dynamics of the elaborating quality of 'enlightened wisdom' (*bodhi prajna*, or *prajna paramita*). Enlightened wisdom (initially realized by Shakyamuni Buddha) is portrayed as being 'transmitted' from the self to the self via the analogy of 'master and apprentice'; as the master transmits the knowledge and skill of a craft to an apprentice, a Buddha transmits the wisdom of enlightenment to a disciple. This analogy presents an image of transmission that is more accessible than images like 'Buddha to Buddha' or 'self and self.'[214]

Now, just as novel expressions/meanings are realized in everyday language through the 'bridging' of two or more different metaphors,[215] novel expressions of self (i.e. dharmas) are realized through the bridging (transmission) of 'expressions of self' with 'self-expressions.'

Accordingly, 'seeing' (with the Dharma-eye) is 'begetting,' 'creating,' or 'fashioning.' When dharmas are seen *as they are*, the 'seeing self' resonates with the 'seen self' in a dynamically creative process that 'rings out *through* space and time,' and 'rings out *as* space and time.' This is the 'actualization of the universe' (*genjokoan*).

To clarify, utilizing the Dharma-eye the self sees its true nature – thus sees its all-inclusiveness and its fathomless infinity. In light of its all-inclusiveness, *total existence-time* (the myriad dharmas) is seen *as a particular form* – *this* dharma here-now and no other. In light of its fathomless infinity, *a particular form* – *this* dharma here-now – is seen *as total existence-time*. This capacity of the Dharma-eye to see 'beyond the many and the one' is graphically presented in *Shobogenzo, Genjokoan* as, 'When one side is illumined, the other side is darkened.' Seeing total existence-time *as* a particular form is seeing what 'is illumined'; seeing a particular form as total existence-time is seeing what 'is darkened.'

To see (illumine) 'this side' of an apple is to see (darken) 'that side' of an apple; seeing 'this side' *depends on* (and therefore *confirms*) the *presence* of 'that side' – thus, seeing 'this side' of the apple is seeing the whole apple *as it is* – illumined/darkened. Likewise, in seeing (illumining) any particular form, the Dharma-eye confirms the (darkened) *presence of* the totality of the self. This illustrates the co-essential and co-extensive nonduality of enlightenment and delusion.

An expansion of enlightenment is precisely matched by an expansion of delusion. No matter how many times, or how fast we turn an apple around, seeing it always *depends on* illuming one side and darkening the other.

Similarly, no matter how intense or expansive enlightenment is, it always depends on illumining one side and darkening the other. Seeing one's true nature is *confirming* this truth; great enlightenment is the normal ability to intelligibly discern whatever is illumined, great delusion is the normal dependence of illumination on darkening – to illumine anything is to darken everything else.

The Double-Edged Sword: Killing and Giving Life, Truth and Falsity

In this light the indexical analogy of "the finger pointing to the moon" is highly misleading, if not altogether wrong, because it draws on a salvifically inefficacious conception of language.
Hee-Jin Kim[216]

This nondual working of illumining/darkening is the reason (*dori*) of the Dharma-eye. This reason is sometimes presented in Zen by the metaphor of a 'double-edged sword' – the 'double-edge' showing its action simultaneously kills *and* gives life.

Expressions and images of death, common in Zen literature, are often used to emphasize that enlightenment (normality) has as much to do with killing as it does with giving life. Like Hades, the Grim Reaper, and Yama, the 'Great Death' of Zen mythology is always alive and vital here-now. Accordingly, the expressions and images of death in Zen ultimately perform the same vital task they do in all the great myths; killing selfish pride (egocentricity); the basis of fear and greed, doubt, confusion, formalism, literalism, and dogmatism.

Zen's method of killing is making normality (thusness) self-evident – evident to the self. Zen's weapon is mythopoeism – expressions that illumine the true nature of reality by clearly revealing what is true *as* true, and clearly revealing what is false *as* false.

All expressions are expressions *of* truth (i.e. dharmas). To see an expression *as it is*, is to see the *true nature of* an expression; thus 'seeing' and 'expression' manifest as an actual instance of enlightenment (normality). To see an expression *as it is not*, is *not* to see the *true nature of* an expression; thus 'seeing' and 'expression' manifest as an actual instance of delusion (abnormality).

That all expressions are expressions of truth means that the reasoning here applies to expressions that assert *erroneous* or *false* notions as well as those that assert accurate or true ones. An expression asserting a false notion is *an expression of truth* that asserts a false notion – *an expression* is a dharma, a manifest form of truth; *what it asserts*, whether true or false, is a *quality of* that dharma. Hence, seeing an expression that asserts something true *as it is*, is an instance of enlightenment; seeing an expression that asserts something false *as it is*, is an instance of enlightenment. And seeing an expression that asserts something true or something false *as it is not*, is an instance of delusion. Hence, an instance of enlightenment is a dharma – an actual, significant, form of existence-time – and an instance of delusion is a dharma.

As a dharma, an instance of enlightenment is a thought, word, or deed that functions harmoniously with reality as it is, thus facilitates one's ability to see/fashion true nature as it is. As a dharma, an instance of delusion is a thought, word, or deed that functions as a divergence from reality as it is, thus negates or hinders one's ability to see true nature as it is. As dharmas, actual instances of both enlightenment and delusion 'abide in their dharma positions.' Killing metaphorically, then, means 'killing false views' by 'bringing them to life' – not eradicating them or dismissing them as illusory, but by *'revealing them as they are'* (i.e. 'real' falsities, 'true' errors). In short, 'giving life' is seeing truth *as* truth and seeing falsity *as* falsity; 'killing' is ceasing to see truth as falsity and ceasing to see falsity as truth.

Since all experience is actualized by illumining/darkening, all literal expressions/readings are inherently biased (partial, one-sided). For 'illumining/darkening' is *literally* a *logical contradiction*. This 'logical contradiction' of literalism is 'paradoxical truth' in mythopoeism. And as the truth of all dharmas *is* paradoxical (illumining/darkening, emptiness/form, enlightenment/delusion), the truth of all expressions *is* paradoxical – hence, beyond the capacity of literal expression or understanding.

Before proceeding I need to clarify what I meant when I stated that the 'truth' or 'falsity' *asserted* by an expression is not a 'dharma' but rather a 'quality' *of* a dharma. Where 'dharmas' are particular *forms of* reality, 'qualities' are particular *attributes* or *characteristics of* dharmas. Blue, sharp, deep, and cold, for example, are *qualities of* blue *dharmas*, sharp *dharmas*, deep *dharmas*, and cold *dharmas* – blue, sharp, deep, and cold are not realities in themselves (dharmas). Likewise, truth and falsity exists only as true thoughts, words, and deeds (dharmas) and false thoughts, words, and deeds (dharmas). Discerning falsity, therefore, always consists of discerning a *particular* falsity. A false view, being a dharma 'as it is' (i.e. a real *false* view), is 'killed' by 'bringing it to life' (clearly revealing its falsity 'as it is').

In harmony with the nature of the self, then, the transmission of enlightened wisdom is paradoxically *ambiguous*. Expressions of truth, having as their reason or function (*dori*) the illumination of the truth of reality, must, by nature, be open, fluid, paradoxical, elusive, unfathomable, subtle, unpredictable, and most significantly, *unfinished*.

Truth and falsity are qualities of things, not things in themselves – thus truth is not a 'thing' that can be learned, discovered, or encountered in a general or definitive law, declaration, description, or explanation. Truth is only and always a *quality of* a particular dharma – truth is *the* 'as it is' quality of *any* and *every* particular dharma.

As every dharma is experienced/exists through illumining/darkening, every expression of truth is inclusive of both the truth *expressed* and the truth *unexpressed* (hence the totality of truth). To illumine *this* truth (this side) is to darken *that* truth (the other side), one that clearly sees an *expressed* truth (illumined) sees the truth that one *does not see* the *unexpressed* truth (darkened) – thus Zen practice-enlightenment (seeing/fashioning truth) is ever *unfinished*.

Popular notions of Zen expressions as 'enigmatic,' 'perplexing,' or 'bewildering,' are largely the result of attempts to read Zen expressions apart from *their context within the unexpressed* (unfinished). To read Zen expressions literally or objectively is to read them 'as they are not.' Notions derived from such readings are not mere errors, they are constraints; such notions immediately obstruct the very truth expressed.

Literal expression and egocentricity are both achieved by constraining or restraining processes; a literal 'this' is achieved by excluding 'that'; self is 'centered' by restraining the 'periphery' or 'distributed' self. Since expressions of truth communicate the whole *truth* to the *whole* self, the truth of expressions is inherently denied to literal expression and inaccessible to an egocentric perspective. This is why Zen insists that the nondual perspective (inclusive of, and going beyond the many and the one) is necessary for the transmission of wisdom.

Expressions of truth, verbal and otherwise, call us to scrutinize our presuppositions, not least of all our presuppositions concerning the nature of our self. This calling is a resonance between self and self, an intimation of enlightenment; *bodhicitta*. Mythopoeic language communicates truth by *exemplifying* truth (rather than defining or representing it). Metaphor communicates significance (*dori*; wisdom, reason) by directly demonstrating the interdependence of various dharmas (e.g. where literal expression says 'A' is 'A', metaphor shows 'A' is 'B' or 'not-A').

Self is the root metaphor of Zen because it exemplifies the truth that all expressions *about* the self are expressions *of* the self (self-expressions). Self as metaphor communicates self-knowledge by directly manifesting as each dharma and all dharmas. All dharmas are expressions (figures, forms, images) of self; self expresses self by ceaselessly abandoning or 'casting-off' universality for individuality, self realizes self by ceaselessly casting-off individuality for universality. Death, the ultimate limitation of the individual self, is and has always been intrinsic to the unlimited universal self. The eternal liberation of all beings from suffering, the ultimate fulfillment of the universal self, is and has always been intrinsic to the limited individual self.

In recognizing the self as its root metaphor, Zen doctrine and methodology provide a perspective from which the myriad dharmas are seen as they are; expressed forms of the nondual activity of the individual self (myriad dharmas) and the universal self (mind alone). This perspective illumines the true nature of the self, revealing the living vitality of the myriad dharmas.

The revelation of the living vitality of the myriad dharmas, or what Dogen calls the 'revaluated world' (*shutsuro*)[217] manifests as an intimate knowledge of the sacred normality of all dharmas. The instruments and institutions of civilization, the inherent striving for and grappling with the great questions concerning justice, morality, and meaning, as well as the infrastructure of housing, transportation, communication, technology, and manufacturing are seen as they are – the sacred manifestations of Buddha, Tao, the normal mind. This metaphorical perspective 'revaluates' the world simply by revealing it as it is; by clearly demonstrating that each and all the myriad dharmas constituting the totality of existence-time here-now is the sole ancestor that is every 'I', every 'I' that is the sole ancestor. Upon encountering this perspective, the dualistic, ego-centered world of external beings, insentient objects, dead matter, and empty space stretching outward and away from the self in all directions, is instantaneously transformed to the true mythopoeic vision of the world wherein trees, lakes, motorcycles, shoes, and figures of speech are sentient beings and even ordinary tiles have hearts:

> If we belittle tiles as being lumps of clay, we will also belittle people as being lumps of clay. If people have a Heart, then tiles too will have a Heart.
> *Shobogenzo, Kokyo*[218]

The 'revaluation' of the world is a 'metaphorical transposition' – the *apocalypse* of the common world that is simultaneously the *revelation* of the Buddha world – wherein the true *valuation* of the world is recognized and actualized by/as authentic Zen practice-enlightenment. From this perspective wherein all dharmas are recognized as unique instances of Buddha, notions of 'superiority and inferiority' give way to the active engagement of discerning and actualizing authenticity. This means, for one thing, that manifest human feelings, interests, and passions are not viewed as more or less 'real' (or important) than mountains, stars, historical facts, or scientific proofs; Melville's Ahab and the carbon dating of a fossil are expressions of the self (self-expressions), equally real, unique instances of Buddha, hence, sacred, eternal, and sentient. The self is the root metaphor of Zen because Zen recognizes that all dharmas are self-actualizations.

Continuous Actualization of Sole-Sitting – The Keystone of Zen

Nevertheless, mediocre persons in recent times are foolish enough to disregard the old tradition and, having no instructions from Buddhas, maintain erroneously that there are five distinct traditions in [Zen] Buddhism. This shows its natural decline. And no one has yet come to save this situation except my teacher, Ju-ching, who was the first one to be greatly concerned with it. Thus humanity has been fortunate; Dharma has deepened.
Shobogenzo, Butsudo[219]

To clearly see is to use the 'eye to read scriptures' or true Dharma-Eye. To use the Dharma-Eye it must first be opened, and thereafter skillfully developed and continuously actualized. This ongoing development and actualization is the keystone of authentic Zen practice-enlightenment, the art of Zen Dogen calls 'solely-seated' or 'wholly sitting' meditation (*shikantaza*, *zazen*-only).

When the Dharma-Eye is active, Zen practice-enlightenment (*zazen*-only) is continuous. Accordingly, practice-enlightenment is not confined to meditation, studying sutras, training with koans, or any other particular form, condition, or activity. To the Dharma-Eye total existence/experience is solely-seated in/as here-now. Going to work, taking out the garbage, mowing the lawn, and eating meals is solely-sitting, is practice-enlightenment. *Shobogenzo* presents detailed examples of the sole-sitting of cooking meals, making robes, cleaning teeth, even wiping one's ass. With the true Dharma-Eye, these are not seen as mundane tasks, as mere cooking, sewing, and cleaning, they are clearly seen as the normal mind, the Tao, authentic Zen practice-enlightenment. In short, when the Dharma-Eye opens one immediately leaves the world of the common (deluded) view.

> Once we find the Way that arrives at Buddha, we leave the area of the common person immediately. The people that have mastered this Way are few.
> *Himitsu Shobogenzo, Bustu-kojo-no-ji*[220]

From the perspective of Zen cosmology, then, Zen practitioners *cannot* engage in ordinary tasks – or engage in extraordinary tasks for that matter. For, to the Dharma-Eye there are neither mundane nor sacred tasks – a task is a task as it is, total existence is Buddha. An authentic Zen practitioner, by definition, *solely* performs Zen practice-enlightenment. In the terms of the doctrine of emptiness, practice-enlightenment *is* not practice-enlightenment, *therefore* practice-enlightenment *is* practice-enlightenment. In other words, when there truly *is* no Zen practice-enlightenment there truly *is* nothing *other than* Zen practice-enlightenment.

In contrast to a popular notions and 'orthodox' interpretations of 'Dogen's *shikantaza*' or 'just sitting' fashioned and adopted by various groups and individuals since Dogen's death, the reality of 'solely sitting' presented by *Shobogenzo* has nothing to do with the kind of 'sitting' that is thought of, spoken about, or performed in the 'area of the common person.'

Because, 'The people that have mastered this Way are *few*,' it is inevitable that the *majority* of notions, definitions, explanations, and interpretations about 'this Way' (*shikantaza*) are erroneous or distorted. As to how such distortions, or those that advocate them, should be seen and treated, we would not go wrong to heed Dogen's guidance here:

> There will be those who dote on what has passed and try to mimic that, and there may even be demons who slander those above them and refuse to learn from them. Do not be attracted to either type or feel resentment towards either. Why do I say not to feel sorry for them or resent them? Because it is said that people who recognize the three poisons of greed, hatred, and delusion to be what they are, are rare enough, so there is no need to feel resentment towards those who do not. Even more importantly, you should not lose sight of the intention that arose when you first took delight in seeking the Way of the Buddhas. It is said that when we first give rise to this intention, we are not seeking the Dharma so that others will praise us, but are discarding thoughts of fame and gain. Without seeking fame or gain, we should simply be persons who hold to the true

course of realizing the Way, never concerning ourselves with expectations of recognition or support from rulers or other officials.

Even though this is the ideal, there are some people today who, alas, are devoid of any fundamental spiritual aspirations, having no spiritual goal that they seek, and are not the least concerned over their delusive entanglements with both ordinary people and those in lofty positions.
Shobogenzo, Keisei Sanshoku[221]

It is worth noting that many who identify themselves as representatives of 'Dogen's Zen' actually do advocate forms of 'practice' characterized as 'goallessness' – suspiciously similar to the 'delusive entanglement' Dogen identifies here as 'having no spiritual goal.'

In any case, our primary concern is what *'shikantaza'* or 'just sitting' is according to *Shobogenzo*. To begin with, the term *'shikan'* (of *shikantaza*), translated as 'solely' or 'just' as in 'just sitting' (*shikan*; just, *taza*; sitting), does not denote 'merely,' or 'simply,' but rather, 'totally' or 'wholly.'

It is worth noticing here that *'shikan'* is a homophone of *'chih-kuan'* (Sanskrit; *samatha-vipassana*) a central notion in the Tendai school, the Buddhist tradition Dogen was initially ordained in and which served as a major influence throughout his career. In Tendai Buddhism, *'chih-kuan'* (*chih*; *samadhi*; tranquil meditation, and *kuan*; *prajna*; enlightened insight) emphasizes the radical nonduality of 'practice' (*shu*) and 'enlightenment' (*sho*). In taking *'shikan'* as connoting both 'soley' and 'meditation/insight,' *'shikantaza'* can be seen as expressing/reading the 'seated human form' (*taza*) as 'practice-enlightenment is the whole of Buddhism itself' (i.e. the sole realization of 'Buddha alone together with Buddha'). The possibility that Dogen intentionally employs *'shikan'* with the Tendai sense of the homophone *'chih-kuan'* intact has been noted by the scholarly community[222] but generally dismissed as unverifiable. In view of Dogen's frequent use of homophones,[223] together with the fact that he was intimately familiar with the connotations of both terms, I take the *intentional* double meaning of *'shikan'* as a 'given' and consider the notion it was *unintended* as extremely unlikely.

Now, while it should go without saying, it often does not, thus I should point out that in *Shobogenzo* the terms *'shikantaza,' 'zazen,'* etc. are, like all Zen expressions (and sacred literature generally) meant mythopoeically, *not* literally. That is, in *Shobogenzo* *'shikantaza'* and *'zazen'* designate 'authentic Zen practice-enlightenment' – they do not mean *literally* 'sitting in meditation.' From the perspective of the Zen tradition, 'Zen' in the term 'zazen' refers to the *Buddha-Dharma* (i.e. Buddhism itself), it does not simply denote its literal meaning, 'meditation.' Likewise the 'za' of 'zazen' and 'taza' of 'shikantaza' designate *practice-enlightenment,* they do not literally denote ordinary 'sitting.'

Next, in harmony with the principals of nonduality, particular Zen practitioners and particular instances of Zen practice-enlightenment (i.e. *shikantaza, zazen*-only) are nondual. Zen practice-enlightenment is solely manifest by and as Zen practitioners, Zen practitioners are solely manifest by and as Zen practice-enlightenment. In short, where authentic practice-enlightenment is manifest, there also authentic practitioners are manifest and vice versa – never one without the other.

It is not difficult to see how *zazen* (or *shikantaza*) functions as a *practical embodiment* and *application* of the truth of nonduality. Accordingly, *zazen* (i.e. Zen practice-enlightenment) is always something *specific* and *particular* – never something vague or general. In short, *zazen* is *always the same* in that it is *always* something *real and particular*, and *zazen* is *never the same* in that it is *never* a *prescribed* form or activity.

Shobogenzo's expressions of *zazen* or *shikantaza* mythopoeically presents (makes present) the Buddha's enlightenment on the 'immovable spot' or 'Bodhi-Seat.'[224] As an *archetypal image*, Shakyamuni Buddha seated in meditation on/at/as the Bodhi-Seat is the here-now (dharma-position) of existence-time wherein the Buddha awakens; the supreme moment-event of Buddhism. In other words, from the perspective of *Shobogenzo* (and Zen generally), *zazen* (*shikantaza*) is the 'axis mundi,' the still point at the center of the cosmos; the hub of the Dharma-Wheel wherein the myriad dharmas ceaselessly rise and set in and as the ceaseless advance of the universe into novelty. As such, *zazen* exemplifies the expression/activity of the three modes of conduct (thoughts, words, and deeds) of a Buddha; a normal (enlightened) human being wholly grounded in, at, and as the immovable spot.

Thus, to be a Zen practitioner is to actualize zazen – to actualize anything other than zazen is not to be a Zen practitioner. Hence, a Zen practitioner is 'solely seated' in and as existence-time here-now. Zen practice-enlightenment is, as it is, 'solely sitting.' From the Zen perspective it is dualistic to regard practice-enlightenment as a distinct, independent reality; a Zen practitioner cannot 'sit in zazen' *and* 'study sutras,' or 'sit in zazen' *and* 'train with koans,' etc., for a Zen practitioner 'solely sits.' As authentic practice-enlightenment is *solely* sitting (i.e. zazen); any and all of a Zen practitioner's thoughts, words, and deeds are *zazen*. Zen practitioners do not teach, work, eat, sleep, *and solely* sit – teaching, working, eating, sleeping are *solely* sitting.

For the Zen practitioner, then, there is *sitting* that is *solely sitting* and there is *walking* that is *solely sitting*; sitting is *not* walking and walking is *not* sitting, but both sitting and walking are *solely sitting*, zazen-only. The thinking of a Zen practitioner is not the speaking or acting of a Zen practitioner, but the thinking, speaking, and acting of a Zen practitioner is *solely sitting*, zazen-only.

> Hence, there is the mind's just sitting there, which is not the same as the body's just sitting there. And there is the body's just sitting there, which is not the same as the mind's just sitting. There is 'just sitting there with body and mind having dropped off', which is not the same as 'just sitting in order to drop off body and mind'. To have already realized such a state is the perfect oneness of practice and understanding that the Buddhas and Ancestors have experienced. Maintain and safeguard your mind's functions of remembering, considering, and reflecting. Thoroughly explore through your training what mind, intent, and consciousness truly are.
> *Shobogenzo, Zammai-o Zammai*[225]

Distorted, superficial, and superstitious notions concerning Dogen's teachings on *zazen* abound. The majority of them result from failing to appreciate the difference between metaphorical or mythopoeic language and the language of literal description, coupled with dualistic views of knowledge and existence. Many factors, including biased views of emptiness and imitation movements attempting to 'cash in' on the success of genuine Zen, have contributed to simplistic notions of seated meditation (*zazen*) over the course of Zen's history. The fallacious notions of zazen embraced by many in the Zen community today are fundamentally the same as those that have dogged Zen throughout its history. As mentioned, most common fallacies combine simplification and superstition; simplifications portraying zazen as '*mere* sitting' (the physical posture), and superstitions that revere zazen (mere sitting) as the '*only* element' essential for Zen liberation. Not infrequently 'mere sitting' is equated with enlightenment *itself*.

Commonly enwrapped in trite slogans about 'no goal,' 'nothing special,' 'everyday,' 'just this,' etc., *zazen* is often pawned off as a simple arrangement of the body-mind in a prescribed posture. *Shobogenzo* asserts what common sense suggests about such prescriptions:

> Even if some appear to understand physical sitting to be what the Buddha taught, they have not yet grasped that 'sitting there' means 'Just sit there!'
> *Shobogenzo, Zammai-o Zammai*[226]

Despite *Shobogenzo's* clear instructions, the classic Zen teachings, and common sense, superficial notions concerning the nature of Zen practice-enlightenment continue to be accepted and applied by groups and individuals far and wide. Routinely arranging their body-minds in an upright, cross-legged sitting postures for measured periods of time, numerous groups and individuals honestly believe they are enacting 'what the Buddha taught,' or at least 'what Dogen taught.' The simple mimicry of the Buddha's enlightenment is, according to their view, what Dogen means by 'sole-sitting' (*zazen*-only, *shikantaza*).

Of course, there is nothing wrong, or even unusual about erroneous understandings and false views; everyone has them, and even sages are compelled to continuously let go of views if they are to advance, expand, and clarify their understanding and skill. And the sages have not been remiss in their warnings about the stagnation and petrifaction inherent to fixed views. Nevertheless, egocentricity, spiritual pride, and allegiance to dogma, are powerful obstacles for even the sincerest and most knowledgeable genuine aspirants.

Promoters of distorted versions of 'Dogen's *zazen*' commonly speak and act *as if* Zen expressions are to be understood in the *literal* sense of descriptive language rather than the *mythopoeic* language common to sacred literature and true art; that 'solely sitting' *literally* means 'just sitting.' To impress the notion that this 'activity' is not only authentic Zen practice-enlightenment, but the *only* 'activity' necessary for actualizing authentic Zen liberation, proponents commonly cite cherry-picked phrases from Dogen's voluminous writings. Not surprisingly, in contradiction to their insistence on 'literal' readings of 'zazen,' etc., the same advocates frequently interpret non-zazen related expressions in Dogen's works as 'metaphors' for the *literal performance* of zazen. Of course, as typical of such advocates in all religious traditions, they commonly assume a very liberal tolerance for their own biases while imposing strict constraints on 'outsiders.' For example, if one of their 'supporting quotes' is contested by an apparently contradictory quote from the same work, the latter is summarily judged 'out of context,' while the former is treated as if its context were self-evident.[227]

In any case, the basic fallacy is that Dogen taught a unique style of Zen (i.e. Japanese Soto Zen) advocating an austere, single method practice (i.e. *zazen*-only) essentially consisting of the *literal* performance of physically sitting still, commonly portrayed as being accompanied with a particularly 'detached' mental attitude. The physical aspects described are technically equivalent to the seated meditation techniques common to nearly all Buddhist traditions; sitting upright in the lotus (or half-lotus) position (a crossed-legged sitting posture). The mental aspect or attitude advocated is often described (again, in *literal* terms) as a kind of intentionally 'goalless,' 'objectless,' or 'detached' state of mind.

When pressed to elaborate, proponents of such notions tend to explain 'goalless' or 'objectless' in negative or apophatic terms; as meaning the abstention or avoidance of utilizing traditional Buddhist techniques such as mindfulness of Buddha, the body, mind, breath, koans, scriptures, etc. – zazen is literally 'just sitting' still with no object in mind, maintaining a detached awareness wherein all thoughts, words, and deeds are to be 'let go of' without arousing questions or even second thoughts. This, it is said, is Dogen's supreme method, which is so effective no other practice is essential for authentic liberation; there is *literally* no need to offer incense, bow, chant, confess, read sutras, or perform any other traditional or nontraditional practice. To support such notions, the most frequently quoted 'authoritative' passage comes from Dogen's writing, *Bendowa*:

> After the initial meeting with a [good] counselor we never again need to burn incense, to do prostrations, to recite Buddha's name, to practice confession, or to read sutras. Just sit and get the state that is free of body and mind. If a human being, even for a single moment, manifests the Buddha's posture in the three forms of conduct, while [that person] sits up straight in *samadhi,* the entire world of Dharma assumes the Buddha's posture and the whole of space becomes the state of realization.
> *Bendowa*[228]

First, how does one that takes Dogen's expression on 'just sitting' literally go about manifesting 'the three forms of conduct (thinking, speech, and action), *while* [that person] sits up straight in samadhi...' literally? Fortunately, Dogen was a Zen master not a delusional zealot, thus his language, like that of all the great sages, is mythical, not historical, mythopoeic not biographic – *Shobogenzo* is an expression of human truth, not a narrative dissertation. If Dogen had truly believed practice-enlightenment consisted in the performance of a particular physical posture/mental attitude, it is unlikely that he would have dedicated his time and energy writing and teaching otherwise. In truth, Dogen understood, acknowledged, and taught that the real form of zazen-only was the myriad dharmas:

> You need to discern and affirm for yourself the underlying meaning of his saying, 'If you wish to see Buddha Nature, you must first rid yourself of your arrogant pride.' It is not that one lacks sight, but the seeing of which he spoke is based on ridding oneself of one's arrogant pride. The arrogance of self is not just of one kind, and pride takes many forms. Methods for ridding oneself of these will also be diverse and myriad. Even so, all of these methods will be 'one's seeing Buddha Nature'. Thus, you need to learn both to look with your eyes and to see with your Eye.
> *Shobogenzo, Bussho*[229]

Apparently the expression conveying the nature and dynamics of zazen-only presented in *Bendowa* had already been misconstrued as a *literal* prescription of 'Zen practice' rather than a mythopoeic expression of truth in Dogen's own day. For in the *Bukkyo* fascicle of *Shobogenzo*, written about a decade after *Bendowa*, Dogen again brought the same expression out, only this time he did so in a manner that could not so easily be superficially misrepresented as a merely formal prescription of practice.

> My late master constantly said, 'In my order, we do not rely on burning incense, doing prostrations, reciting names of buddhas, practicing confession, or reading sutras. Just sit, direct your energy into pursuing the truth, and get free of body and mind.'
>
> Few people clearly understand an expression like this. Why? Because to call 'reading sutras' 'reading sutras' is to debase it, and not to call it 'reading sutras' is to be perverse. 'You are not allowed to talk and not allowed to be mute: say something at once! Say something at once!' We should learn this truth in practice. Because this principle [of reading sutras] exists, a man of old has said, 'To read sutras we must be equipped with the eyes of reading sutras.'
> *Shobogenzo, Bukkyo*[230]

Obviously, if this expression was meant literally, more than a 'few people' would have clearly understood it. Calling it 'reading sutras' debases it because it cuts it out of the whole reality of its existence (i.e. reading sutras/not-reading sutras); not calling it 'reading sutras' is perverse because it ignores the truth of its real form (i.e. 'reading sutras'). For those 'few' that clearly understand, 'reading sutras' is *just sitting*, along with offering incense, bowing, chanting, and confessing. To clearly understand just sitting, reading sutras, or any other aspect of the Buddha Dharma, we must activate the Dharma-Eye. To read sutras, the ordinary eyes of literal description are simply not the appropriate tools; we must be equipped with the eye to read sutras.

There is a reliable rule for distinguishing the 'zazen' that is Dogen's archetypal image of Zen actualization, and the 'zazen' of ordinary seated meditation that is routinely practiced by Buddhists and non-Buddhists alike (which Dogen elucidates in his meditation manuals). Whenever 'zazen' (or just sitting etc.) is treated or regarded as a *separate* activity or *distinct* action, as *one* activity *among* others (e.g. working, reading, eating, etc.), it is definitely *not* the *zazen*-only illumined and presented by *Shobogenzo*. As the formal or literal practice of seated meditation, zazen is simply *one* form of activity *among* many forms of activity. As the actualization of the universe (i.e. *genjokoan*), however, zazen is not only wholly inclusive of 'the three forms of human conduct' (thinking, speech, and action), it is total existence itself, the myriad dharmas as they are.

> In this way, you need to thoroughly explore through your training the thousands of aspects, nay, the hundreds of thousands of aspects of just sitting.
> Shobogenzo, Zammai-o Zammai[231]

Fashioning a Moon and Fashioning a Rice Cake

If a person looks for buddha outside of life and death, that is like pointing a cart north and making for [the south country of] Etsu, or like facing south and hoping to see the North Star. It is to be amassing more and more causes of life and death, and to have utterly lost the way of liberation. When we understand that only life and death itself is nirvana, there is nothing to hate as life and death and nothing to aspire to as nirvana. Then, for the first time, the means exist to get free from life and death. To understand that we move from birth to death is a mistake. Birth is a state at one moment; it already has a past and will have a future. For this reason, it is said in the Buddha-Dharma that appearance is just nonappearance. Extinction also is a state at one moment; it too has a past and a future. This is why it is said that disappearance is just non-disappearance. In the time called "life," there is nothing besides life. In the time called "death," there is nothing besides death. Thus, when life comes it is just life, and when death comes it is just death; do not say, confronting them, that you will serve them, and do not wish for them.

This life and death is just the sacred life of buddha. If we hate it and want to get rid of it, that is just wanting to lose the sacred life of buddha. If we stick in it, if we attach to life and death, this also is to lose the sacred life of buddha.
Shobogenzo, Shoji[232]

Consciousness, Speculation, and Actualization

Because the fundamental elements of reality (i.e. dharmas) are recognized as form/essence unities constituted of particular instances of experience, Zen cosmology recognizes that the *form experienced* is the *reality encountered*. No division exists between the *appearance* of dharmas and the *reality* of dharmas. The form of a dharma is the true nature of a dharma, the true nature of a dharma is the form of a dharma; therefore, the form of a dharma is the form of a dharma, the true nature of a dharma is the true nature of a dharma.

As dualistic systems grant existence to unexperienced realities, they grant independent status to aspects of experienced realities. Where the former *bestows reality on* purely hypothetical notions, the latter *bestows independence on* elements of interdependent realities. More specifically, the latter conceptually abstracts – hence *subtracts* – qualities from dharmas and grants them status as independent existents. For example, the color white is abstracted from a cloud or snowflake and conceived of as an independent reality called 'white' or 'whiteness.' But in reality 'white' or 'whiteness' exists only as a *quality* or *attribute* of dharmas. 'White' is something that does not exist; one cannot encounter general 'whiteness' or imagine 'white' apart from a dharma. 'White' is not a thing, being, or event (i.e. a dharma) but an *attribute* or *quality of* things, beings, or events.

Within the contemporary Zen community, many grant independent existence to 'realities' that are just as nonexistent as 'white.' For example, *qualities* like form, emptiness, practice, right-views, and true nature are commonly spoken of and regarded as if they were actual things, *independent realities* that exist in and of themselves. Conceptualization, abstract speculation, generalization, and the like are fine as far as they go, indeed these are capacities Zen encourages us to develop, refine, and put to good use – however, to see abstractions and similar derivatives as independent entities is to see them *as they are not*; to be deluded. Within the Zen community, false views concerning the existent nature of 'enlightenment' and 'delusion' are probably second only to fallacies about the independent nature of 'emptiness' and 'form.' When delusion and enlightenment are thus reified, their true nature – as *attributes of* particular dharmas – is obscured, thus their liberating *potential* is effectively subverted into the *actualization of bondage*. Thus the refrain in Zen literature not to mistake concepts or generalizations for independently existent realities, for example, Dogen reminds us:

> Delusion, remember, is something that does not exist. Realization, remember, is something that does not exist.
> *Shobogenzo, Yui-butsu-yo-butsu*[233]

From the Zen perspective, the particular quality exhibited by a dharma is far less important than the particularity of the dharma itself. For example, clearly seeing the particular form/essence demonstrated by an enlightened thought, word, or deed is the fundamental point – not the fact that it possesses the quality of enlightenment. In other words, the significance and value of a dharma is its existence as a *distinct instance* of reality, not the presence of a quality it does or does not possess. In short, Zen practice-enlightenment is more concerned with the actual *particularity* of a dharma, and less concerned with the qualities or characteristics that one dharma might share with others. To see a particular enlightened deed as it is, is to actualize reality (*genjokoan*), to see that one particular deed and another particular deed share the quality of enlightenment, is to conceptualize about reality. The former 'makes' a deed as it is, the latter 'makes' an abstract concept from two deeds. Recall that Zen recognizes 'seeing' or 'experiencing' dharmas as corollary with 'fashioning' or 'making' dharmas.

> The emphasis in Dogen's Zen thus deepens the meaning of "*seeing things as they are*" by construing it as "*changing/making* things as they are."
> Hee-Jin Kim[234]

While abstract notions are useful, to see them *as they are not*, is not only a failure to see them *as they are*, but to obstruct *one's ability to see the reality they are derived from*, thus fashion it as it should be. For example, the abstract concept of 'enlightenment' derived from various enlightened thoughts, words, and deeds (i.e. dharmas) might be useful for communicating to others, or clarifying one's understanding, but if it is seen as identifying 'enlightenment' as an independent thing, being, or event, it fails to see the abstract concept as it is, *and* it bars one from seeing enlightenment as it is.

This is in accordance with the nondual nature of existence and experience; the fact that 'appearance' and 'reality' are not two. The *reality* of a dharma is proportional to *how clearly and comprehensively* it is *discerned as it is*. The clearer, more fully it is seen, the greater is its realization. Experience is existence because discerning is creating. To *see* dharmas as they are, is to *make* dharmas as they are (thus, as they should be); the clearer and more comprehensively dharmas are discerned, the realer they are.

To see dharmas *as they are not*, is *not* to make them *as they are* or *as they are not*, but rather, to obstruct our view, to mask dharmas behind 'false views.' To see a tadpole as it is – that particular tadpole – is to make that tadpole as it is. To see a tadpole *as it is not* – to see it as a leaf, say – is not only to fail to make *that* tadpole *as it is*, it is to obscure its true nature with a 'false view' (e.g. the view, 'that is a leaf'). Thus, to see a dharma *as it is not*:

- Is to fail to see it *as it is* (thus, fail to make it *as it is*).
- Is to obscure it behind a false view.

From there the task is no longer simply to see the dharma as it is, but first to see the *false view* that obscures it *as it is*. To see a false view as it is, is to see it as *a real* false view. Thus it is not to be vanquished or eradicated from existence, but rather to be revealed as it truly is – a *false* view. The fact that it is 'false' does not mean it is bad, wrong, evil, illusory, or inferior in any way to any other dharma. Insofar as it is a real false view, it is a dharma, a manifest form of Buddha, an instance of Buddha-nature. To see a false view as it is (a false view) is to make it as it is (thus, as it should be – a *false* view). To see a false view *as it is not* (e.g. a true view, an illusion, an evil, etc.) is only to 'add delusion to delusion' – to *beget* false views (dharmas) *from* false views.

The fact that many such dharmas – false views – are beget in this way is evinced, for example, by explanations in popular 'Zen' books that portray enlightenment as 'ineffable,' 'incommunicable,' 'undifferentiated,' and similar ambiguous vagaries.

As experience is existence, there are no vague or arbitrary realities; any and all experience consists of real, particular sights, sounds, smells, tastes, tactile sensations, and thoughts. While the extent of the realization of forms, sounds, fragrances, flavors, feelings, and cognitions is proportional to the extent they are experienced as they are, no reality, no matter how small, is vague or arbitrary. There are certainly vague ideas – but even their reality is exactly and distinctly *what it is*. There are arbitrary actions, but their existence too, is only *as it is* – and not otherwise.

This is why the experiential encounter is the standard in Zen; it is the *only* standard that is completely reliable. Theoretical knowledge, systems of thought, concepts, generalizations, and so on can and should be effectively employed and utilized – which means, in accordance with what they are; theories, systems, concepts, generalizations, and so on. Seen *as they are*, they are seen as (thus fashioned as) intrinsic qualities of existence-time itself, reliable characteristics of existence that, when treated in harmony with their normality, contribute to the normal human capacity for the realization of universal liberation and fulfillment that Zen calls '*genjokoan*' (i.e. the actualization of the universe).

In light of this we can see that Zen cosmology agrees with the claim by scientific cosmology that experiment (experientially observed empirical evidence) is the only reliable standard for truth. Zen, however, insists on the *radical* adherence to *all* the implications of this standard. For Zen, applying this standard means unequivocally accepting and accounting for *all the actual evidence* of experiment – *all* of which is as dependent on *subjective* reality as it is *objective* reality. If *subjective* experience is unreliable then *objective* existence is unreliable – for whether the findings of experiments are realized through the naked eye, a telescope, a computer, a particle collider, a mathematical theorem, or any other means, they are *only* realized through a *human subject*. Clearly, if reality can be considered as *constituted* of any kind of 'substance' or 'material,' that material must first and foremost be identified as sentient *experience*. For the 'material' of the self and the world is only and always encountered as *particular* instances of subjective experience; *specific* objects of consciousness actualized in and as *definite* place-times here-now. Just as any and all actual instances of consciousness are only and always encountered as particular forms at specific place-times of total existence-time.

Experience As It Is: Existence As It Is

It is obvious that there is a significant difference between our subjective sense of self and our objective sense of self. Our subjective sense of self is as of an isolated, private experience; a self that is privy to ourselves alone. Our objective sense of self is as of a public, non-concealable appearance; a self that is out there for all to see. Here I want to consider some implications concerning these two distinct senses of self in order to help clarify Zen's view that objective existence is *dependent on* subjective experience. More specifically, I want to address an implication that naturally presents itself in light of our discussion this far; if all dharmas are actualized (formed or fashioned) by subjective experience, then our existence as an 'objective' human being must be actualized by (thus *interconnected* with) one or more *particular* subjective being's experience (hence existence).

There is no need to argue about *which* (subjective or objective) of the selves 'I' experience as 'myself' is the *real* 'I'; it is clear they *both* are. Also, there is no denying that 'my' two senses of self demonstrate significant differences. My task, then, is to highlight the most significant characteristics of each of these two aspects of self experience. That is, to clearly distinguish the *differences* between the two by clarifying the particular qualities *unique* to each – to come to a clear vision of the attributes that qualify them to be accurately characterized as either subjective *or* objective, but not both at once.

First, insofar as a self is an *experienced* object, it is a *form*; a phenomenal appearance. This 'form' of self is commonly called a 'body.' Here it should be stressed that insofar as a self is *experienced as* a subject it is an *object* (i.e. something experienced) – thus also falls under the same terms; an *experienced* experiencer is a 'form' or 'body.' Next, insofar as a self is an *experiencing subject*, it is a *former*; an *actualizer* of phenomenal appearances. This 'former' of self is commonly called a 'mind.'

Here I hasten to add it is important to remember this discussion assumes the principles of nonduality; both 'body' and 'mind' refer to a *whole* self; when 'body' is illumined, 'mind' is eclipsed (i.e. present as shadowed) and vice versa.

Now if dharmas are actualized by/as sentient experience, as Zen contends, then each individual sentient being must experience a self/world that is *unique* to their self alone. 'Seeing the moon,' for instance, is an actualization of a 'seer' and a 'seen.' In the absence of either a seer or seen there could be no 'seeing the moon' – no 'seer' (of the moon) and no (moon) 'seen.' When I see the moon, a particular instance of 'seeing the moon' is actualized; when you see the moon, another particular instance of 'seeing the moon' is actualized. Each instance is a particular dharma, a particular location-time – you do not see my 'seeing the moon,' I do not see your 'seeing the moon.' My 'seeing the moon' is me/moon, your 'seeing the moon' is you/moon. The actual 'moon seen' is totally unique in either case, even if you and I are standing side by side at the same time. This is an experientially verifiable truth that is transmitted via a variety of Zen expressions, for example, the Zen koan 'You Don't See My Not Seeing':

> The *Surangama* scripture says, "When I do not see, why do you not see my not seeing? If you see my not seeing, naturally that is not the characteristic of not seeing. If you don't see my not seeing, it is naturally not a thing – how could it not be you?"[235]

'You' don't see 'my' not seeing, 'I' don't see 'your' not seeing. Of course this applies as well to 'my' *seeing*, as Yuanwu (compiler of the Zen classic

Hekiganroku) underscores by citing some context from the scripture that is the source of this koan:

> "If seeing were a thing, then you could also see my sight..."[236]

In any case, the main point is, if dharmas consist of sentient experience, each dharma must be *unique* to a *particular sentient being*. The moon that I see and the moon that you see are not *the same moon*. In fact, the moon that I see *tonight* is not even the same moon I saw *yesterday*:

> So although the moon was there last night, tonight's moon is not yesterday's moon.
> *Shobogenzo, Tsuki*[237]

This does not mean that Zen denies the *unity* or *oneness* of reality; the moon that I see and the moon that you see are undoubtedly real, manifest forms of one and the same reality. The sense in which they are the same will be taken up shortly; here I am focusing on how they are different. For the moment, then, the point is that the moon's actual existence consists only in and of its actualization by you, me, or another sentient being – in the absence of a 'moon experiencer' there is no 'experienced moon.' At the same time, and in harmony with the same reasoning (*dori*), the very instant that the moon is seen by you, me, or another sentient being, the moon is actualized in and as total existence-time; the whole of space and time actualize that particular instance of 'seeing the moon', that particular instance of seeing the moon actualizes the whole of space and time – as the totality of existence-time and as all the particular experiential instances of total existence-time:

> An eternal buddha says, "One mind is the whole Dharma, and the whole Dharma is one mind." So the mind is the whole Dharma, and the whole Dharma is the mind. And, because the mind is the moon, it may be that the moon is the moon. Because the whole Dharma as the mind is totally the moon, the whole world is the whole moon, and the "thoroughly realized body" is in its entirety the thoroughly realized moon. Even among the "three and three before and after"—which belong directly to eternity—is any not the moon? The sun-faced buddhas and moon-faced buddhas which are the present body-mind or object-subject may all be in the moon. Living-and dying, coming-and-going, are both "in the moon." The whole universe in ten

directions may be the top, bottom, left, and right of "in the moon." Daily functions now are the hundred things being utterly clear "in the moon," and are the mind of the ancestral masters being utterly clear "in the moon."
Shobogenzo, Tsuki[238]

This brings us to the next point; just as dualists grant independent existence to qualities abstracted from dharmas, so too they bestow independent existence to qualities abstracted from self. The emotional capacity, for instance, is commonly regarded as an aspect of self separate and distinct from the reasoning capacity of self; the intuitional and the instinctual qualities of self are seen and treated as independent of the former capacities as well as each other, and so on. Once such qualities are abstracted from the whole of human subjectivity, they are conceptually defined, evaluated, classified, and put in their 'places' so as not to interfere with one another. Thus the lover is supposed to be guided by the 'heart' (emotional capacity) not the 'head' (reasoning capacity) which is seen as unreliable in romantic matters. The opposite is assumed in 'more practical' affairs; only cold reason can be trusted with necessities; here the separate domain of emotion is out of its element. The instinctual aspects of self are not only separated from more 'civilized' capacities, but often far removed from them – at least in polite company. Intuition, déjà vu, synchronicity, and other less visually 'apparent' phenomena are commonly given a wide berth, not by seeing them as unfortunate 'matters of fact' like the 'lower,' 'reptilian' brain (i.e. instinct), but by seeing them as persistent but whimsical notions; common enough to be widely recognizable, but too far divergent from the 'factual' actualities allowed by the consensus of the common worldview to be seriously entertained.

In recognizing that *all* existence is *experienced* existence, Zen cosmology evades the entangling complications corollary with all such abstract compartmentalizing gobbledygook. Experience as it is, is existence as it is; and as all experience is particular, every experience is *uniquely* as it is. This is why true wisdom cannot be applied prior to verifying the true nature of reality. Only from the nondual perspective is it clear that, just as 'whiteness' is not something that exists, there is no such a thing as a 'sentimental feeling' an 'instinctual impulse' or an 'objective view.' A particular person can be emotionally moved by an actual sunset, a specific being might dive for cover at the sound of a gunshot, or an actual scholar might observe specific data from a particular viewpoint, but every such reality will inevitably involve a whole subjective self – a particular being wholly inclusive of their intellectual, emotional, instinctual, and other experiential capacities.

Totally objective scientists, emotional artists, or instinctual killers might be convincing on paper or screen, but no actual being – or experience – is so simplistic. Only real beings complete with *understanding* and *knowledge* can experience or express real *emotion*. Chaucer and Shakespeare would have been unable to affect real *emotional* responses without a real *knowledge* and *understanding* of human *existence*. Likewise, every true *thinker* is only able to achieve true *profundity* by possessing true *passion* and *aspiration*; Plato, Dogen, or Einstein could never have achieved their expressions if they had been totally objective, detached, or unconcerned.

Clearly, in the particular world we actually inhabit instinct and intuition are as essential to each thought, word, and deed as are sensation, emotion, and the intellect. Reason is as crucial to the poet as it is the philosopher, the sexual impulse is as necessary to the mother as it is to the lover. From the Zen perspective every real thought, word, and deed has its source in the whole self, thus the more the whole self is involved in one's thoughts, words, or deeds, the realer (both truer and more existent) one's thoughts, words, or deeds are. Accordingly, the depths and heights of the world and the self experienced vary in proportion to the clarity of each being's unique capacity. That is to say, not only do 'all beings not see water in the same way,' as Dogen says (*Shobogenzo, Sansuigyo*), but the level or degree of the reality of the water seen (hence actualized) differs among individual beings.[239] Therefore, the path of the Zen practitioner follows a course of continuous advancement; ever-increasing the clarity and degree of reality they actualize by developing and refining their ability to put more of their self into their activities (i.e. thoughts, words, and deeds).

In *Shobogenzo, Bussho,* Dogen provides an evocative illustration of the unity/differentiation of sentient experience by appealing to an event from Buddhist mythology wherein the ancestral master Nagarjuna 'manifests' his body in the form of the 'full moon.' In the course of his commentary, Dogen distinguishes between an 'ordinary being' and a 'Buddha' by describing the difference between their experiences of the 'moon.' The ordinary being is said to experience the moon as a 'round disc-like' circle in the sky that is somewhat like a 'coin' or 'rice-cake.' The Buddha, on the other hand is said to experience the moon as endowed with a great multitude of qualities and characteristics, including, for example, the ability to 'blink the eyes and twirl a flower' (a famous 'sermon' by the

Buddha) and to 'crack a smile' (one disciple's response to the 'famous sermon').

Now, the 'eye-winking, flower-twirling, face-smiling moon,' seen/fashioned in the *Bussho* fascicle , in context of our present discussion, is *realer* and *more significant* than the 'round rice-cake moon' precisely because Dogen manages to muster more of his whole being into the seeing/fashioning of that moon.

Because the common worldview is grounded on dualism its adherents are obliged to assert an unverifiable hypothesis. In this case, that the moon exists independent of subjective experience. To 'explain' what this independent moon 'really' is, advocates are compelled to reductionism; subtracting all but its most commonly experienced characteristics – thus arriving at the 'real moon' which is something like a 'round rice-cake' in the sky. In this way, the common view essentially grants final authority concerning the validity of an individual's knowledge to consensus; the 'round rice-cake moon' is a *generalization*; a 'composite-sketch' arrived at by *averaging* a multitude of various experiences. Everyone can see the white, disc-like, round rice-cake-like moon; these are apparent to even the most passive observer. Indeed, it is these *obvious* qualities that initially allow us to discern the moon as a *normal* element of our reality in the first place.

When Dogen testifies to the flower-twirling, face-smiling qualities, he is not *denying* the round, disc-like qualities, but *elaborating* upon them – *expanding* the experience (hence existence) of the moon and oneself. To see/fashion the flower-twirling moon is to 'increase the sacred life of the Buddha.' To reduce the moon to its 'common denominators' or, as is common in pseudo-Zen, 'just sit' and 'let go of' whatever is evoked in one's encounter with the moon, is to passively accept the 'rice-cake moon,' thus to 'waste one's life in vain.' On the other hand, to see/make the 'flower-twirling moon' is to recognize that *the normal mind is the Tao*.

Just as Zen recognizes the real distinctions between subjective experience and objective existence without denying their essential unity, Zen recognizes differences between conscious and unconscious functions without disregarding their unity. It is the recognition of the differentiated yet essential unity of consciousness that testifies to and informs the reasoning of Zen's insight concerning the various levels of profundity of existence/experience among individual beings – often referred to in terms of unique 'innate capacities.'

To clarify, we recognize the difference between voluntary and involuntary bodily functions; we can raise our arms or not raise them, but we cannot circulate our blood or not circulate it. From the common perspective the difference between what is voluntary and what is not is *practically* viewed as the difference between what is 'ourself' and what is 'other than ourself' – 'I' raise my arms or do not, but 'I' do not circulate my blood or not do so, rather the 'heart,' 'circulatory system,' or something else 'other than me' does that. Thus the reasoning of the common view *begins* from an assumption that identifies 'ourself' with voluntary functions and 'other than ourself' with involuntary functions – eating jalapeno bean dip with ice-cream is something 'I do,' indigestion is something that 'happens to me.'

Zen, on the other hand, recognizes that *both* 'self' *and* 'other' are coessential elements of both voluntary and involuntary functions – eating jalapeno bean dip with ice-cream is actualized by and as 'I and not I,' indigestion is realized by and as 'self and other.' At the level of this example the significance may appear minor, but when this unity of 'self' and 'other' is recognized in context of the more sophisticated capacities of human creativity its import is vast.

If I recognize perception, for example, as both something 'I do' *and* something that 'happens to me,' my experience, understanding, and conduct will significantly differ from what it will if I see perception as *either* something 'I do' *or* something that 'happens to me,' (or *partly* what 'I do' and *partly* what 'happens to me'). From the nondual perspective, for example, perceiving the cry of a hawk is both what 'I do' *and* what 'happens to me' – at that dharma-position the cry of the hawk is the whole of existence-time; there is no gap between 'cry,' 'me,' or 'the universe.'

From the perspective of dualism, the cry of the hawk is one reality and my perception another, independent reality. Perceiving the cry is *partly* something I do and *partly* something that happens to me, *partly* 'self' and partly 'other.' Now, if perceiving the cry of the hawk is only 'partly' something that *happens to me* – thus partly *not* 'me' – then perception, and by extension, experience in general, is *ultimately involuntary*. Even if perceiving is something 'I do,' I can have no actual choice in the matter; if a hawk cries I *can't help* but hear it, if instead a dog yelps, *I am compelled to hear that instead.* If I cover my ears I have no choice but to perceive the muffling sound of my hands against my ears or the blood surging in my head. In short, to accept the tenets of dualism is to see oneself as a victim of circumstances; 'I' may have the power to perceive, but perception itself is involuntary, hence, something that *happens to* me. When this line of reasoning is carried to its conclusion it amounts to a species of fatalism or predestination – even if the 'things' that constitute our experience of a self and a world are random (undetermined), our 'life' is ultimately something that *happens to* us, not something we 'do.'

Thus, owing to the widespread, longstanding acceptance of the fallacy of dualism the majority of the global population (consciously or unconsciously) uncritically presupposes that everything they 'know' – all sights, sounds, tastes, smells, tactile sensations, and thoughts – consists of arbitrary phenomena (appearances in the mind/brain, according to the representationalists) involuntarily engendered by the sense organs in reaction to happenstance occurrences in the external world. In short, concerning the experience/existence of phenomena, the self ('I,' 'me,' 'you') is ultimately a reflexive process; everything the self encounters (hence its *total* experience) is involuntarily perceived, cognized, conceived, or felt. Therefore, 'the moon' I see is unequivocally 'the moon' – not 'me.' Nothing 'I' do makes or influences what the moon is or does.

In contrast, by recognizing the reality of forms is dependent on the 'self' directed outward as well as the 'other' directed inward, the Zen perspective reveals that 'the moon' I see makes me what I am and I make it what it is. The moon is the self, and the self is the moon.

> What has been described like this is that life is the self, and the self is life.
> *Shobogenzo, Zenki*[240]

In sum, the moon perceived reflexively, involuntarily, or representationally is bound to appear (thus be experienced) as a flat whitish disc, somewhat like a rice-cake in the sky. Being perceived through an eye obscured by the scales of dualism, the moon could hardly appear otherwise. Perceiving the smiling, flower-twirling moon revealed by Dogen is dependent on the intentional, voluntary exercise of the Dharma-Eye, the normal human capacity of actualization.

The ordinary being sees dualistically, thus is plagued by fear and greed – fear of what is loathed, greed for what is desired – hence denies their identity with 'the other,' and denies 'the other' identity with their self. The normal being clearly sees that experiencing 'other' is fashioning and being fashioned by 'other' and cultivating the experiential capacities of one's self is self-actualization – increasing the sacred life of Buddha. At the place-time the hawk cries, there is nothing besides the cry of the hawk. The same reason (*dori*) applies to all dharmas, including those of 'life' and 'death.' Such is the sacred life of Buddha.

In the time called "life," there is nothing besides life. In the time called "death," there is nothing besides death. Thus, when life comes it is just life, and when death comes it is just death; do not say, confronting them, that you will serve them, and do not wish for them.

This life and death is just the sacred life of buddha. If we hate it and want to get rid of it, that is just wanting to lose the sacred life of buddha. If we stick in it, if we attach to life and death, this also is to lose the sacred life of buddha.
Shoji[241]

Consciously Actualizing the Universe (genjokoan)

If the doors of perception were cleansed every thing would appear to man as it is, Infinite. For man has closed himself up, till he sees all things thro' narrow chinks of his cavern.
William Blake[242]

The task is...not so much to see what no one has yet seen; but to think what nobody has yet thought, about that which everybody sees.
Erwin Schrödinger[243]

Contrary to notions about the possible dangers of conveying knowledge concerning self-actualization to novice students or those with less than honorable intentions, expressing the truth that the individual and the universe participate in a mutually coordinated process of self-actualization is never inappropriate. This is knowledge that should be assimilated along with Mother's milk. Those that argue the contrary do so from an egocentric perspective. Identifying the 'self' that fashions its reality as the 'personal' or 'ego' self, such proponents conclude that immature or malicious individuals might misuse their creative capacities for foolish or evil ends. There is no need to worry however; the measure of one's capacity for self-actualization is exactly the measure of one's normality. Thus the effectiveness of one's intentions is directly proportional to the enlightenment governing one's conduct. Any intention to actualize dharmas (things, beings, or events) that could hinder, restrain, mislead, or otherwise injure oneself or another would, being delusional by nature, be futile. For, in a nondual reality there can be no foolish or evil dharmas; folly and evil are not manifestations or actions, but failures to manifest or act.[244]

Two points I want to get at here are, sentient existence/experience (i.e. consciousness) is not fashioned *by* the world, but is the fashioner *of* the world; and, each sentient being is a unique and essential fashioner of the world.

The first point means, for one thing, that sentient experiences are not arbitrary forms or haphazard processes incidentally produced by or from an independent reality. Our realm does possess limitations –inherent restrictions on what can or cannot be actualized – and our realm can condition our existence (i.e. our experience of life), but it cannot *determine* or *alter* our essential nature. The second point means that each sentient being is responsible (has the ability to respond) to and for the condition or circumstances of their ever-advancing dharma-position, their particular here-now in existence-time. In this, no particular sentient being is superior or inferior to any other. Thus the differences in the degree of reality actualized by various sentient beings are difference in degrees of enlightened experience, not differences of better and worse or more or less essential.

Enlightenment, insofar as it is a measure of self-awareness, is what I call the 'integral character' of an individual's experiential capacity. By 'integral character' I mean the specific quality and quantity of the force that determines the nature and significance of the dharmas one experiences, as well as the patterns in which they are arranged. Experience is only experience when *someone* is experiencing *something* – in the absence of a pattern or arrangement (even if only an order of 'I' and 'not-I') nothing can be experienced as existent. What *can be experienced* as existent is dependent on *what is discerned* as existent – what *is experienced* as existent is dependent on what *can be discerned* as existent. One's 'integral character' at any give place-time (dharma-position) is one's *actual capacity to discern the dharmas* constituting that particular place-time *as they are*. One whose integral character is 'less developed' will, for example, discern (thus experience) the moon as having qualities 'somewhat like a rice-cake,' one whose integral character is 'more developed' will discern the moon as having qualities 'myriad and particular.' The integral character of the former and latter beings is as it is in each case; neither is better or worse, more or less essential.

Sentience, the normal capacity (i.e. enlightenment) to experience existence, is inherent to the human condition, thus even the least enlightened being is able to discern some qualities of reality, the rice-cake moon for instance. Those more profoundly awakened to their true nature (having further developed their normal capacities) are able to discern more qualities of reality, the flower-twirling moon for instance. The rice-cake moon can be discerned simply by virtue of being in the human condition; discerning the flower-twirling moon, however, requires the increased experiential capacities developed through sustained effort in systematic cultivation.

Zen practitioners, in accord with the normal human aspiration for full actualization (*bodhicitta*), consciously strive to engage their perceptual and cognitive abilities in the way that is here-now most efficacious for universal liberation and fulfillment. They recognize that their experience (hence existence) here-now is determined by their ability to respond (responsibility) here-now with wisdom and compassion – their ability to actualize enlightenment. Awake to the truth that all real enlightenment is particular, Zen practitioners engage solely in actualizing particular enlightened thoughts, words, and deeds in, at, and as particular location-times, all of which are experienced in, at, and as here-now.

The actual fruits of enlightenment are expressions of Buddha, real instances of true nature actualized as the things, beings, and events experienced as existence-time. And the medium through which expressions of Buddha are realized is that of human conduct, the enlightened thoughts, words, and deeds that are the products of normal human existence. Expressions of Buddha are actualized by the normal mind – that is, the whole unified being of the enlightened individual.

The average or common mind, habituated to abstraction and generalization, is easily perplexed by authentic expressions of Buddha, and is quick to agree with superficial explanations or interpretations that offer the safety and assurance of consensus opinion. Explanations and interpretations of the function or meaning of koans is one obvious example of this in the realm of Zen. In reality there is nothing complicated about expressions of Buddha; instances of reality are only and always *as they are*; particular, novel phenomena in and of existence-time. The confusions and dilemmas are imposed on them; commonly by inappropriate attempts to arrange novel instances of reality according to presuppositions, abstractions, or generalizations. Consider this Zen expression:

> The monks of the East hall and the monks of the West hall are arguing about a cat.

Zen Master Nansen happens by, a knife in his hand. Snatching up the cat, he says, "If you can say a word the cat will be spared. If you can't say a word I will kill it."

The monks are unable to say a word. Nansen cut the cat in two.[245]

An expression of Buddha presenting wisdom through the image of a Zen master bisecting a live kitten can hardly be classified as good or bad, comedy or tragedy, compassion or cruelty – clearly, all of these elements and more are present in such an expression. The composition of a koan (as well as its resolution) cannot be classified as a mental act or a physical act, as emotional or intellectual – it can only be produced (or resolved) by someone's whole being. Expressions of Buddha are fashioned from the whole cloth of experience – sights, sounds, smells, tastes, tactile sensations, and thoughts – and it is the normal capacities of sentient beings that arrange and order that fabric into the actual things, beings, and events encountered as the self and the world, existence and time.

Even the most enlightened beings are compelled to sift and sort, invent and experiment with the endless stream of unshaped potential ever actualizing their experience – the raw material with which they must strive to actualize the reality of their deepest aspiration. In Zen it is said, 'Shakyamuni Buddha has been practicing for 2500 years and he is only halfway there.'

Nonthinking

Composing a poem consists in the creative arrangement of various particular words and experiential elements. Normally the poet will only be distracted by random lists of words or unmediated forays down memory lane – hence needs to develop the ability to remain focused on the task at hand while maintaining access to their store of words and experiences. For similar reasons, Zen methodology incorporates the development and cultivation of the capacity to 'think not-thinking,' also called 'nonthinking.'

Nonthinking describes a normal human capacity; the ability to think (i.e. fashion rational thoughts) without losing awareness of the ever-present reality of not-thinking (essential nature, emptiness). All expressions of Buddha are dependent on clear (normal or enlightened) thought (form), and all clear thought is dependent on no-thought (emptiness). To clearly see (see/fashion) thought, is to see it *as it is* – that is, as *inclusive of* the 'presence of what is present' (illumined) *and* 'the presence of what is absent' (eclipsed). What is thought apart from its coessential context with what is not-thought is inevitably partial (biased), hence unclear and unreliable.

What is thought/expressed is explicate, what is not-thought/unexpressed is implicate; explicate and implicate are coessential and coextensive.[246] The absence, lack, space, silence, emptiness, background, and everything else that constitutes what *is* 'not-expressed,' embodies and *gives body* (form, appearance) to what *is* 'expressed.'

No real expression ever presents a general reality; every actual expression presents a definite, precise form. The directness and clarity of actual expressions, compared to general ideas, basic notions, or vague senses has its reason in the truth that particular forms demonstrate (thus possess) greater reality than abstract concepts or generalizations.

In learning to discern the nature of dharmas, the Buddha nature of expressions, we come to recognize the things, beings, and events ceaselessly-experienced as self-and-other here-now are vastly greater, more significant, and realer than a general or abstract system, theory, or formula could ever be. This is the reasoning that informs the Zen expression, 'The normal mind is the Tao.' To clearly see is to see *accurately*, to see dharmas are only and always specific, particular – normal 'as they are.' This is why *normality* is identified with *Buddha* or the *enlightened* mind rather than the *ordinary being* or *common* mind, and why enlightenment is identified with the transformative, liberating quality of Buddhahood – the summum bonum of the Buddha Way. In sum, realizing universal liberation is achieved through accurate discernment which is realized through the activation, development, cultivation, and utilization of the normal mind.

If objective existence is dependent on, and determined in accordance with subjective experience then the objects encountered by a greatly enlightened being are greater, thus realer than the objects encountered by a lesser enlightened being – the *realest* moon is that experienced (hence actualized, fashioned, or expressed) by the *most enlightened* being. Thus the skeptic that says, 'I will only believe it when I see it,' is *thereby* bound by their own rope. By preemptively denying reality to everything but their own doubt, such skeptics relinquish their capacity to realize (make real) truth. The folly of such a move has been well testified to by visionaries of all times and places, for example, by William Blake:

> What is now proved was once only imagined.[247]

In biblical terms, "...faith is the *substance* of things hoped for, the *evidence* of things not seen."[248] In harmony with all realities, *real* faith is always *particular*, never general; nobody can muster true conviction in an unknown whatcha-ma-call-it, an unimaginable something, an inconceivable pure being, an esoteric experience, a 'not this, not this,' or ineffable enlightenment. *Genuine* faith is only and always faith in *a specific* thing, being, or event; real faith *requires* a *clear, accurate understanding* or *vision of* whatever that faith is invested in. William Blake also pointed out that:

Truth can never be told as to be understood, and not be believ'd.[249]

Zen agrees, and would only add that something not understood can never be believed, never be told (expressed) – and never be *true* (existent). For, our actual *understanding* or *vision* of the things, beings, and events we *hope for* is the *very substance* (i.e. reality) of those things, beings, and events – the more comprehensive our understanding and clearer our vision, the greater and realer the substance.

Existence is experience, experience is existence – seeing is believing, believing is seeing.

Seeing is fashioning and fashioning is expressing; the clearer the seeing the more effective the fashioning and the greater the reality expressed. Dogen says, "Total existence is Buddha-nature" (*Shobogenzo, Bussho*) – every expression is an expression of Buddha, an instance of Buddha-nature.

As each instance of experience is a unique instance of existence-time, every expression is a novel expression – including the expression being recited from memory for the ten-thousandth time or read from an ancient scripture for the ten-millionth time. The words presently being formed in your mind, are neither entities that have endured from the past nor representations; they are novel realities coming into being – *becoming* – particular instances of existence illuminating your particular mind at this particular here-now; instances of Buddha being born in and as your experience/existence here-now.

A Buddha is one that sees *normally*, not through some supernormal power, but through *seeing as it is*. One that *clearly sees* through seeing, *truly hears* through hearing, *actually smells* through smelling; has verified that 'flavor' is *what* the tongue tastes, and the *means* whereby the tongue tastes.

To experientially verify the truth that the 'image' is the *means* as well as the object of eye-consciousness is to verify that nondual (normal) seeing is not seeing that sees *beyond* not-seeing (great delusion), but seeing that sees *by means of* not-seeing. Likewise, to verify that the 'thought' is the *means* as well as the object of mind-consciousness is to verify that normal thinking is thinking that thinks *by means of* not-thinking (great delusion). This is what Dogen means when he identifies Zen practice-enlightenment as 'thinking not-thinking' (or 'nonthinking). This is also the reason of the passage in *Shobogenzo, Genjokoan* that identifies Buddhas as beings "enlightened about delusion."

This Goes Along With That

In light of our discussion here it should be clear that the authentic Zen practitioner is one that directly and unconditionally faces whatever the world presents, no matter how difficult, uninviting, demanding, tedious, terrifying, or horrific. Contemporary 'Zen' doctrines or methods that encourage submission to and or detachment from the world as it is diverge widely from the classic Zen teachings which insist on giving focused attention to all aspects of reality 'as *it is*' and an unremitting commitment to *make* every aspect all 'it *can be*.'

If we are to experience the myriad dharmas 'as they are' then, obviously, our experiential capacities must be able to acquaint us with reality. To give credence to dualists or pseudo-Zen cultists that claim 'we do not experience reality as it is,' we would need to be convinced that such a claim was valid, or at least that it *could be* valid. To qualify as 'valid' (by the standards of Zen or science) the proposition should be experimentally – that is, experientially – *verifiable*. In short, to *validate* the claim that 'we do not experience reality as it is' would *invalidate* itself. Thus, the claim is not only *unverifiable*; if it were true it would deny its own validity.

The reason such an absurd proposition is nevertheless commonly asserted within pseudo-Zen groups, is because from their perspective (dualism), it is the logical conclusion of Zen teachings that affirm the infinite and eternal nature of 'the myriad dharmas' ('one mind' or 'Buddha'). From the perspective of dualism, such an affirmation means that we, being *independent of* the myriad dharmas, are *finite* and *temporary* and, therefore, *cannot* experience reality *as it is*; infinite and eternal.

From the nondual perspective, however, the logical conclusion to this affirmation is quite different. If reality is infinite and eternal 'we,' being *interdependent with* the myriad dharmas, *must be* infinite and eternal – to verify Zen's affirmation that reality is infinite and eternal would be to, *thereby,* verify our experiential capacity (our human normality) is infinite and eternal. If it were not, we could not experience it to be so.

The implications here may be subtle, but they are clear and unambiguous. Perhaps Dogen's treatment of this in the *Shobogenzo, Inmo* fascicle can help clarify the point. Dogen begins by citing a koan in which Master Kokaku of Ungo-zan mountain says:

> "If you want to attain the matter which is it, you must be a person who is it. Already being a person who is it, why worry about the matter which is it?"
> *Shobogenzo, Inmo*[250]

Dogen goes on to clarify the primary implications of the koan asserting:

> In other words, those who want to attain the matter which is it must themselves be people who are it. They are already people who are it: why should they worry about [attaining] the matter which is it? The point of this is that directing oneself straight for the supreme truth of bodhi is described, for the present, as 'it.'
> *Shobogenzo, Inmo*[251]

And a little further along Dogen sets out the heart of the matter:

> Remember, it happens like this because we are people who are it. How do we know that we are people who are it? We know that we are people who are it just from the fact that we want to attain the matter which is it.
> *Shobogenzo, Inmo*[252]

To recognize that reality is infinite and eternal is to, *thereby,* recognize that our experiential capacities (thus we ourselves) are infinite and eternal – if they were not so, we could not recognize reality to be so.

To experience sights, sounds, smells, tastes, tactile sensations, and thoughts is to fashion sights, sounds, smells, tastes, tactile sensations, and thoughts. Sights, sounds, smells, tastes, tactile sensations, and thoughts exhaust the modes in which reality manifests. A Zen practitioner is one that continuously strives to increase their capacities to fashion these six ever-advancing streams of novel existence-time into a Buddha within a Buddha realm.

Zen practice-enlightenment is a particular skillful means/ends, a particular Way, established and refined through sincere wholehearted effort and discipline, of actualizing universal enlightenment (normality) through the normal (enlightened; accurate, adequate, appropriate) arrangement of particular instances of experience (dharmas). A normal arrangement is an arrangement that advances, elaborates, or otherwise enhances the arbitrary, haphazard arrangement of experience realized by the reflexive or passive mind. This advanced ordering of dharmas is what Dogen means by, "increasing the sacred life of Buddha" (*Shoji*).

True seeing is active, intentional seeing; seeing that *sees* seeing *as it is*; *sees* that seeing is seeing/not-seeing. Likewise, true thinking is thinking that knows (thinks) thinking is thinking/not-thinking – called 'nonthinking,' and 'right-thinking' in *Shobogenzo*.

When the dualist points to the moon and proclaims the moon does not wink, twirl flowers or smile, the Zen master may point out that it is no 'rice-cake' either; more likely, the master will simply wink, twirl a flower, or smile. For Dogen's part, he offers up the *Shobogenzo, Bussho* fascicle, thus inviting us to experience the winking, smiling, flower-twirling moon for ourselves – that is, if we *are* people that *want to* experience it.

In light of this reason, it is worth noticing why those that describe the 'great Bodhisattva vows' or '*annuttara-samyak-sambodhi*' as 'ideals' of Buddhism misrepresent the Buddha-Dharma. Expressions are phenomena, instances of existence-time, not ideals, actualizations, not potentials. To accurately *express* the Buddha-Dharma, one *must* accurately *see* (understand, think) the Buddha-Dharma, to accurately *see* the Buddha-Dharma is to accurately *fashion* the Buddha-Dharma.

This reasoning also harmonizes with the fact that authentic aspiration for enlightenment (*bodhicitta*) only manifests as *particular instances* of *genuine desire* to deliver *all* beings from suffering, realize liberation from *all* greed, hatred, and ignorance, awaken to *all* truths, and *fully* embody the Buddha Way. In short, a person who genuinely aspires for enlightenment *must* 'already be a person who is it.'

In failing to clearly see that our mythopoeic capacity embodies our thinking mind or intellect, rather than being *embodied* (or *produced*) *by* our mind or intellect, we thereby obstruct our genuine desire (*bodhicitta*) by subjecting it to the realm of abstract speculation thus confining it to the limitations of literalism and generalization.

The myriad dharmas are not arbitrary occurrences, but instances of existence-time — expressions of Buddha — to be ordered and arranged actively by the enlightened mind or passively by the deluded mind. The enlightened mind is the normal human capacity to intentionally discern and distinguish, hence concentrate and unify, the ceaseless-stream of sights, sounds, smells, tastes, tactile sensations, and thoughts ever-advancing into the novelty that has never been hidden:

> Total Existence is the Buddha's words, the Buddha's tongue, the Buddhist patriarchs' eyes, and the nostrils of a patch-robed monk. The words "Total Existence" are utterly beyond beginning existence, beyond original existence, beyond fine existence, and so on. How much less could they describe conditioned existence or illusory existence? They are not connected with "mind and circumstances" or with "essence and form" and the like. This being so, object-and-subject as living beings-and-Total Existence is completely beyond ability based on karmic accumulation, beyond the random occurrence of circumstances, beyond accordance with the Dharma, and beyond mystical powers and practice and experience. If the Total Existence of living beings were [ability] based on karmic accumulation, were the random occurrence of circumstances, were accordance with the Dharma, and so on, then the saints' experience of the truth, the buddhas' state of bodhi, and the Buddhist patriarchs' eyes, would also be ability based on karmic accumulation, the occurrence of circumstances, and accordance with the Dharma. That is not so. The whole Universe is utterly without objective molecules: here and now there is no second person at all. [At the same time] "No person has ever recognized the direct cutting of the root"; for "When does the busy movement of karmic consciousness ever cease? [Total Existence] is beyond existence that arises through random circumstances; for "The entire Universe has never been hidden."
> *Shobogenzo, Bussho*[253]

This yellow flower, that melodious bird-song, this particular doubt, that specific memory — this very life-and-death — *as it is* here-now is the sacred life of Buddha; thus *Shobogenzo* presents and elucidates the nondual nature of aspiration and realization, desire and fulfillment. The conceptual division of aspiration and rationality is as dualistic — hence, as untenable — as the independent existence of form and essence, appearance and reality, self and not-self, and every other dualistic notion exhibited by the hesitant, fearful, and repressed forms of passivity, often in the guise of scientific rationalism or radical skepticism.

Until one clearly sees the 'true falsity' of dualism, one is obstructed from seeing that true 'rationality' (*dori*) can only be achieved by a being with true 'aspiration' to achieve it, and that true 'aspiration' can only be realized by a being that exercises true 'rationality' in pursuit of it. Insofar as it is real, 'reason' is only actualized as particular thoughts, words, and deeds by particular beings in and as particular place-times. No rational thought, word, or deed has ever been realized apart from a particular being's aspiration to realize it. No aspiration has ever been realized apart from a particular being's ability to rationally conceive of its attainability. The sentient mind experiences the reality it sees/fashions, and since *bodhicitta* is intrinsic to the normal mind, the realm we genuinely aspire for – the Buddha realm – is more authentic then the realm experienced by the detached passivity of the 'ordinary' reflexive mind.

While I speak of practice-enlightenment in the terms of Zen Buddhism I do not mean to suggest that authentic practice-enlightenment is confined to a specific mythology, or any other system or sphere of interest. Insofar as science, religion, philosophy, agriculture, politics, carpentry, or other realm or activity are conducted in harmony with the normal mind – thus genuinely actualize their dharma-position in the homeland of the self – they certainly qualify as, indeed *amount to*, authentic practice-enlightenment.

To clarify, the Zen practitioner assimilates and utilizes the findings and methods of science, for example, as specific instances of existence-time, expressions effective for advancing liberation and fulfillment, not as fixed laws or infallible techniques. Such assimilation and use is simply the natural conduct of one that recognizes existence-time as constituted of particular forms actualized by particular beings. Scientific institutions are consensual, thus conservative; their tenets are relinquished only through a long, gradual, painstaking process. Zen is individual and fluid; truths are cast-off in the very process through which they are realized. Zen's relation to science is 'adaption' rather than 'adoption.' Similarly, Zen assimilates and utilizes religion, philosophy, medicine, law, and any other realm that may serve to increase the sacred life of Buddha.

Every being sees it differently, but the fact that they all see 'it' demonstrates the nature of universal normality. Each being sees 'it' in accordance with their unique integral character, thus fashions a realm of the self-same homeland that is novel from the realm of any other. As the various great mythologies are various dialects of the expression of the one mind or universal Buddha, the various sentient beings are various members of 'one good person' – the sole ancestor.

Zen Cosmology: Summary Expression

The term "buddhas" means Sakyamuni Buddha. Sakyamuni Buddha is just "mind here and now is buddha." When all the buddhas of the past, present, and future become buddha, they inevitably become Sakyamuni Buddha, that is, "mind here and now is buddha."
Shobogenzo, Soku-shin-ze-butsu[254]

Zen recognizes as self-evident the nonduality of existence, experience, and realization.[255] Consciousness of existence is manifest as experience; thus existence and experience exhaust the reality of self and other.[256] Clearly seeing[257] the true nature[258] of existence and experience actualizes universal liberation and fulfillment; *annuttara-samyak-sambodhi*.[259]

Experientially verifying the truth of the Buddhist vision of the nonduality of self[260] and other[261], self cognizes its true identity as Buddha[262] thereby realizing liberation from fear and greed.[263] Cognizing its identity with the myriad dharmas[264] makes the true nature of unity and separation[265] self-evident; self and other are inherently united[266] – nothing can be added, nothing taken away; no basis for fear or greed exists.

'Enlightenment by oneself without a teacher' (*mushi dokugo*)[267] is Zen's only standard of truth.[268] A notion, view, teaching, or understanding, even if a basic principle of Buddhism heard face to face from Buddha, is true only when verified in one's actual experience – such verification is authentic practice-enlightenment (*shusho*).

Authentic practice-enlightenment verifies the truth that the *experience* of self and other is actualized by the *existence* of self and other, and the *existence* of self and other is actualized by the *experience* of self and other. Focused attention[269] on the experience of self and other experientially verifies the truth that neither self nor other possess independent existence. *Other* is experienced *as not-self*. *Self* is experienced *as not-other*. Thus, the existence of self is verified as *dependent on*[270] not-self (i.e. other), the existence of other is verified as *dependent on* not-other (i.e. self) – only with this experience is the true nature of self clearly seen *as it is*, and the true nature of other clearly seen *as it is*.

The true nature of reality is experientially verified by the Zen practitioner as nondual; equally demonstrating plurality *and* oneness, differentiation *and* unity; self and other are simultaneously *distinct*, *unique*, and *particular*, and *united*, *coessential*, and *interdependent*. Singular experience is actualized by and as differentiated existence; singular existence is actualized by and as differentiated experience. A variety of sights, sounds, smells, tastes, tactile sensations, and thoughts[271] are *experienced as* existence, and *exist as* experience.

To experience the existence of other is to experience the existence of self. To exist as the experience of other is to exist as the experience of self. To clearly see the true nature of self is to identify with the true nature of other. To identify with the true nature of other is to experience existence as self *and* other. To experience existence as self and other is to be liberated from delusion about self and other[272] – thus dharmas are actualized as dharmas. When dharmas are actualized as dharmas, dharmas continuously rise and set[273] in the ceaseless advance of the universe into novelty. The dharmas that set are not transformed into the dharmas that rise; the dharmas that rise do not obstruct the dharmas that set. The dharmas that set are the dharmas that set, the dharmas that rise are the dharmas that rise. Each and all dharmas *are* dharmas *as they are*; particular phenomenal expressions of the whole universe, actual instances of total existence-time; each dharma contains and is contained by each other dharma, and each dharma contains and is contained by total existence-time.

Self and other exist as/of the continuous rising and setting of sights, sounds, smells, tastes, tactile sensations, and thoughts. The self and other that sets does not become the self and other that rises; the self and other that rises does not obstruct the self and other that sets. The self and other that sets is the self and other that sets, the self and other that rises is the self and other that rises. Clearly seeing this truth verifies that life does not become death, death does not obstruct life. Life is a dharma, death is a dharma, thus life is not-life, death is not-death – therefore life is truly life, death is truly death. Life *is* total existence-time as it is, death *is* total existence time as it is; life is unborn and imperishable, death is unborn and imperishable.

Clearly seeing self and other, self cognizes its homeland,[274]actualizing the universe (*genjokoan*). The homeland of the self neither endures from the past nor is just now arising.

Clearly seeing the true nature of reality, self verifies the truth that experiencing a single dharma is experiencing total existence-time. Experience here-and-now exists as the whole universe; the existence of the whole universe is experience here-and-now. Existence is only and always existence here-and-now, experience is only and always experience here-and-now. Here-and-now is the existence/experience of the whole universe ceaselessly advancing into novelty.

Great enlightenment is what illuminated here-and-now is. Great delusion is what eclipsed here-and-now is. Enlightenment and delusion are nondual; empty and interdependent – infinite and eternal.

True nature continuously rises and continuously sets here-and-now *as* here-and-now. Here-and-now is the ceaseless advance of the universe into novelty, the ever-becoming of self-and-other, enlightenment-and-delusion, form-and-emptiness, existence-and-time. This is the infinite and eternal actualization of the whole universe, the sentient-being that is the ever-becoming Buddha. Total Existence, Buddha-nature, True Self, and sentient-being are synonymous with the experience of existence here-and-now *solely becoming*, the existence of experience here-and-now *solely becoming*.

Notes

[1] Hee-Jin Kim, *Dogen on Meditation and Thinking: A Reflection on His View of Zen*, State University of New York Press (November 9, 2006), p. 124

[2] Tarnas, Richard, *Cosmos and Psyche: Intimations of a New World View*, Plume; Reprint edition (April 24, 2007), p.16

[3] Northrop Frye, *The Educated Imagination and Other Writings on Critical Theory*, 1933-1963, University of Toronto Press, Scholarly Publishing Division (December 9, 2006), p.307; Frye is commenting on the nature of cosmology proposed by Paul Valery (1871-1945)

[4] Ludwig Wittgenstein, *Tractatus Logico-Philosophicus*, Chiron Academic Press (January 11, 2016), 5.6

[5] Alfred North Whitehead, *Process and Reality* (Gifford Lectures Delivered in the University of Edinburgh During the Session 1927-28) Free Press; 2nd edition (July 1, 1979), p.28

[6] From this standpoint, Dogen deeply imbibed *hongaku* discourse as radical phenomenalism, which became the crux of his soteriological vision. In fact, his entire religion may be safely described as the exploration and explication of this radical phenomenalism in terms of its linguistic, rational, and temporal dimensions, as well as the endeavor to overcome its ever-threatening religio-ethical perils. Hee-Jin Kim, *Eihei Dogen: Mystical Realist,* Wisdom Publications; 3 Revised edition (January 1, 2000), p. xx

Contrary to the conventional view that language is no more than a means of communication, it is profoundly internal to an individual's life as well as to the collective life. Language flows individually and collectively through the existential bloodstream, so much so that it is the breath, blood and soul of human existence. Herein lies the essence of Dogen's radical phenomenalism. Hee-Jin Kim, *Dogen on Meditation and Thinking: A Reflection on His View of Zen*, State University of New York Press (November 9, 2006), p.64

[7] J.C. Cleary, *Zen Dawn: Early Zen Texts from Tun Huang* (Shambhala Dragon Editions) Paperback – November 13, 2001, p.39-40

[8] Hee-Jin Kim, *Dogen on Meditation and Thinking: A Reflection on His View of Zen*, State University of New York Press (November 9, 2006), p. ix

[9] David Bohm, *Wholeness and the Implicate Order,* Routledge; First Edition edition (July 1980), pp.1-2

[10] Brian Greene, *The Fabric of the Cosmos: Space, Time, and the Texture of Reality*, Vintage (February 8, 2005), p.122

[11] Hee-Jin Kim, *Eihei Dogen: Mystical Realist,* Wisdom Publications; 3 Revised edition (January 1, 2000), p.98

[12] Rupert Sheldrake, *The Science Delusion*, Coronet Books; First edition & printing in this form edition (December 6, 2012), p.6

[13] Thich Nhat Hạnh, *The Heart of Understanding: Commentaries on the Prajnaparamita Heart Sutra,* Parallax Press (November 24, 1964), p.6

[14] Hee-Jin Kim, *Eihei Dogen: Mystical Realist,* Wisdom Publications; 3 Revised edition (January 1, 2000), p.117

[15] Galileo Galilei, *Letter to the Grand Duchess Christina* (1615), *Discoveries and Opinions of Galileo*: including *The starry messenger* (1610), *Letter to the Grand Duchess Christina* (1615), and excerpts from *Letters on sunspots* (1613), *The assayer* (1623) Mass Market Paperback – 1957

[16] Marcus Tullius Cicero, *On the laws, Cicero: Selected Works Penguin Classics*; 1St Edition edition (September 30, 1960)

[17] Hee-Jin Kim, *Dogen on Meditation and Thinking: A Reflection on His View of Zen*, State University of New York Press (November 9, 2006), p.10

[18] The 'truth of suffering' (*dukkha*) is the first of Buddhism's 'Four Noble Truths'

[19] Attributed to Swift in *Scientific American*, Vol. 7 (Munn & Company, 1851), p. 338

[20] Eihei Dogen, *Shobogenzo, Bukkyo, Eihei Dogen: Mystical Realist*, Hee-Jin Kim, Wisdom Publications; 3 Revised edition (January 1, 2000), p.53

[21] David Bohm, *Wholeness and the Implicate Order,* Routledge; First Edition

edition (July 1980), p.xi

[22] Gudo Nishijima, Chodo Cross, trans. Shōbōgenzō: The True Dharma-Eye Treasury2, Berkeley: Numata Center for Buddhist Translation and Research, 2008. http://www.bdk.or.jp/document/dgtl-dl/dBET_T2582_Shobogenzo2_2008.pdf (accessed August 5, 2016), p.4

[23] Erwin Schrodinger, *Mind and Matter: The Tarner Lectures* delivered at Trinity College, Cambridge, in October 1956, Cambridge University Press; 1st edition (1958)

[24] Werner Heisenberg, *Physics from Wholeness: Dynamical Totality As a Conceptual Foundation for Physical Theories* (Uppsala Dissertations from the Faculty of Science & Technology), Uppsala University (December 30, 2005), Barbara Piechocinska

[25] Niels Bohr, Volume I - *Atomic Theory and the Description of Nature* (Philosophical Writings of Niels Bohr Series, Vol 1), Ox Bow Press (June 15, 1987), p.54

[26] David Bohm, *On the Intuitive Understanding of Nonlocality as Implied by Quantum Theory*, Foundations of Physics Vol 5 (1975)

[27] Robert Lanza is an American medical doctor, scientist, Chief Scientific Officer of Ocata Therapeutics, formerly named Advanced Cell Technology and Adjunct Professor at the Institute for Regenerative Medicine, Wake Forest University School of Medicine

[28] Robert Lanza, *Biocentrism: How Life and Consciousness Are the Keys to Understanding the True Nature of the Universe*, Robert Lanza and Bob Berman

[29] Alfred North Whitehead, *Modes of Thought*, The Free Press (February 1, 1968), p.130

[30] Alfred North Whitehead, *Modes of Thought*, The Free Press (February 1, 1968), pp.130-131

[31] Alfred North Whitehead, *Modes of Thought*, The Free Press (February 1, 1968), p.131

[32] Alfred North Whitehead, *Modes of Thought*, The Free Press (February 1, 1968), p.132

[33] Richard Tarnas, *Cosmos and Psyche: Intimations of a New World View*, Plume; Reprint edition (April 24, 2007), p.29

[34] Richard Tarnas, *Cosmos and Psyche: Intimations of a New World View*, Plume; Reprint edition (April 24, 2007), pp.29-30

[35] Heisenberg, Werner, *Physics and Philosophy: The Revolution in Modern Science*, Harper Torchbooks (June 1958)

[36] Often cited, but I have been unable to trace the source

[37] Hee-Jin Kim, *Dogen on Meditation and Thinking: A Reflection on His View of Zen*, State University of New York Press (November 9, 2006), p.38

[38] Hee-Jin Kim, *Dogen on Meditation and Thinking: A Reflection on His View of Zen*, State University of New York Press (November 9, 2006), p.64

[39] Because the real particular existence (ontology) of dharmas is interdependent [*dependent* on and *depended* on – thus constituted by their *relative* 'position' to each other] the *interaction* and *coordination* (mutual *influence*) of 'multiple' dharmas is actualized without obstructing, altering, or otherwise interfering with the individual sovereignty of any particular dharma involved. That is, the influence of the spatial-temporal *distinction* (distance in space and time separating/connecting individual dharmas) exerted, enacted, or displayed by any dharma (say, 'tonight's moon') and accommodated, felt, or experienced by any other dharma (say, 'yesterday's moon') is exerted and accommodated *by means of* the very *sovereignty* of each, without which *neither* would (or could) exist. For example, 'tonight's moon' exists *as* 'tonight's moon' *only because* 'yesterday's moon' exists *as* 'yesterday's moon' (and vice versa).

In *Shobogenzo*, 'dharma-positions' – the reason (*dori*) of the 'sovereignty' or 'uniqueness' of dharmas – are accounted for and illuminated in terms of 'dharmas abiding in their dharma-position' or 'abiding at their place in the Dharma.' The dynamic significance and implications of dharma-positions is most comprehensively treated by *Shobogenzo's* vision of the 'nonobstruction,' 'self-obstruction,' or 'total exertion of an individual dharma' *(ippo-gujin)*.

[40] Some examples of Dogen's use of the term *dori* include:

"the reason of the true nature of things" or "reason of things as they are" (*honi dori*)

"the reason of Dharma-nature" (*hossho no dori*)

"the reason of words and letters" *(monji no dori)*

"the reason of total surrender" (*ninnin no dori*)

"the reason of the Buddha-Dharma" (*buppo no dori*)

"the reason of the time of my self" *(jiko no toki naru dori)*

"the reason of the skin, flesh, bones and marrow entwining with each other as vines" *(hiniku-kotsuzui no katto suru dori)*

"the reason of no reason" (*mugi o motte gi to su* or *gi naki o gi to su*)

"the reason of arising and perishing from moment to moment (*stsuna shometsu no dori*)

"the reason of relation" *(kandai-dori)*

"the reason of causation" *(sayu-dori)*

"the reason of cause and effect" (*inga no dori*)

"the reason of karmic retribution" (*goppo no dori*)

"the reason of recognition" *(shojo-dori)*

[41] Hee-Jin Kim, *Eihei Dogen: Mystical Realist*, Wisdom Publications; 3 Revised edition (January 1, 2000), pp.108-109

[42] Hee-Jin Kim, *Eihei Dogen: Mystical Realist*, Wisdom Publications; 3 Revised edition (January 1, 2000), p.137

[43] Hee-Jin Kim, *Eihei Dogen: Mystical Realist*, Wisdom Publications; 3 Revised edition (January 1, 2000), 165

[44] Hee-Jin Kim, *Dogen on Meditation and Thinking: A Reflection on His View of Zen*, State University of New York Press (November 9, 2006), p.101

[45] Hee-Jin Kim, *Dogen on Meditation and Thinking: A Reflection on His View of Zen*, State University of New York Press (November 9, 2006), pp.102-103

[46] Hee-Jin Kim, *Dogen on Meditation and Thinking: A Reflection on His View of Zen*, State University of New York Press (November 9, 2006), p.103

[47] Hee-Jin Kim explains Dogen's coining of the term thus:

> He quoted the statement of Yueh-shan Wei-yen (745-828), but modified it in such a way that "a particular time" *(arutoki)*, from Yueh-shan's original, was interpreted as "existence-time" *(uji)*. Hee-Jin Kim, *Eihei Dogen: Mystical Realist*, Wisdom Publications; 3 Revised edition (January 1, 2000), p.149

[48] Hee-Jin Kim, *Eihei Dogen: Mystical Realist*, Wisdom Publications; 3 Revised edition (January 1, 2000), p.150

[49] Gudo Nishijima, Chodo Cross, trans. Shōbōgenzō: The True Dharma-Eye Treasury1, Berkeley: Numata Center for Buddhist Translation and Research, 2009. http://www.bdk.or.jp/document/dgtl-dl/dBET_T2582_Shobogenzo1_2009.pdf (accessed August 5, 2016), p.144

[50] Gudo Nishijima, Chodo Cross, trans. Shōbōgenzō: The True Dharma-Eye Treasury1, Berkeley: Numata Center for Buddhist Translation and Research, 2009. http://www.bdk.or.jp/document/dgtl-dl/dBET_T2582_Shobogenzo1_2009.pdf (accessed August 5, 2016), p.144

[51] Gudo Nishijima, Chodo Cross, trans. Shōbōgenzō: The True Dharma-Eye Treasury1, Berkeley: Numata Center for Buddhist Translation and Research, 2009. http://www.bdk.or.jp/document/dgtl-dl/dBET_T2582_Shobogenzo1_2009.pdf (accessed August 5, 2016), p.144

[52] Hee-Jin Kim brings some relevant implications concerning the term 'sho' to light in a discussion on various terms for 'satori' (enlightenment) – go, kaku, and sho. After summarizing the connotations of 'go' (as stressing intuitive insight into true nature) and 'kaku' (as stressing awakening or becoming aware of a previously unknown truth), Kim writes:

> By contrast, sho (which means "to prove," "to bear witness to," "to verify") signifies the direct, personal verification of salvific reality/truth through the body-mind (shinjin), one's whole being. A crucially important point here is, namely, "that which verifies" and "that which is verified" are inseparably intertwined via the body-mind. In this context, sho is typically coupled with shu ("practice") as in shusho ("practice and enlightenment"). Although go, kaku, and sho are used interchangeably in Zen Buddhism, as well as in Dogen, his most favored term is undoubtedly sho. Thus in speaking of enlightenment (sho), Dogen always presupposes the process of verification in which enlightenment entails practice, and vice versa. To put it differently, enlightenment (nonduality) makes it incumbent upon practitioners to put the unitive vision of all things into practice, in terms of duality of the revisioned world. Hee-Jin Kim, *Dogen on Meditation and Thinking: A Reflection on His View of Zen*, State University of New York Press (November 9, 2006), pp.21-22

[53] For a comprehensive elucidation on Kim's use of 'foci,' see *Dogen on Meditation and Thinking: A Reflection on His View of Zen*, State University of New York Press (November 9, 2006), pp. 4, 19, 24-26, 27-28, and esp. 34-38

[54] Nondual foci frequently confused or distorted include:

   atman/anatman (self/no-self)

   subject/object

   one/many

form/emptiness

delusion/enlightenment

appearance/reality

ordinary (unenlightened) beings/Buddhas

expressible/inexpressible ('inside words and letters'/'outside words and letters')

acquired enlightenment/original enlightenment (gradual cultivation/sudden awakening)

practice/enlightenment

[55] According to Professor Funayama Toru:

> "The Sanskrit term *tathata* 'suchness,' signifying 'the condition of (entities) as they are' or a state of true reality in the broad sense, is popularly known as *zhenru* 'thusness' in Chinese Buddhism." Funayama Toru, *Thusness (zhenru) - A Case of the Sinicized Interpretation of Buddhist Terms* (http://hcbss.stanford.edu/event/thusness-zhenru-case-sinicized-interpretation-buddhist-terms)

[56] Gudo Nishijima, Chodo Cross, trans. Shōbōgenzō: The True Dharma-Eye Treasury2, Berkeley: Numata Center for Buddhist Translation and Research, 2008. http://www.bdk.or.jp/document/dgtl-dl/dBET_T2582_Shobogenzo2_2008.pdf (accessed August 5, 2016), p.52

[57] Hee-Jin Kim, *Eihei Dogen: Mystical Realist*, Wisdom Publications; 3 Revised edition (January 1, 2000), p.117

[58] 'Knowledge' is something (accurately or erroneously) known by someone – all actual knowledge exists as an actual object or objects of consciousness; a subjective *knower* and an objective *known* are coessential foci of all knowledge. The 'true nature of reality' means *reality as it is* (thusness). 'Accurate knowledge' is true knowledge; knowledge that harmonizes with reality as it is. 'Erroneous knowledge' is false knowledge; knowledge that diverges from reality as it is. 'Accessible' means present, recognizable, and available (tangible, intelligible) to a subjective knower. 'Experientially verifiable' means amenable to reliable discernment and evaluation through experiential capacities – the actuality, significance, and value of knowledge can be accurately and adequately determined in and through the experiential capacities of human beings. Thus, while knowledge (experience) can be (exist) true or false, the difference between accurate and erroneous knowledge can be reliably discerned by human beings – what is true about reality can be clearly distinguished

from what is false about reality.

[59] i.e. 'nonduality' is nonduality/duality, 'duality' is duality/nonduality.

[60] Here the terms 'enlightenment' and 'delusion' are used in the context specific to the nondual foci of 'enlightenment/delusion.' Thus 'enlightenment' is 'great enlightenment' (*daigo*) and 'delusion' is 'great delusion' (*daimei*) – this is discussed further in the 'Clarifications' section immediately following this section.

For an excellent overview of the significant factors of nonduality specific to delusion and enlightenment in Dogen's vision of Zen see Hee-Jin Kim, *Dogen on Meditation and Thinking: A Reflection on His View of Zen*, State University of New York Press (November 9, 2006), pp.1-20

[61] The meaning of 'emptiness' (*sunyata*) here is comprehensively treated in a discussion on the Zen/Buddhist doctrines of emptiness and interdependence taken up later in this study.

[62] While accounts of Zen commonly portray emptiness (*sunyata*) as the fundamental essence of reality, the notion of emptiness *presupposes* a *prior* recognition of dharmas (i.e. thus dharmas, not emptiness, are primary and primordial). Indeed, the very reason and value of the *notion* (as well as the *experience*) of emptiness exists in/as its capacity to adequately account for the experience/existence of dharmas. It is worth noticing that the same reasoning applies to the Zen/Buddhist notion of 'no-self' or '*anatman*'; the notion of no-self *presupposes* a *prior* recognition of self; the reason and value of no-self exists in/as its capacity to adequately account for the experience/existence of self.

[63] 'Appearance' and 'form' denote the 'total appearance' of dharmas experienced by sentient beings (i.e. the total influence of dharmas on human experience), thus is not confined to *visual* experience, but applies to *every* mode in which dharmas are present, consciously and unconsciously, in/as/to human experience; sight, sound, taste, smell, tactile sensation, thought – the *reality* [ontological existence] of a dharma and the *experience* of a dharma are nondual.

[64] As phenomenal forms, dharmas can generally be understood as appearing/manifesting as one or more of the six 'objects of consciousness' – sights, sounds, tastes, smells, tactile sensations, and thoughts – recognized in traditional Buddhist notions of sensation, perception, mental formulation, and consciousness.

[65] The existence of each dharma is dependent on the existence of 'all dharmas' [the totality of all dharmas] *and* the existence of 'each *other* dharma' [each particular dharma 'other than' it]; *all* dharmas are dependent on

each dharma).

[66] The 'universal normality of dharmas' means that *all* dharmas are *normal as they are*. 'As they are' means the (ontological) true nature of dharmas – the *real* reality of dharmas that Buddhism calls 'thusness' *(immo* or *tathata)*.

[67] That the normality of dharmas is 'universal' means that *all* dharmas are *normal*, and that the *particular normality* (or thusness) of any individual dharma is the *same* for/to *all* individual beings. For example, the normality of a particular tree experienced by a particular individual being is the same for/to all particular beings. The dharma realized by/as one being's experience of/as a particular dharma at a particular place-time *is what* it is, *as* it is, in the totality of existence-time. Thus, while Zen agrees with Blake that 'A fool sees not the same tree that a wise man sees' (*Marriage of Heaven and Hell*), for Zen the fool's tree is as actual, significant, and valuable as the wise man's tree. The same reasoning (*dori*) applies to all dharmas and all beings.

[68] 'Mythopoeism' is the noun form of 'mythopoeic' (coined in the mid 1800s by combining 'mythos' and 'poetic'): pertaining to the making of myths; causing, producing, or giving rise to myths; the source of myths, mythos, etc. In common usage (primarily in religious studies and literary criticism) 'mythopoeic' differentiates visionary, figurative, imagistic, or metaphorical expression (i.e. mythos; mythical language and works, mythic things, beings, and events) from ordinary narrative accounts or literal descriptions (e.g. technical, historical, and biographical explanations, reports, records, etc.).

[69] 'Dharma-transmission' is the communication of enlightened wisdom by 'Buddha alone together with Buddha,' and should not be confused with contemporary ceremonies (also called 'Dharma-transmission') certifying new 'Zen teachers' as 'Dharma-heirs' by formally acknowledging their views (understanding) as conforming to the standards of a specific lineage, sect, or individual.

[70] The self ('I', 'me') and the world ('other than I', 'not me') have been identified with dharmas since the earliest days of Buddhism. Buddhist expressions on the nature of this identification has been continuously elaborated, developed, and refined for millennia. The terms, details, and emphasis of Buddhist expressions on the identification of dharmas with self/other vary, but the fundamental tenet stands – self/other is *constituted of* and *actualized by* dharmas; dharmas are *what* self/other is and the *means* whereby self/other manifests.

[71] We have already noted that in Zen cosmology 'existence' is synonymous with

'time' and 'existence-time,' and is constituted of dharmas. Here the significance of 'existence' (ontology) is expanded by noting its nondual unity with 'experience' already intimated in our observations on the nature of dharmas and the significance of nonduality. This, along with other previous observations sheds light on the essential significance of experience; the actual existence (ontology) of both subjectivity and objectivity is intrinsically *dependent on*, thus *constituted of* experience (epistemology). The *existence* of a 'self' (subjective experiencer) and the *existence* of an 'other than self' (experienced object) are *coessential* foci in and of each and all actual instances of experience.

According to Zen doctrine anyone can verify the nondual unity of existence and experience. By focusing attention on one's own actual experience here-now it becomes self-evident that *all* experience is constituted of *both* an (existent) experiencer *and* an experienced (existent) – *never* of anything *else*, and *never* of one *without* the other. Thus it is self-evident that existence *is* experience, and experience *is* existence, therefore, existence is (truly) existence, and experience is experience.

72 While Zen does not *deny* the existence of realities transcendent to human experiential capacities (perhaps undetectable universes *do* exist), it does discourage futile activity and disparages views that presuppose abstract speculation to be *more reliable* than experiential evidence. The reason for Zen's stance is practical; a reality that *can* be experienced (i.e. the self/world) is more likely *to be* experienced than a reality that *cannot* be experienced.

73 The particular significance of 'consciousness' herein is harmonious with the term for consciousness identified in Sanskrit as '*vijnana*.' Vijnana, like many Buddhist terms, has a great variety of possible meanings (e.g. the fifth of the five skandhas, the third of the twelve links of causation, etc.). In the context of 'objects of consciousness,' *vijnana* identifies the (sixth) 'sense organ' associated with 'objects of mind consciousness' – but *vijnana* also identifies the 'consciousness' associated with the other five types of objects (i.e. sights, sounds, tastes, smells, tactile sensations). Therefore, it should be noted that in the former case (i.e. as a 'sense organ') *vijnana* is *specific* to that role, hence of *equal status* with the other five sense organs; while in the latter case (i.e. as a 'shared' type of 'consciousness') *vijnana* is more *general*. In this study I attempt to distinguish this *specific* sense from the *general* by identifying '*vijnana*' as 'mind' when speaking of it as a sense organ. For example, when discussing the 'six modes of consciousness,' I write 'mind consciousness,' rather than 'consciousness-consciousness.' This is not crucial to understanding, and is noted only for the sake of thoroughness.

74 To exist (i.e. *to be* a dharma) is *to be* (subjectively) *experienced*; *to be experienced* is *to exist*. Existence and experience are nondual spatial-temporal appearances/manifestations in/of reality (the universe, true nature, or Buddha-nature). Hence, all dharmas necessarily appear (manifest) nondually *with* and *as* particular instances of the consciousness (interdependently inclusive of a *sense field, sense faculty*, and *sense organ*) of *particular* sentient beings, at *particular* places (or spaces) and *particular* moments of time.

75 Zen/Buddhist literature often treats of consciousness in systems that describe it in accordance with a variety of 'modes,' in this study I confine my discussion to the most common system of 'six modes' of consciousness. The six modes of consciousness are eye-consciousness, ear-consciousness, nose-consciousness, tongue-consciousness, body-consciousness, and mind-consciousness.

This Buddhist vision of dharmas as objects (things, beings, or events) integral to one or more of 'six types' or 'modes' of consciousness provides a perspective from which to accurately observe and communicate about the process whereby dharmas manifest experience. The six types of 'objects of consciousness' (i.e. dharmas) generally correspond to the five sense faculties common to western systems, plus a 'sixth sense faculty' that 'senses' (discerns, reads, experiences, cognizes) thought. The 'sense organ' associated with this 'sixth sense' is identified as 'mind.' In harmony with the nonduality of experience and existence (epistemology and ontology), Zen/Buddhism recognizes the six modes of experience as the very process in which, and of which the universe (totality of self/world) is actualized.

76 In no case is Zen expression intelligible through the language of literal narrative description or definition alone.

77 This is in accord with the reason (*dori*) of 'dharmas communicating dharmas with dharmas' or 'Buddha alone together with Buddha.' As the 'myriad dharmas' are the 'one Buddha,' there is only and always 'Buddha alone' (al-one; *all-one*); as the 'one Buddha' is the 'myriad dharmas,' there is only and always 'together with' (to-gather with) Buddha. Accordingly, 'Buddha alone' *is the normality of* 'together with Buddha' and 'together with Buddha' *is the normality of* 'Buddha alone.' Likewise, 'dharmas communicating dharmas with dharmas,' is the normality of dharmas. As particular *expressions* (i.e. dharmas) of reality (one Buddha), encountered by particular *sentient beings* (i.e. dharmas) communicating (presenting; making present) particular *forms, sounds, smells, tastes, tactile sensations*, and *thoughts* (i.e. dharmas) all particular dharmas (things, beings, events) communicate particular dharmas with particular

dharmas.

[78] That the single greatest characteristic distinguishing Dogen's vision of Zen is its profound insight into the true nature and dynamics of language first received the emphasis it warranted in 1975 by Hee-Jin Kim in his groundbreaking, *Dogen Kigen: Mystical Realist* (revised and reissued as, *Eihei Dogen: Mystical Realist*, Wisdom Publications; 3 Revised edition (January 1, 2000). While his findings have been greatly elaborated and vastly reinforced by scholarship ever since, Kim's works remain at the forefront in giving adequate emphasis to the crucial significance of accounting for this fact to accurately understand Dogen's writings (hence, Zen/Buddhism). In his most recent work (2007), for example, Kim writes:

> As I have often noted in the present work and elsewhere, the single most original and seminal aspect of Dogen's Zen is his treatment of the role of language in Zen soteriology. Hee-Jin Kim, *Dogen on Meditation and Thinking: A Reflection on His View of Zen*, State University of New York Press (November 9, 2006), p.59

[79] Despite the clarity and emphasis of the scholarship by Hee-Jin Kim and others, Zen/Buddhism's insight into and utilization of language continues to be seriously neglected, obscured, and misunderstood. In diametric opposition to nominalist and instrumentalist propositions of popular (and 'orthodox') institutions, Dogen (hence, Zen) presents a vision wherein language (hence, thinking and reason) demonstrates universal significance. Accordingly, words and letters are not only *intrinsically real* and *meaningful*, but, as Kim writes, "alive and active 'in flesh and blood.'"

> Words and letters, however socially constructed, are never mere signs in the abstract, theoretical sense, but alive and active 'in flesh and blood.' Contrary to the conventional view that language is no more than a means of communication, it is profoundly internal to an individual's life as well as to the collective life. Language flows individually and collectively through the existential bloodstream, so much so that it is the breath, blood and soul of human existence. Herein lies the essence of Dogen's radical phenomenalism. Thus knowledge becomes ascesis, instead of gnosis or logos — 'seeing things as they are' now means 'making things as they are.' In this light the indexical analogy of 'the finger pointing to the moon' is highly misleading, if not altogether wrong, because it draws on a salvifically inefficacious conception of language. Hee-Jin Kim, *Dogen on Meditation and Thinking: A Reflection on His View of Zen*, State University of New York Press (November 9, 2006), p.64

[80] 'Self,' whether used in reference to the individual or the world, communicates to and about both. Thus, Zen expressions to or about 'self' communicate truth relevant to the particular or individual self and to the universal or world self; what is true of *either* is and must be true of *both*.

[81] All expressions, terms, and notions concerning human subjectivity ('self') in Zen cosmology presuppose the Buddhist tenets of no-self (*anatman*). The experiential reality of human subjectivity is regarded and treated in light of the principles of nonduality as illuminated by the Buddhist doctrines of emptiness and interdependence. Briefly, self and no-self are recognized as co-essential and co-extensive elements, or nondual foci, of a unified reality – 'self' always presupposes 'no-self,' and 'no-self,' always presupposes 'self.' 'Self' should not, in any way, be identified with 'selfhood' (i.e. an independent entity). A view, usage, or understanding of 'self' as an independent entity is a fallacy, misuse, or misunderstanding, respectively.

[82] The nondual nature of the individual and the world self presented here should not be understood as meaning the *individual* and the *world* self are *identical*. 'Nondual' means 'not-two' or 'not separate,' it does not mean 'uniform' or 'undifferentiated.' The *individual* self and the *world* self constitute a *unified*, but *differentiated* reality. When illumined in light of the principles of nonduality *the differences* between the individual and world self do not alter or obstruct their *unity*; rather, their differences *facilitate* their unity, and their unity *facilitates* their differences.

[83] Metaphor communicates through *exemplification* (rather than explanation, definition, or representation). The function or reason (*dori*) of metaphor demonstrates (rather than explains) the interdependent nature of dharmas; where literal expression *explains* that 'A' is 'A' not 'B,' and 'B' is 'B' not 'A,' metaphor *demonstrates* that 'A' *is* 'B' (i.e. is 'not-A"), and therefore 'A' is (truly) 'A' and 'B' is 'B.' Stating that the self is the root metaphor of Zen *exemplifies* the truth that all expressions are expressions *of* self (self-expressions). Self as metaphor communicates self-knowledge – wisdom of Buddha alone together with Buddha – by manifesting *itself* as each dharma and all dharmas according to the nature and dynamics of interdependence.

[84] The archetypal image of 'eternal-return' as presented, for example by the enso, circle, or ouroboros, appears in Zen/Buddhist literature in a manner presenting the truth that dharmas are expressions (figures, forms, images) of self. In context of our present discussion this can be envisioned as the self expressing itself by abandoning (or 'casting off') universality for individuality, and self realizing self by abandoning individuality for universality. Such expressions of truth or archetypal

images reveal death, the ultimate limitation of the individual self, as being intrinsic to the universal self, and immortality, the ultimate fulfillment of Buddhahood, as being intrinsic to the individual self.

85 As the oxymoronic structure of the term 'polycentric' suggests, the notion of a thing, being, or event possessing a *plurality* of *centers* seems to be contrary to actual experience. Nevertheless, when the true nature of reality is discerned in light of the reason (*dori*) of emptiness and interdependence the truth that the world/self is 'polycentric' is self-evident. One way this can be expressed is to appropriate the definition of God attributed to Alain of Lille and say: Reality (self/world) is an intelligible (communicable, expressible, knowable, etc.) sphere whose center is everywhere and circumference nowhere.

'God is an intelligible sphere, whose center is everywhere, and whose circumference is nowhere.' Alain of Lille

86 From the Zen perspective, forms (dharmas) are not good or bad, sacred or profane, but rather they are (each and all) particularly unique and significant *as they are*. Thus, to abstain from the judgments (assessments, evaluations) they evoke, for instance in an attempt to be 'objective,' demonstrates the deluded notion (dualistic presumption) that dharmas are objective (independent) entities. As fundamental elements of reality (i.e. dharmas), judgments are both the 'what' that is experienced *as* judgments and the 'means' whereby the experience *of* judging is realized. Thus, the failure to accurately utilize judgments evoked by/as dharmas is a failure to see dharmas as they are.

The authentic Zen practitioner recognizes the judgments evoked by dharmas as *integral* to and *revelatory of* the normality of those dharmas. The capacity for such recognition is realized through the activation of the True Dharma-eye in concert with the skill acquired and sustained through discipline and effort in the art of nonthinking or ceasing conceptualization. By 'ceasing conceptualization' is meant, for one thing, the ability to avoid being sidetracked by abstract speculation and generalization in the here-now of encountering dharmas *as they are*, inclusive of the judgments they evoke. As conceptualization and generalization arises endlessly, the skill or art (*upaya*) to encounter dharmas without distorting the judgments (discernments) evoked by them here-now with acquired prejudices (preconceptions) is a skill that can always be improved. As dharmas are only and always particular, their true nature can only be obscured by discerning them *as they are not*, which commonly results from reducing them to the generalizations or preconceptions acquired from systematic theories, sectarian schemes, dogmatic codes, or fixed formulas.

[87] Idolatry has long proven to be a particularly tenacious hindrance to accurately seeing the true nature of reality (self/world). The perspective of the idolater commonly is similar to what archetypal psychology recognizes as the 'perspective (or stance) of spirit' (in contrast to 'soul'). This similarity is particularly evident in Zen's portrayal of attachment to doctrines, codes, formulaic fixation, or dogmatic order (e.g. scholars that count words and letters, board carrying fellows, etc.). The hindering nature of the 'stance of spirit' in archetypal psychology is, for all practical purposes, identical to the hindering effect of this idolatry in Zen, that is, the stance of the 'egocentric' self to the 'polycentric' self. The hindrance to truth described by archetypal psychology as the 'conventional perspective of science and religion,' for example, corresponds to the hindrance to true nature described by Zen as 'attachment to doctrines.' In light of this, the observations of James Hillman, who deeply studied the issue for many years, merit our close attention:

At times the spirit position with its rhetoric of order, number, knowledge, permanency, and self-defensive logic has been discussed as 'senex' and Saturnian (Vitale 1973; Hillman 1975d); at other times, because of its rhetoric of clarity and detached observation, it has been discussed as Apollonic (Hillman 1972c); on other occasions, because of its rhetoric of unity, ultimacy, identity, it has been termed 'monotheistic"; and in yet other contexts, 'heroic' and also 'puer' (1967b).

While recognizing that the spirit perspective must place itself above (as the soul places itself as inferior) and speak in transcendent, ultimate, and pure terms, archetypal psychology conceives its task as one of imagining the spirit language of 'truth,' 'faith,' 'law,' and the like as rhetoric of spirit, even if spirit is obliged by this same rhetoric to take its stance truthfully and faithfully, i.e. literally. James Hillman, *Archetypal Psychology: A Brief Account* (Uniform Edition Vol. 1), Spring Publications (December 1, 2004), p.25

The general significance of the 'hindering perspective' can be glimpsed in light of the particular terms and phrases Hillman uses to illumine the 'stance of spirit' – order, number, knowledge, permanency, self-defensive logic, clarity, detached observation, unity, ultimacy, identity, truth, faith, and law. The implications of 'attachment to doctrine' is even clearer when we consider what is *illumined* in context of what is *darkened*, that is, in context of what is necessarily *unexpressed* to convey what *is* expressed. In this sense, consider this sample of what Hillman is compelled to leave *unexpressed* in order to accurately describe the stance of spirit (i.e. delineate 'spirit' from 'not-spirit").

Order [chaos, randomness, ailment, freedom], number [guess, intuition, infinity], knowledge [unknown, fiction, novelty], permanency [change, becoming, activity], self-defensive logic [common sense, humility, open-mindedness, wisdom], clarity [ambiguity, mystery, privacy, possibility], detached observation [relationship, concern, involvement, passion], unity [distinction, differentiation, variation, uniqueness], ultimacy [partiality, boundary, innovation, increase], identity [individuality, character, eccentricity], truth [imaginary, fantasy, romance], faith [experience, reason, validation, rationale], law [potential, fortune, risk].

[88] Generally, 'suffering' (*dukkha*) in Buddhism is identified with the painful inevitabilities of the human condition; old age, sickness, and death.

[89] Conscious awareness of the immunity of truth to literal expression and egocentricity demonstrates one of the most significant differences between the Zen view and the common view of consciousness. The difference between Zen's view of consciousness as the 'normal mind' *itself*, and the prevailing view of consciousness as a *product of* the mind (often equated with the brain) is a difference between resolving the problem of suffering and exacerbating it. Like its Christian cousin, the 'doctrine of original sin,' the 'truth of ṣuffering' both affirms the real existence of suffering, and reveals its true nature. Insofar as expressions on the truth of suffering (or original sin) are *authentic*, they *resolve* the question of suffering (provided they are read with the True Dharma-eye).

In sum, the 'truth of suffering' (or 'original sin') is the truth of the limits of the human condition which *provides for*, or more precisely, *amounts to*, the experiential capacity of human subjectivity (self-consciousness) which is itself the very thing that provides for the opportunity to experience the limitlessness of the human condition (Buddhahood). If it is true that, 'He who seeks to save his life must lose it' it is because both saving life and losing life *are* life *itself* – "This very 'life-and-death' is the sacred life of the Buddha." Eihei Dogen, *Shoji*

[90] Percy Bysshe Shelley, *The Necessity of Atheism and Other Essays,* Prometheus Books; 1St Edition edition (June 1, 1993)

[91] 'Nominalism' is commonly used in one of two distinct ways, one in which the existence of abstract objects is denied, and one in which the existence of universals is denied. My usage conforms more to the latter than the former – though not exactly (due to differences between the dualistic worldview in which the term originates and the nondual worldview being presented here). More particularly, my usage closely coincides

with its meaning in archetypal psychology, for example, with James Hillman's explanation here:

This is nominalism which too has been instrumental in de-personifying our existence. Nominalism empties out big words; nominalists consider universal laws and general types to be only names (nomina). Words have no inherent substance of their own. Re-Visioning Psychology, William Morrow Paperbacks; Reissue edition (June 19, 1997), p.5

[92] In this, Zen's vision of existence-time is remarkably similar to Alfred North Whitehead's notion of the 'ceaseless advance into novelty' (of the universe). Alfred North Whitehead, *Process and Reality* (Gifford Lectures Delivered in the University of Edinburgh During the Session 1927-28) Free Press; 2nd edition (July 1, 1979)

[93] Rupert Sheldrake, *The Science Delusion*, Coronet Books; First edition & printing in this form edition (December 6, 2012), p.116

[94] George Lakoff and Mark Johnson, *Philosophy in the Flesh: the Embodied Mind & its Challenge to Western Thought,* Basic Books (October 8, 1999), pp.9-10

[95] David Bohm, *Wholeness and the Implicate Order,* Routledge; First Edition edition (July 1980), p.6

[96] N. Lee Swanson, *The Religion of Science*, (2012), pp.19-20

[97] N. Lee Swanson, *The Religion of Science*, (2012), p.20

[98] *New World Encyclopedia* http://www.newworldencyclopedia.org/entry/Perception

[99] Hee-Jin Kim, *Dogen on Meditation and Thinking: A Reflection on His View of Zen*, State University of New York Press (November 9, 2006), pp.100-101

[100] Richard Tarnas, *Cosmos and Psyche: Intimations of a New World View*, Plume; Reprint edition (April 24, 2007), p.19

[101] James Hillman, *Re-Visioning Psychology*, William Morrow Paperbacks; Reissue edition (June 19, 1997), p.1

[102] Hubert Nearman, *SHOBOGENZO The Treasure House of the Eye of the True Teaching* by Eihei Dogen, Translated by Reverend Master Hubert Nearman, Order of Buddhist Contemplatives, (Shasta Abbey Press, Mount Shasta, California 2007 ISBN: 978-0-930066-27-7), p.229

[103] Richard Tarnas, *Cosmos and Psyche: Intimations of a New World View*, Plume; Reprint edition (April 24, 2007), p.17

[104] James Hillman, *Re-Visioning Psychology*, William Morrow Paperbacks; Reissue

edition (June 19, 1997), pp.1-2

[105] N. Lee Swanson, *The Religion of Science*, (2012), p.19 (emphasis in the original)

[106] The particular presuppositions upon which the first principles of scientific method depend essentially consist of a consensus as to what qualify as 'viable' hypotheses. Whatever 'hypotheses' are thereby established must then be treated (by scientists) as having absolute authority for any 'fact' arrived at by scientific method to be considered 'valid.' For example, if we presuppose (hypothesize) that a cup contains water at 1600 and we find at 1604 the cup contains oil, according to scientific method, the proposition that 'water was replaced by oil between 1600 and 1604' is 'scientifically valid,' but the proposition that 'oil was there all along' is 'scientifically invalid' because it violates the standard of scientific method by denying the initial presupposition.

Notice too, that once a proposition is 'validated' (e.g. 'water was replaced by oil'), that 'hypothesis' becomes a scientifically valid 'fact' upon which further scientific investigations can be based. Thus, 'scientific facts' consist as much of 'subjective presuppositions' as they do of 'objective empirical evidence.' And, of course, a *presupposition* is ultimately a species of *blind faith*; to presuppose is to *accept* what *could be* true 'as if' it *actually is* true. Finally, while scientific method *formally* denies the validity of presuppositions that are contrary to empirical evidence or are inherently unverifiable, in actual practice validity is sometimes asserted and accepted despite empirical evidence or an absence of falsiafibility.

While the precise criteria qualifying as 'scientific method' varies among particular fields of science and specific contexts, even its most liberal forms require some manner of 'empirical evidence' (e.g. independently observable, repeatable experimental results, accurate predictions, etc.) and 'falsiafibility' (i.e. an explanation or argument whereby a proposition could be demonstrably refuted. For example, 'nothing can travel faster than light,' is falsifiable; it could be refuted by observing something travelling faster than light). The proposition that 'objective reality exists' (independent of subjective experience) inherent to the representational theory of knowledge is supported by *neither* empirical evidence nor falsiafibility – indeed, this proposition is *both contrary to* empirical evidence and *inherently* unverifiable (hence, *unfalsifiable*).

[107] Rupert Sheldrake, *The Science Delusion*, Coronet Books; First edition & printing in this form edition (December 6, 2012), p.13

[108] Gudo Nishijima, Chodo Cross, trans. Shōbōgenzō: The True Dharma-Eye Treasury1, Berkeley: Numata Center for Buddhist Translation and

Research, 2009. http://www.bdk.or.jp/document/dgtl-dl/dBET_T2582_Shobogenzo1_2009.pdf (accessed August 5, 2016), p.144

[109] Richard Tarnas, *Cosmos and Psyche: Intimations of a New World View*, Plume; Reprint edition (April 24, 2007), p.18

[110] Gudo Nishijima, Chodo Cross, trans. Shōbōgenzō: The True Dharma-Eye Treasury2, Berkeley: Numata Center for Buddhist Translation and Research, 2008. http://www.bdk.or.jp/document/dgtl-dl/dBET_T2582_Shobogenzo2_2008.pdf (accessed August 5, 2016), p.4

[111] Brian Greene, *The Fabric of the Cosmos: Space, Time, and the Texture of Reality*, Vintage (February 8, 2005), p.94

[112] N. Lee Swanson, *The Religion of Science*, (2012), p.138

[113] Hubert Nearman, *SHOBOGENZO The Treasure House of the Eye of the True Teaching* by Eihei Dogen, Translated by Reverend Master Hubert Nearman, Order of Buddhist Contemplatives, (Shasta Abbey Press, Mount Shasta, California 2007 ISBN: 978-0-930066-27-7), p.153

[114] John Steinbeck, *East of Eden*, Penguin Classics; Reissue edition (1952)

[115] N. Lee Swanson, *The Religion of Science*, (2012), pp.19-20

[116] Henry David Thoreau, Journal, 6 May 1854, *The Writings of Henry David Thoreau* (Boston: Houghton Mifflin Co., 1906)

[117] Garma C.C. Chang, *The Buddhist Teaching of Totality: The Philosophy of Hwa Yen Buddhism*, Penn State University Press (May 4, 2001), p.64

[118] Hee-Jin Kim, *The Flowers of Emptiness: Selections from Dogen's Shobogenzo*, Edwin Mellen Press (1985), p.61

[119] Red Pine, *The Platform Sutra: The Zen Teaching of Hui-neng*, Counterpoint (November 28, 2008), p.178

[120] Hee-Jin Kim, *The Flowers of Emptiness: Selections from Dogen's Shobogenzo*, Edwin Mellen Press (1985), p.61

[121] Translated by Robert Aitken Roshi of the Diamond Sangha Zen Buddhist Society

[122] Gudo Nishijima, Chodo Cross, trans. Shōbōgenzō: The True Dharma-Eye Treasury2, Berkeley: Numata Center for Buddhist Translation and Research, 2008. http://www.bdk.or.jp/document/dgtl-dl/dBET_T2582_Shobogenzo2_2008.pdf (accessed August 5, 2016), p.4

[123] Hee-Jin Kim, *The Flowers of Emptiness: Selections from Dogen's Shobogenzo*,

Edwin Mellen Press (1985), p.61

[124] The five skandhas are: form, sensation, conception, volition, and consciousness. As characteristic of Buddhist categorizations, *each* of the five skandhas is *interdependent* with *all* and *each of the other* five skandhas; each presupposes *all* and *each* of the five. What is true of one is true of all five skandhas. Accordingly, Zen/Buddhist expressions (e.g. the *Heart Sutra*) frequently employ 'form' as an abbreviation for all five skandhas; for that matter, 'form' is often employed as an abbreviation for any and all phenomena.

[125] Translated by Hee-Jin Kim (*Flowers of Emptiness*, p.61)

[126] Hee-Jin Kim, *The Flowers of Emptiness: Selections from Dogen's Shobogenzo*, Edwin Mellen Press (1985), p.63 (note 5 to the translation of *Shobogenzo, Maka-hannya-haramitsu*)

[127] Translation by Hee-Jin Kim (*Flowers of Emptiness*, p.61)

[128] Hee-Jin Kim, *The Flowers of Emptiness: Selections from Dogen's Shobogenzo*, Edwin Mellen Press (1985), p.64 (note 7 to the translation of *Shobogenzo, Maka-hannya-haramitsu*)

[129] Gudo Nishijima, Chodo Cross, trans. Shōbōgenzō: The True Dharma-Eye Treasury1, Berkeley: Numata Center for Buddhist Translation and Research, 2009. http://www.bdk.or.jp/document/dgtl-dl/dBET_T2582_Shobogenzo1_2009.pdf (accessed August 5, 2016), p.32

[130] Gudo Nishijima, Chodo Cross, trans. Shōbōgenzō: The True Dharma-Eye Treasury1, Berkeley: Numata Center for Buddhist Translation and Research, 2009. http://www.bdk.or.jp/document/dgtl-dl/dBET_T2582_Shobogenzo1_2009.pdf (accessed August 5, 2016), p.149

[131] Gudo Nishijima, Chodo Cross, trans. Shōbōgenzō: The True Dharma-Eye Treasury2, Berkeley: Numata Center for Buddhist Translation and Research, 2008. http://www.bdk.or.jp/document/dgtl-dl/dBET_T2582_Shobogenzo2_2008.pdf (accessed August 5, 2016), p.356

[132] Gudo Nishijima, Chodo Cross, trans. Shōbōgenzō: The True Dharma-Eye Treasury2, Berkeley: Numata Center for Buddhist Translation and Research, 2008. http://www.bdk.or.jp/document/dgtl-dl/dBET_T2582_Shobogenzo2_2008.pdf (accessed August 5, 2016), p.356

[133] Gudo Nishijima, Chodo Cross, trans. Shōbōgenzō: The True Dharma-Eye Treasury1, Berkeley: Numata Center for Buddhist Translation and

[133] Research, 2009. http://www.bdk.or.jp/document/dgtl-dl/dBET_T2582_Shobogenzo1_2009.pdf (accessed August 5, 2016), p.32

[134] Gudo Nishijima, Chodo Cross, trans. Shōbōgenzō: The True Dharma-Eye Treasury1, Berkeley: Numata Center for Buddhist Translation and Research, 2009. http://www.bdk.or.jp/document/dgtl-dl/dBET_T2582_Shobogenzo1_2009.pdf (accessed August 5, 2016), pp.32-33

[135] Gudo Nishijima, Chodo Cross, trans. Shōbōgenzō: The True Dharma-Eye Treasury1, Berkeley: Numata Center for Buddhist Translation and Research, 2009. http://www.bdk.or.jp/document/dgtl-dl/dBET_T2582_Shobogenzo1_2009.pdf (accessed August 5, 2016), p.33

[136] Gudo Nishijima, Chodo Cross, trans. Shōbōgenzō: The True Dharma-Eye Treasury1, Berkeley: Numata Center for Buddhist Translation and Research, 2009. http://www.bdk.or.jp/document/dgtl-dl/dBET_T2582_Shobogenzo1_2009.pdf (accessed August 5, 2016), p.33

[137] Gudo Nishijima, Chodo Cross, trans. Shōbōgenzō: The True Dharma-Eye Treasury1, Berkeley: Numata Center for Buddhist Translation and Research, 2009. http://www.bdk.or.jp/document/dgtl-dl/dBET_T2582_Shobogenzo1_2009.pdf (accessed August 5, 2016), p.33

[138] Translation by Hee-Jin Kim (*Flowers of Emptiness*, p.62)

[139] Translation by Hee-Jin Kim (*Flowers of Emptiness*, p.66)

[140] Translation by Hee-Jin Kim (*Flowers of Emptiness*, pp.62-63)

[141] Hee-Jin Kim, *The Flowers of Emptiness: Selections from Dogen's Shobogenzo*, Edwin Mellen Press (1985), p.66

[142] Translation by Thomas Cleary, *Book of Serenity: One Hundred Zen Dialogues*, Shambhala; 1st edition (August 6, 1998), p. 206

[143] Statement made in 1986, quoted in *Towards a Theory of Transpersonal Decision-Making in Human-Systems* (2007) by Joseph Riggio, p. 66

[144] As quoted in *The Observer* (11 January 1931); also in *Psychic Research* (1931), Vol. 25, p. 91

[145] Translation by Hee-Jin Kim (*Flowers of Emptiness*, p.61)

[146] Hubert Nearman, *SHOBOGENZO The Treasure House of the Eye of the True Teaching* by Eihei Dogen, Translated by Reverend Master Hubert Nearman, Order of Buddhist Contemplatives, (Shasta Abbey Press, Mount Shasta, California 2007 ISBN: 978-0-930066-27-7), p.87

[147] *The Diamond Sutra & The Sutra of Hui-Neng*, A. F. Price & Wong Mou-lam,

Shambhala Publications Inc; 1 edition (2004-10-31) (1800) p.144

[148] Translation by Thomas Cleary, *Classics of Buddhism and Zen, Volume 4: The Collected Translations of Thomas Cleary*, p.796

[149] Translation by Thomas Cleary, *Classics of Buddhism and Zen, Volume 3: The Collected Translations of Thomas Cleary*, p.299

[150] Translation by John Blofeld, *The Zen Teaching of Huang Po: On the Transmission of Mind,* p.121-122

[151] Gudo Nishijima, Chodo Cross, trans. Shōbōgenzō: The True Dharma-Eye Treasury4, Berkeley: Numata Center for Buddhist Translation and Research, 2008. http://www.bdk.or.jp/document/dgtl-dl/dBET_T2582_Shobogenzo2_2008.pdf (accessed August 5, 2016), p.331

[152] *The Lotus Sutra*

[153] Gudo Nishijima, Chodo Cross, trans. Shōbōgenzō: The True Dharma-Eye Treasury3, Berkeley: Numata Center for Buddhist Translation and Research, 2008. http://www.bdk.or.jp/document/dgtl-dl/dBET_T2582_Shobogenzo2_2008.pdf (accessed August 5, 2016), p.113

[154] Gudo Nishijima, Chodo Cross, trans. Shōbōgenzō: The True Dharma-Eye Treasury3, Berkeley: Numata Center for Buddhist Translation and Research, 2008. http://www.bdk.or.jp/document/dgtl-dl/dBET_T2582_Shobogenzo2_2008.pdf (accessed August 5, 2016), p.114

[155] Gudo Nishijima, Chodo Cross, trans. Shōbōgenzō: The True Dharma-Eye Treasury3, Berkeley: Numata Center for Buddhist Translation and Research, 2008. http://www.bdk.or.jp/document/dgtl-dl/dBET_T2582_Shobogenzo2_2008.pdf (accessed August 5, 2016), p.114

[156] Gudo Nishijima, Chodo Cross, trans. Shōbōgenzō: The True Dharma-Eye Treasury3, Berkeley: Numata Center for Buddhist Translation and Research, 2008. http://www.bdk.or.jp/document/dgtl-dl/dBET_T2582_Shobogenzo2_2008.pdf (accessed August 5, 2016), p.114

[157] Gudo Nishijima, Chodo Cross, trans. Shōbōgenzō: The True Dharma-Eye Treasury3, Berkeley: Numata Center for Buddhist Translation and Research, 2008. http://www.bdk.or.jp/document/dgtl-dl/dBET_T2582_Shobogenzo2_2008.pdf (accessed August 5, 2016), p.114

[158] Translation by Thomas Cleary, *Teachings of Zen*, Shambhala; 1st edition (December 16, 1997), p.51

[159] Translation by J.C. Cleary, *Zen Dawn: Early Zen Texts from Tun Huang* (Shambhala Dragon Editions) Paperback – November 13, 2001, p.53

[160] Translation by Thomas Cleary, *Instant Zen: Waking Up in the Present,* North Atlantic Books (October 12, 1994), p.46

[161] Translation by Robert Buswell, *Tracing Back the Radiance* (Classics in East Asian Buddhism), University of Hawaii Press; Third Impression edition (May 1, 1991), p.151-152

[162] Plotinus, *Enneads*, II, 3, 7, "*Are the Stars Causes?*" (c. 268), quoted in Eugenio Garin, *Astrology in the Renaissance*, trans. C. Jackson and J. Allen, rev. C. Robertson (London: Arkana, 1983), p. 117

[163] Gudo Nishijima, Chodo Cross, trans. Shōbōgenzō: The True Dharma-Eye Treasury1, Berkeley: Numata Center for Buddhist Translation and Research, 2009. http://www.bdk.or.jp/document/dgtl-dl/dBET_T2582_Shobogenzo1_2009.pdf (accessed August 5, 2016), p.144

[164] Gudo Nishijima, Chodo Cross, trans. Shōbōgenzō: The True Dharma-Eye Treasury3, Berkeley: Numata Center for Buddhist Translation and Research, 2008. http://www.bdk.or.jp/document/dgtl-dl/dBET_T2582_Shobogenzo2_2008.pdf (accessed August 5, 2016), pp.4-5

[165] Hee-Jin Kim, *Eihei Dogen: Mystical Realist*, Wisdom Publications; 3 Revised edition (January 1, 2000), p.117

[166] Translated by Thomas Byrom, *Dhammapada* (Shambhala Pocket Classics), Shambhala; New edition edition (November 9, 1993)

[167] Gudo Nishijima, Chodo Cross, trans. Shōbōgenzō: The True Dharma-Eye Treasury1, Berkeley: Numata Center for Buddhist Translation and Research, 2009. http://www.bdk.or.jp/document/dgtl-dl/dBET_T2582_Shobogenzo1_2009.pdf (accessed August 5, 2016), p.65

[168] Gudo Nishijima, Chodo Cross, trans. Shōbōgenzō: The True Dharma-Eye Treasury1, Berkeley: Numata Center for Buddhist Translation and Research, 2009. http://www.bdk.or.jp/document/dgtl-dl/dBET_T2582_Shobogenzo1_2009.pdf (accessed August 5, 2016), p.68

[169] Gudo Nishijima, Chodo Cross, trans. Shōbōgenzō: The True Dharma-Eye Treasury1, Berkeley: Numata Center for Buddhist Translation and Research, 2009. http://www.bdk.or.jp/document/dgtl-

dl/dBET_T2582_Shobogenzo1_2009.pdf (accessed August 5, 2016), p.69

[170] Gudo Nishijima, Chodo Cross, trans. Shōbōgenzō: The True Dharma-Eye Treasury1, Berkeley: Numata Center for Buddhist Translation and Research, 2009. http://www.bdk.or.jp/document/dgtl-dl/dBET_T2582_Shobogenzo1_2009.pdf (accessed August 5, 2016), p.69

[171] *The Oneness of Mind*, as quoted/translated in *Quantum Questions: Mystical Writings of The World's Great Physicists*, Shambhala; 1st edition (June 12, 1984) edited by Ken Wilber

[172] Ockham's Razor is the 'scientific' rule or principle which basically asserts that among competing hypotheses the one with the fewest necessary assumptions should be selected; *pluralitas non est ponenda sine necessitate*, "plurality should not be posited without necessity." coined by William of Ockham (c. 1287–1347).

[173] Notice that authentic conceptualization is, like all genuine human capacities, a normal and necessary aspect of Zen practice-enlightenment. Zen's rejection concerns the activity of 'purely speculative conceptualization' – conceptualization *based on* entirely abstract or unverifiable concepts – which is accurately recognized as *inherently unreliable*; not only inapplicable to authentic conceptualization, but a hindrance to it.

[174] Gudo Nishijima, Chodo Cross, trans. Shōbōgenzō: The True Dharma-Eye Treasury2, Berkeley: Numata Center for Buddhist Translation and Research, 2008. http://www.bdk.or.jp/document/dgtl-dl/dBET_T2582_Shobogenzo2_2008.pdf (accessed August 5, 2016), p.90

[175] *Shōbōgenzō, Jinzū,* Gudo Nishijima & Mike Cross

[176] Gudo Nishijima, Chodo Cross, trans. Shōbōgenzō: The True Dharma-Eye Treasury2, Berkeley: Numata Center for Buddhist Translation and Research, 2008. http://www.bdk.or.jp/document/dgtl-dl/dBET_T2582_Shobogenzo2_2008.pdf (accessed August 5, 2016), p.152

[177] Gudo Nishijima, Chodo Cross, trans. Shōbōgenzō: The True Dharma-Eye Treasury4, Berkeley: Numata Center for Buddhist Translation and Research, 2008. http://www.bdk.or.jp/document/dgtl-dl/dBET_T2582_Shobogenzo2_2008.pdf (accessed August 5, 2016), p.292

[178] The six sense organs are eyes, ears, nose, tongue, body (tactile sense), and mind. The six sense fields are sights, sounds, smells, tastes, tactile sensations, and thoughts (inclusive of all 'mental phenomenon', e.g. ideas, memories, fantasies, etc.). The six sense capacities are seeing,

hearing, smelling, tasting, feeling, and thinking.

[179] Sensorium; noun sen·so·ri·um \sen-'sȯr-ē-əm\: the parts of the brain or the mind concerned with the reception and interpretation of sensory stimuli; broadly: the entire sensory apparatus http://www.merriam-webster.com/dictionary/sensorium

[180] Dan Lusthaus, *Buddhist Phenomenology: A Philosophical Investigation of Yogacara Buddhism and the Ch'eng Wei-shih Lun* (Routledge Critical Studies in Buddhism), Routledge (January 8, 2003), p.56

[181] Dan Lusthaus, *Buddhist Phenomenology: A Philosophical Investigation of Yogacara Buddhism and the Ch'eng Wei-shih Lun* (Routledge Critical Studies in Buddhism), Routledge (January 8, 2003), p.56

[182] In Buddhism, sensing and actualizing are not two different things – we do not have sense capacities because there are things to sense, there are things to sense because we have sense capacities. For an excellent overview of this see *Buddhist Phenomenology: A Philosophical Investigation of Yogacara Buddhism and the Ch'eng Wei-shih Lun* (Routledge Critical Studies in Buddhism), Routledge (January 8, 2003), Dan Lusthaus, pp.52-82

[183] Gudo Nishijima, Chodo Cross, trans. Shōbōgenzō: The True Dharma-Eye Treasury2, Berkeley: Numata Center for Buddhist Translation and Research, 2008. http://www.bdk.or.jp/document/dgtl-dl/dBET_T2582_Shobogenzo2_2008.pdf (accessed August 5, 2016), p.356

[184] Hubert Nearman, *SHOBOGENZO The Treasure House of the Eye of the True Teaching* by Eihei Dogen, Translated by Reverend Master Hubert Nearman, Order of Buddhist Contemplatives, (Shasta Abbey Press, Mount Shasta, California 2007 ISBN: 978-0-930066-27-7), p.84

[185] Hee-Jin Kim, *The Flowers of Emptiness: Selections from Dogen's Shobogenzo*, Edwin Mellen Press (1985), p.66

[186] Gudo Nishijima, Chodo Cross, trans. Shōbōgenzō: The True Dharma-Eye Treasury3, Berkeley: Numata Center for Buddhist Translation and Research, 2008. http://www.bdk.or.jp/document/dgtl-dl/dBET_T2582_Shobogenzo2_2008.pdf (accessed August 5, 2016), pp.257-258

[187] Hubert Nearman, *SHOBOGENZO The Treasure House of the Eye of the True Teaching* by Eihei Dogen, Translated by Reverend Master Hubert Nearman, Order of Buddhist Contemplatives, (Shasta Abbey Press, Mount Shasta, California 2007 ISBN: 978-0-930066-27-7), p.109

[188] Alfred North Whitehead, *Modes of Thought*, The Free Press (February 1, 1968), p.47

[189] The fact that every assertion or belief in the 'nonexistence' of anything *independent of* 'experience' is *also* false does not deny the accuracy of this observation. Any concept or notion not grounded on experiential evidence is, by definition, *hypothetical*. A claim or belief that treats a *hypothesis* as a *verified truth* or *fact* is, by default, false.

[190] Gudo Nishijima, Chodo Cross, trans. Shōbōgenzō: The True Dharma-Eye Treasury3, Berkeley: Numata Center for Buddhist Translation and Research, 2008. http://www.bdk.or.jp/document/dgtl-dl/dBET_T2582_Shobogenzo2_2008.pdf (accessed August 5, 2016), pp.349-350

[191] Northrop Frye, *Fearful Symmetry, a Study of William Blake By Northrop Frye*, princeton university press; 1 edition (1972), pp.20-21

[192] Hee-Jin Kim, *Eihei Dogen: Mystical Realist*, Wisdom Publications; 3 Revised edition (January 1, 2000), p.100

[193] *The Heart of Dogen's Shobogenzo*, State University of New York Press; annotated edition edition (January 24, 2002), by Norman Waddell (Translator), Masao Abe (Translator), pp.7-30

[194] Translated by Hee-Jin Kim, *Dogen on Meditation and Thinking: A Reflection on His View of Zen*, State University of New York Press (November 9, 2006), p.21

[195] Hee-Jin Kim, *Dogen on Meditation and Thinking: A Reflection on His View of Zen*, State University of New York Press (November 9, 2006), p.21

[196] Translation by Red Pine, *The Zen Teaching of Bodhidharma* (English and Chinese Edition), North Point Press (November 1, 1989), p.29

[197] Gudo Nishijima, Chodo Cross, trans. Shōbōgenzō: The True Dharma-Eye Treasury3, Berkeley: Numata Center for Buddhist Translation and Research, 2008. http://www.bdk.or.jp/document/dgtl-dl/dBET_T2582_Shobogenzo2_2008.pdf (accessed August 5, 2016), p.261

[198] Gudo Nishijima, Chodo Cross, trans. Shōbōgenzō: The True Dharma-Eye Treasury3, Berkeley: Numata Center for Buddhist Translation and Research, 2008. http://www.bdk.or.jp/document/dgtl-dl/dBET_T2582_Shobogenzo2_2008.pdf (accessed August 5, 2016), p.338

[199] Gudo Nishijima, Chodo Cross, trans. Shōbōgenzō: The True Dharma-Eye

Treasury3, Berkeley: Numata Center for Buddhist Translation and Research, 2008. http://www.bdk.or.jp/document/dgtl-dl/dBET_T2582_Shobogenzo2_2008.pdf (accessed August 5, 2016), p.109

[200] *The Marriage of Heaven and Hell*, William Blake, *The Complete Poetry & Prose of William Blake,* Paperback – March 5, 1997, William Blake (Author), David V. Erdman (Author), Harold Bloom (Author), William Golding (Author), Anchor; Revised edition (April 16, 1982)

[201] Gudo Nishijima, Chodo Cross, trans. Shōbōgenzō: The True Dharma-Eye Treasury4, Berkeley: Numata Center for Buddhist Translation and Research, 2008. http://www.bdk.or.jp/document/dgtl-dl/dBET_T2582_Shobogenzo2_2008.pdf (accessed August 5, 2016), p.332

[202] Gudo Nishijima, Chodo Cross, trans. Shōbōgenzō: The True Dharma-Eye Treasury1, Berkeley: Numata Center for Buddhist Translation and Research, 2009. http://www.bdk.or.jp/document/dgtl-dl/dBET_T2582_Shobogenzo1_2009.pdf (accessed August 5, 2016), pp.364-365

[203] Translated by Urs App, *Master Yunmen: From the Record of the Chan Master "Gate of the Clouds"*, Kodansha America; First Edition first Printing edition (September 1994), p.127

[204] Translated by James Green, James, *The Recorded Sayings of Zen Master Joshu*, Shambhala (September 18, 2001)

[205] *Seeing Voices,* Vintage; Reprint edition (November 28, 2000)

[206] Gensha Shibi (835–907), see; *Shōbōgenzō Ikka-no-myōju*

[207] Hubert Nearman, *SHOBOGENZO The Treasure House of the Eye of the True Teaching* by Eihei Dogen, Translated by Reverend Master Hubert Nearman, Order of Buddhist Contemplatives, (Shasta Abbey Press, Mount Shasta, California 2007 ISBN: 978-0-930066-27-7), p.38

[208] Hubert Nearman, *SHOBOGENZO The Treasure House of the Eye of the True Teaching* by Eihei Dogen, Translated by Reverend Master Hubert Nearman, Order of Buddhist Contemplatives, (Shasta Abbey Press, Mount Shasta, California 2007 ISBN: 978-0-930066-27-7), p.765

[209] Translation by Hee-Jin Kim, *Eihei Dogen: Mystical Realist*, Wisdom Publications; 3 Revised edition (January 1, 2000), p.168

[210] See *Process and Reality* (Gifford Lectures Delivered in the University of Edinburgh During the Session 1927-28) Free Press; 2nd edition (July 1,

1979), pp.18-20

[211] Translation by Hee-Jin Kim, *Eihei Dogen: Mystical Realist*, Wisdom Publications; 3 Revised edition (January 1, 2000), pp.168-169

[212] Richard Tarnas, *Cosmos and Psyche: Intimations of a New World View*, Plume; Reprint edition (April 24, 2007), p.33

[213] Gudo Nishijima, Chodo Cross, trans. Shōbōgenzō: The True Dharma-Eye Treasury2, Berkeley: Numata Center for Buddhist Translation and Research, 2008. http://www.bdk.or.jp/document/dgtl-dl/dBET_T2582_Shobogenzo2_2008.pdf (accessed August 5, 2016), p.356

[214] Unfortunately the clarity of this image has made the doctrine of transmission vulnerable to simplistic interpretations fostering idolatry. Literalistic simplifications (i.e. distortions) of this doctrine has long plagued Zen, however, attention to its true (metaphorical) significance may have never been as profoundly absent as it is today – contemporary discussion of 'transmission' is almost exclusively confined to formal rituals of sectarian succession (the official sanctioning of sectarian teachers).

[215] For example, see *Philosophy in the Flesh: the Embodied Mind & its Challenge to Western Thought,* Basic Books (October 8, 1999) by George Lakoff and Mark Johnson, pp. 60-73

[216] Hee-Jin Kim, *Dogen on Meditation and Thinking: A Reflection on His View of Zen*, State University of New York Press (November 9, 2006), p.64

[217] *Bendowa*, See Hee-Jin Kim, *Dogen on Meditation and Thinking: A Reflection on His View of Zen*, State University of New York Press (November 9, 2006), p.21

[218] Hubert Nearman, *SHOBOGENZO The Treasure House of the Eye of the True Teaching* by Eihei Dogen, Translated by Reverend Master Hubert Nearman, Order of Buddhist Contemplatives, (Shasta Abbey Press, Mount Shasta, California 2007 ISBN: 978-0-930066-27-7), p.229

[219] Translation by Hee-Jin Kim, *Eihei Dogen: Mystical Realist*, Wisdom Publications; 3 Revised edition (January 1, 2000), p.34

[220] Gudo Nishijima, Chodo Cross, trans. Shōbōgenzō: The True Dharma-Eye Treasury4, Berkeley: Numata Center for Buddhist Translation and Research, 2008. http://www.bdk.or.jp/document/dgtl-dl/dBET_T2582_Shobogenzo2_2008.pdf (accessed August 5, 2016), p.329

[221] Hubert Nearman, SHOBOGENZO The Treasure House of the Eye of the True Teaching by Eihei Dogen, Translated by Reverend Master Hubert Nearman, Order of Buddhist Contemplatives, (Shasta Abbey Press, Mount Shasta, California 2007 ISBN: 978-0-930066-27-7), p.73

[222] For example, see Takashi James Kodera's *Dogen's Formative Years in China: An Historical Study and Annotated Translation of the Hokyo-Ki*, Prajna Press (May 1980), p.58

[223] See Hee-Jin Kim's *The Reason of Words and Letters: Dogen and Koan Language*, in *Dogen Studies* (Studies in East Asian Buddhism, No 2), Edited by William R. LaFleur, University of Hawaii Press; Enlarged ed. edition (May 1, 1985), pp.73-74

[224] For more on the archetypal or prototypical aspect of zazen in Dogen see Hee-Jin Kim, Eihei Dogen: Mystical Realist, pp.37-39, 58-67, Hee-Jin Kim, Dogen on Meditation and Thinking, , pp.23-26, and *Studies in East Asian Buddhism No. 2, Dogen Studies*, Edited by William R. LaFleur, pp.55-61

[225] Hubert Nearman, SHOBOGENZO The Treasure House of the Eye of the True Teaching by Eihei Dogen, Translated by Reverend Master Hubert Nearman, Order of Buddhist Contemplatives, (Shasta Abbey Press, Mount Shasta, California 2007 ISBN: 978-0-930066-27-7), pp.779-780

[226] Hubert Nearman, SHOBOGENZO The Treasure House of the Eye of the True Teaching by Eihei Dogen, Translated by Reverend Master Hubert Nearman, Order of Buddhist Contemplatives, (Shasta Abbey Press, Mount Shasta, California 2007 ISBN: 978-0-930066-27-7), p.779

[227] Some classic Zen records may superficially appear to support claims that Zen advocates meditation techniques that are literally supposed to be void of 'objects.' Upon closer examination, however, the classic records *do not* support such claims, indeed they explicitly refute them. First, techniques for 'objectless meditation' that fail to account for the fact that an 'objectless state' can only be pursued by making such state an 'object' in the first place are flawed for obvious reasons. Further, when carefully considered it becomes clear that most of the actual expressions in the classics only appear to support such notions when given a *literal* (rather than mythopoeic) reading. Finally, every actual manifestation of authentic practice-enlightenment – whether actualized in seated meditation (zazen, shikantaza), koan training, mindfulness, hauling water, driving a school bus, or changing a diaper – is actualized in/as the (nondual) activity Dogen calls 'nonthinking' wherein *both* subject *and* object are cast-off in/as the actualization of the self/world (*genjokoan*).

[228] Gudo Nishijima, Chodo Cross, trans. Shōbōgenzō: The True Dharma-Eye

Treasury1, Berkeley: Numata Center for Buddhist Translation and Research, 2009. http://www.bdk.or.jp/document/dgtl-dl/dBET_T2582_Shobogenzo1_2009.pdf (accessed August 5, 2016), p.5

[229] Hubert Nearman, SHOBOGENZO The Treasure House of the Eye of the True Teaching by Eihei Dogen, Translated by Reverend Master Hubert Nearman, Order of Buddhist Contemplatives, (Shasta Abbey Press, Mount Shasta, California 2007 ISBN: 978-0-930066-27-7), p.259

[230] Gudo Nishijima, Chodo Cross, trans. Shōbōgenzō: The True Dharma-Eye Treasury3, Berkeley: Numata Center for Buddhist Translation and Research, 2008. http://www.bdk.or.jp/document/dgtl-dl/dBET_T2582_Shobogenzo2_2008.pdf (accessed August 5, 2016), pp.142-143

[231] Hubert Nearman, SHOBOGENZO The Treasure House of the Eye of the True Teaching by Eihei Dogen, Translated by Reverend Master Hubert Nearman, Order of Buddhist Contemplatives, (Shasta Abbey Press, Mount Shasta, California 2007 ISBN: 978-0-930066-27-7), p.779

[232] Gudo Nishijima, Chodo Cross, trans. Shōbōgenzō: The True Dharma-Eye Treasury4, Berkeley: Numata Center for Buddhist Translation and Research, 2008. http://www.bdk.or.jp/document/dgtl-dl/dBET_T2582_Shobogenzo2_2008.pdf (accessed August 5, 2016), pp.299-300

[233] Gudo Nishijima, Chodo Cross, trans. Shōbōgenzō: The True Dharma-Eye Treasury4, Berkeley: Numata Center for Buddhist Translation and Research, 2008. http://www.bdk.or.jp/document/dgtl-dl/dBET_T2582_Shobogenzo2_2008.pdf (accessed August 5, 2016), p.290

[234] Hee-Jin Kim, Dogen on Meditation and Thinking: A Reflection on His View of Zen, State University of New York Press (November 9, 2006), p.52

[235] The Blue Cliff Record, Shambhala (April 12, 2005), Translated by Thomas Cleary & J.C Cleary, p.514

[236] The Blue Cliff Record, Shambhala (April 12, 2005), Translated by Thomas Cleary & J.C Cleary, p.515

[237] Gudo Nishijima, Chodo Cross, trans. Shōbōgenzō: The True Dharma-Eye Treasury3, Berkeley: Numata Center for Buddhist Translation and Research, 2008. http://www.bdk.or.jp/document/dgtl-dl/dBET_T2582_Shobogenzo2_2008.pdf (accessed August 5, 2016), p.4

[238] Gudo Nishijima, Chodo Cross, trans. Shōbōgenzō: The True Dharma-Eye Treasury3, Berkeley: Numata Center for Buddhist Translation and

Research, 2008. http://www.bdk.or.jp/document/dgtl-dl/dBET_T2582_Shobogenzo2_2008.pdf (accessed August 5, 2016), p.5

[239] While the actual amount or degree of reality actualized is relative to the individual being, the significant difference between the 'enlightened being' and the 'ordinary being' is that the former experiences a *continuously increasing* capacity for actualization (hence experiences a continuously expanding reality).

[240] Gudo Nishijima, Chodo Cross, trans. Shōbōgenzō: The True Dharma-Eye Treasury2, Berkeley: Numata Center for Buddhist Translation and Research, 2008. http://www.bdk.or.jp/document/dgtl-dl/dBET_T2582_Shobogenzo2_2008.pdf (accessed August 5, 2016), p.356

[241] Gudo Nishijima, Chodo Cross, trans. Shōbōgenzō: The True Dharma-Eye Treasury4, Berkeley: Numata Center for Buddhist Translation and Research, 2008. http://www.bdk.or.jp/document/dgtl-dl/dBET_T2582_Shobogenzo2_2008.pdf (accessed August 5, 2016), pp.299-300

[242] *The Marriage of Heaven and Hell, The Complete Poetry & Prose of William Blake,* Paperback – March 5, 1997, William Blake (Author), David V. Erdman (Author), Harold Bloom (Author), William Golding (Author), Anchor; Revised edition (April 16, 1982)

[243] *What Is Life? with Mind and Matter and Autobiographical Sketches*, by Erwin Schrödinger, Roger Penrose (Foreword)

[244] For a discussion of Zen's perspective concerning the nature of 'Good and Evil' see *Good (doing) and Evil (nondoing) in Zen* by Ted Biringer

[245] Classic Zen Koan

[246] The terms 'explicit' and 'implicit' here are used in the sense employed by David Bohm in his landmark book, *Wholeness and the Implicate Order,* Routledge; First Edition edition (July 1980)

[247] *The Marriage of Heaven and Hell, The Complete Poetry & Prose of William Blake,* Paperback – March 5, 1997, William Blake (Author), David V. Erdman (Author), Harold Bloom (Author), William Golding (Author), Anchor; Revised edition (April 16, 1982)

[248] *Hebrews* 11:1, KJV

[249] *The Marriage of Heaven and Hell, The Complete Poetry & Prose of William Blake,* Paperback – March 5, 1997, William Blake (Author), David V. Erdman (Author), Harold Bloom (Author), William Golding (Author),

Anchor; Revised edition (April 16, 1982)

[250] Gudo Nishijima, Chodo Cross, trans. Shōbōgenzō: The True Dharma-Eye Treasury2, Berkeley: Numata Center for Buddhist Translation and Research, 2008. http://www.bdk.or.jp/document/dgtl-dl/dBET_T2582_Shobogenzo2_2008.pdf (accessed August 5, 2016), p.151

[251] Gudo Nishijima, Chodo Cross, trans. Shōbōgenzō: The True Dharma-Eye Treasury2, Berkeley: Numata Center for Buddhist Translation and Research, 2008. http://www.bdk.or.jp/document/dgtl-dl/dBET_T2582_Shobogenzo2_2008.pdf (accessed August 5, 2016), p.151

[252] Gudo Nishijima, Chodo Cross, trans. Shōbōgenzō: The True Dharma-Eye Treasury2, Berkeley: Numata Center for Buddhist Translation and Research, 2008. http://www.bdk.or.jp/document/dgtl-dl/dBET_T2582_Shobogenzo2_2008.pdf (accessed August 5, 2016), p.152

[253] Gudo Nishijima, Chodo Cross, trans. Shōbōgenzō: The True Dharma-Eye Treasury2, Berkeley: Numata Center for Buddhist Translation and Research, 2008. http://www.bdk.or.jp/document/dgtl-dl/dBET_T2582_Shobogenzo2_2008.pdf (accessed August 5, 2016), p.4

[254] Gudo Nishijima, Chodo Cross, trans. Shōbōgenzō: The True Dharma-Eye Treasury1, Berkeley: Numata Center for Buddhist Translation and Research, 2009. http://www.bdk.or.jp/document/dgtl-dl/dBET_T2582_Shobogenzo1_2009.pdf (accessed August 5, 2016), p.70

[255] Existence, experience, and realization here are meant in the sense of ontology, epistemology, and soteriology respectively:

Ontology; existence-time; objectivity, other, the universe, the myriad dharmas

Epistemology; knowledge, sentience; subjectivity, self

Soteriology; liberation, salvation, enlightenment

[256] The totality of existence-time; the mind-alone/myriad dharmas, Buddhas alone together with Buddhas

[257] Experientially verifying

[258] Nonduality; emptiness, interdependence

[259] The soteriological goal of Zen/Buddhism

[260] Subjective experience, not-other

[261] Objective existence, not-self

[262] Existence-time; the mind-alone/myriad dharmas

[263] Ignorance (*lack* of right views) and delusion (*presence* of wrong views) are the roots of all fear and greed; fear and greed are the roots of all anguish and distress. The experience of fear depends on the possibility of being separated from what one loves or united with what one hates; the experience of greed depends on the possibility of being united with what one loves or separated from what one hates. Seeing the truth of nonduality enlightens one to the truth that one is not 'separated' from anything and there is nothing apart from oneself that one could become 'united' with.

[264] Buddha; the universe

[265] The dynamics of nonduality

[266] Nondual; empty, interdependent

[267] Experiential verification

[268] Criterion or measure for accuracy, (or 'right view')

[269] Actualized through practice-enlightenment

[270] Hence inclusive of

[271] Dharmas; phenomenal forms, objects of consciousness, instances of existence-time

[272] As possessing independent existence

[273] Continuously arise and fall away, appear and disappear

[274] Its dharma-position, its place-and-time in/as existence-time

Bibliography

Abe, Masao. "Dogen on Buddha Nature." *The Eastern Buddhist,* vol. 4, no. 1 (May 1971), pp. 28–71.

——. *A Study of Dogen: His Philosophy and Religion*. Albany, NY: State University of New York Press, 1992.

——. *Zen and Western Thought*. Honolulu, HI: University of Hawaii Press, 1985.

Aitken, Robert, trans. *The Gateless Barrier: The Wu-men kuan (Mumonkan)*. San Francisco, CA: North Point Press, 1991.

——. *Original Dwelling Place: Zen Buddhist Essays*. Washington, DC: Counterpoint, 1997.

——. *The Practice of Perfection: The Paramitas from a Zen Buddhist Perspective*. Washington, DC: Counterpoint, 1997.

——. *Taking the Path of Zen*. San Francisco, CA: North Point Press, 1985.

App, Urs, *Master Yunmen: From the Record of the Chan Master "Gate of the Clouds"*, Kodansha America; First Edition first Printing edition (September 1994)

Benoit, Hubert. *The Supreme Doctrine: Psychological Studies in Zen Thought.* New York: The Viking Press, 1959.

Bielefeldt, Carl. Dogen's Manuals of Zen Meditation. Berkeley, CA: University of California Press, 1988.

Biringer, Ted. *The Flatbed Sutra of Louie Wing: The Second Ancestor of Zen in the West*, American Book Publishing; 1st edition (August 13, 2009)

——. Recarving the Dragon: History and Dogma in the Study of Dogen, in Dogen Studies, Lafleur, William R. Lafleur, ed., Honolulu, HI: University of Hawaii Press, 1985.

Blake, William, *The Complete Poetry & Prose of William Blake,* Paperback – March 5, 1997, William Blake (Author), David V. Erdman (Author), Harold Bloom (Author), William Golding (Author), Anchor; Revised edition (April 16, 1982)

Blofeld, John, The Zen Teaching of Huang Po, Grove Press, New York, 1958.

———. The Zen Teaching of Instantaneous Awakening, Buddhist Publishing Group Leicester, England, 1974.

Bodiford, William M., *Soto Zen in Medieval Japan* (Studies in East Asian Buddhism), University of Hawaii Press; 1 edition (June 1, 2008)

Bohm, David, *Wholeness and the Implicate Order* Routledge; First Edition edition (July 1980)

———. *On the Intuitive Understanding of Nonlocality as Implied by Quantum Theory, Foundations of Physics* Vol 5 (1975)

Bohr, Niels, Volume I - *Atomic Theory and the Description of Nature* (Philosophical Writings of Niels Bohr Series, Vol 1), Ox Bow Press (June 15, 1987)

Buswell, Robert, *Tracing Back the Radiance* (Classics in East Asian Buddhism), University of Hawaii Press; Third Impression edition (May 1, 1991)

Byrom, Thomas, Dhammapada (Shambhala Pocket Classics), Shambhala; New edition edition (November 9, 1993)

Campbell, Joseph. The Hero With a Thousand Faces. Princeton, New Jersey, Princeton University Press; 2nd edition (1973)

———. The Inner Reaches of Outer Space. New York, NY: Harper Perennial (November 1988)

———. The Masks of God. New York, NY: Penguin Books (1976)

———. The Mythic Image. Princeton, New Jersey: Princeton University Press (November 1, 1981)

———. The Power of Myth. New York, NY:Anchor, June 1, 1991.

Chang Chung-yuan. Original Teachings of Ch'an Buddhism. New York: Grove Press, 1982.

Chang, Garma C.C., *The Buddhist Teaching of Totality: The Philosophy of Hwa Yen Buddhism*, Penn State University Press (May 4, 2001

Cicero, Marcus Tullius, *On the laws, Cicero: Selected Works Penguin Classics*; 1St Edition edition (September 30, 1960)

Cleary, J.C., *Zen Dawn: Early Zen Texts from Tun Huang* (Shambhala Dragon Editions) Paperback – November 13, 2001

———. Swampland Flowers: The Letters and Lectures of Zen Master Ta Hui. New York: Grove Press, 1977.

Cleary, Thomas, *Book of Serenity: One Hundred Zen Dialogues*, Shambhala; 1st edition (August 6, 1998)

———. *Classics of Buddhism and Zen* (5 Volumes): *The Collected Translations of Thomas Cleary,* Shambhala; 1 edition (April 12, 2005)

———. *Teachings of Zen*, Shambhala; 1st edition (December 16, 1997)

———. *Instant Zen: Waking Up in the Present,* North Atlantic Books (October 12, 1994)

———. (With Cleary, J.C.) *The Blue Cliff Record*, Shambhala (April 12, 2005)

———. *Shobogenzo: Zen Essays by Dogen*. Honolulu, HI: University of Hawaii Press, 1986.

———. *Timeless Spring: A Soto Zen Anthology*. New York: Weatherhill, 1980.

Conze, Edward. *Buddhist Wisdom Books*. New York & San Francisco: Harper & Row, 1958.

Cook, Francis Dojun, trans. *The Record of Transmitting the Light: Zen Master Keizan's Denkoroku*. Boston, MA: Wisdom, 2004.

Conze, Edward. *Buddhism: Its Essence and Development.* Harper Torchbooks edition. New York: Harper & Row, 1959.

———. *Buddhist Meditation.* London: George Allen & Unwin, Ltd., 1956.

Foster, Nelson, and Shoemaker, Jack, *The Roaring Stream: A New Zen Reader*, New Jersey, The Ecco Press, 1996.

Frye, Northrop, *The Educated Imagination and Other Writings on Critical Theory*, 1933-1963, University of Toronto Press, Scholarly Publishing Division (December 9, 2006)

———. *Fearful Symmetry, a Study of William Blake By Northrop Frye*, princeton university press; 1 edition (1972)

Galilei, Galileo, *Discoveries and Opinions of Galileo*: including *The starry messenger* (1610), *Letter to the Grand Duchess Christina* (1615), and excerpts from *Letters on sunspots* (1613), *The assayer* (1623) Mass Market Paperback – 1957

Garin, Eugenio, *Astrology in the Renaissance*, trans. C. Jackson and J. Allen, rev. C. Robertson (London: Arkana, 1983)

Green, James, *The Recorded Sayings of Zen Master Joshu*, Shambhala (September 18, 2001)

Greene, Brian, *The Fabric of the Cosmos: Space, Time, and the Texture of Reality*, Vintage (February 8, 2005)

Gregory, Peter G., *Sudden and Gradual: Approaches to Enlightenment in Chinese*

Thought. Honolulu: University of Hawaii Press, 1987.

———. *Tsung-Mi and the Sinification of Buddhism.* Honolulu: University of Hawaii Press, 2002.

Griffiths, Paul J., *On Being Mindless: buddhist meditation and the mind-body problem.* Delhi, India: Sri Satguru Publications, 1986.

Hakeda, Yoshito S., trans. *The Awakening of Faith.* New York: Columbia University Press, 1967.

Hanh, Thich Nhat, *The Heart of Understanding: Commentaries on the Prajnaparamita Heart Sutra,* Parallax Press (November 24, 1964)

Hawking, Stephen, The Universe in a Nutshell, Bantam; 1St Edition edition (2000)

Heine, Steven and Dale S. Wright, eds. *The Koan: Texts and Contexts in Zen Buddhism.* Oxford, UK: Oxford University Press, 2000.

Heine, Steven. *Did Dogen Go to China? What He Wrote and When He Wrote It.* New York, NY: Oxford University Press, Inc., 2006.

———. *Dogen and the Koan Tradition.* Albany, NY: State University of New York Press, 1994.

———. *Dogen and Soto Zen*, Oxford University Press; 1 edition (February 26, 2015)

———. *Zen Skin, Zen Marrow: Will the Real Zen Buddhism Please Stand up.* New York, NY: Oxford University Press, Inc., 2008.

Heisenberg, Werner, *Physics and Philosophy: The Revolution in Modern Science*, Harper Torchbooks (June 1958)

Hillman, James, Re-Visioning Psychology, William Morrow Paperbacks; Reissue edition (June 19, 1997)

———. *Archetypal Psychology: A Brief Account* (Uniform Edition Vol. 1), Spring Publications (December 1, 2004)

Kim, Hee-Jin, *Dogen on Meditation and Thinking: A Reflection on His View of Zen*, State University of New York Press (November 9, 2006)

———. *Eihei Dogen: Mystical Realist*, Wisdom Publications; 3 Revised edition (January 1, 2000)

———. *The Flowers of Emptiness: Selections from Dogen's Shobogenzo*, Edwin Mellen Press (1985)

———. *The Reason of Words and Letters: Dogen and Koan Language*, Dogen Studies (Studies in East Asian Buddhism, No 2), Edited by William R. LaFleur, University of Hawaii Press; Enlarged ed. edition (May 1, 1985)

Kodera, Takashi James, *Dogen's Formative Years in China: An Historical Study and Annotated Translation of the Hokyo-Ki*, Prajna Press (May 1980)

Kraft, Kenneth. Eloquent Zen: Daito and Early Japanese Zen. Honolulu, HI: University of Hawaii Press, 1992.

——. Zen: Traditions and Transition. New York: Grove Press, 1992.

LaFleur, William R.(editor), *Dogen Studies* (Studies in East Asian Buddhism, No 2), University of Hawaii Press; Enlarged ed. edition (May 1, 1985)

Lakoff, George and Johnson, Mark, *Philosophy in the Flesh: the Embodied Mind & its Challenge to Western Thought,* Basic Books (October 8, 1999)

Lanza, Robert, *Biocentrism: How Life and Consciousness Are the Keys to Understanding the True Nature of the Universe*, Robert Lanza and Bob Berman, BenBella Books; 1 edition (May 18, 2010)

Leighton, Daniel and Yi Wu. Cultivating the Empty Field: The Silent Illumination of Zen Master Hongzhi. Rutland, VT: Charles E. Tuttle, 2001.

——. and Okumura, Shohaku, Dogens Extensive Record: A Translation of the Eihei Koroku, Wisdom Publications, 2004.

Lipton, Bruce, The Biology of Belief: Unleashing the Power of Consciousness, Matter, & Miracles, Hay House; Revised edition (2008)

Luk, Charles (Lu K'uan Yu). Ch'an and Zen Teaching, 3 Vols. Boston, MA: Red Wheel/Weiser, 1993.

——. *The Secret of Chinese Meditation.* London: Rider & Co., 1964.

Lusthaus, Dan, *Buddhist Phenomenology: A Philosophical Investigation of Yogacara Buddhism and the Ch'eng Wei-shih Lun* (Routledge Critical Studies in Buddhism), Routledge (January 8, 2003)

McRae, John R. The Northern School and the Formation of Early Ch'an Buddhism. Honolulu, HI: University of Hawaii Press, 1986.

——. Seeing through Zen: Encounter, Transformation, and Genealogy in Chinese Chan Buddhism, University of California Press; 1 edition (January 19, 2004)

Murti, T.R.V. *The Central Philosophy of Buddhism.* London: George Allen & Unwin, Ltd., 1955.

Nearman, Hubert "SHOBOGENZO The Treasure House of the Eye of the True Teaching" by Eihei Dogen, Translated by Reverend Master Hubert Nearman, Order of Buddhist Contemplatives, (Shasta Abbey Press, Mount Shasta, California 2007 ISBN: 978-0-930066-27-7)

Nishijima, Gudo, and Cross, Chodo, trans. *Shōbōgenzō: The True Dharma-Eye Treasury1*, Berkeley: Numata Center for Buddhist Translation and Research, 2009. http://www.bdk.or.jp/document/dgtl-dl/dBET_T2582_Shobogenzo1_2009.pdf (accessed August 5, 2016)

——. *Shōbōgenzō: The True Dharma-Eye Treasury2*, Berkeley: Numata Center for Buddhist Translation and Research, 2008. http://www.bdk.or.jp/document/dgtl-dl/dBET_T2582_Shobogenzo2_2008.pdf (accessed August 5, 2016)

——. *Shōbōgenzō: The True Dharma-Eye Treasury3*, Berkeley: Numata Center for Buddhist Translation and Research, 2008. http://www.bdk.or.jp/document/dgtl-dl/dBET_T2582_Shobogenzo2_2008.pdf (accessed August 5, 2016)

——. *Shōbōgenzō: The True Dharma-Eye Treasury4*, Berkeley: Numata Center for Buddhist Translation and Research, 2008. http://www.bdk.or.jp/document/dgtl-dl/dBET_T2582_Shobogenzo2_2008.pdf (accessed August 5, 2016)

Noe, Alva, Out of Our Heads: Why You Are Not Your Brain, and Other Lessons from the Biology of Consciousness, Hill and Wang; 1 edition (February 2, 2010)

Ogata, Sohaku, trans., *The Transmission of the Lamp: Early Masters*. Wolfeboro, NH: Longwood Academic, 1988.

Okubo Dosho, ed. *Dogen zenji zenshu*. 2 vols. Tokyo: Chikumu shobo, 1969, 1970.

Piechocinska, Barbara, *Physics from Wholeness: Dynamical Totality As a Conceptual Foundation for Physical Theories* (Uppsala Dissertations from the Faculty of Science & Technology), Uppsala University (December 30, 2005)

Pine, Red, *The Platform Sutra: The Zen Teaching of Hui-neng*, Counterpoint (November 28, 2008)

——. The Diamond Sutra: Text and Commentaries Translated from Sanskrit and Chinese. Washington, DC: Counterpoint, 2001.

——. *The Zen Teaching of Bodhidharma* (English and Chinese Edition), North Point Press (November 1, 1989)

Powell, William F. *The Record of Tung-shan*. Honolulu, HI: University of Hawaii Press, 1986.

Price, A. F., & Mou-lam, Wong, *The Diamond Sutra & The Sutra of Hui-Neng*, Boston, MA: Shambhala, 1990.

Schrodinger, Erwin, *Mind and Matter: The Tarner Lectures* delivered at Trinity College, Cambridge, in October 1956, Cambridge University Press; 1st edition (1958)

Scientific American, Vol. 7 (Munn & Company, 1851)

Sheldrake, Rupert, *The Science Delusion*, Coronet Books; First edition & printing in this form edition (December 6, 2012)

Shelly, Percy Bysshe, *The Necessity of Atheism and Other Essays,* Prometheus Books; 1St Edition edition (June 1, 1993)

Stambaugh, Joan. *Impermanence is Buddha-Nature: Dōgen's Understanding of Temporality*. Honolulu, HI: University of Hawaii Press, 1990.

Steinbeck, John, *East of Eden*, Penguin Classics; Reissue edition (1952)

Stone, Jacqueline. *Original Enlightenment and the Transformation of Medieval Japanese Buddhism*. Honolulu, HI: University of Hawaii Press, 1999.

Suzuki, Daisetz Teitaro. *Essays in Zen Buddhism.* 3 vols. London: Luzac, 1927, 1933, and 1934.

———. *Manual of Zen Buddhism.* Evergreen edition. New York: Grove Press, 1960.

———. *Studies in the Lankavatara sutra.* London: Routledge & Kegan Paul, Ltd., 1930.

———. *Studies in Zen.* London: Rider, 1955.

———. *The Zen Doctrine of No-Mind.* London: Rider and Company, 1949, and 1958.

———. *Zen and Japanese Culture.* New York: Pantheon Books, Inc., 1959.

Swanson, N. Lee, *The Religion of Science*, (2012)

Tanahashi, Kazuaki, ed. *Enlightenment Unfolds: The Essential Teachings of Zen Master Dogen*, Boston, MA: Shambhala, 1999.

———. *Moon in a Dewdrop: Writings of Zen Master Dogen*. San Francisco, CA: North Point Press, 1985.

———. *Treasury of the True Dharma Eye: Zen Master Dogen's Shobo Genzo*, Shambhala (May 14, 2013)

———. *The True Dharma Eye: Zen Master Dogen's Three Hundred Koans*, Shambhala Publications (October 4, 2011)

Tarnas, Richard, *Cosmos and Psyche: Intimations of a New World View*, Plume; Reprint edition (April 24, 2007)

———. *The Passion of the Western Mind: Understanding the Ideas that Have

Shaped Our World View, Ballantine Books; Reprint edition (March 16, 1993)

Thoreau, Henry David, *The Writings of Henry David Thoreau* (Boston: Houghton Mifflin Co., 1906)

Thurman, Robert A. F. *The Holy Teachings of Vimalakirti: A Mahayana Scripture*. University Park, Pennsylvania: Pennsylvania State University Press, 1976.

Waddell, Norman, *Wild Ivy: The Spiritual Autobiography of Zen Master Hakuin*, Shambhala (July 13, 2010)

———. and Abe, Masao, trans. "Dogen's Bendowa." *The Eastern Buddhist,* vol. 4, no. 1 (May 1971), pp. 124–57.

———. trans. "Dogen's Fukanzazengi and *Shobogenzo zazengi*." *The Eastern Buddhist,* vol. 6, no. 2 (October 1973), pp. 115–28.

———. trans. "Dogen's Shobogenzo Zenki 'Total Dynamic Working' and *Shoji* 'Birth and Death.'" *EB,* vol. 5, no. 1 (May 1972), pp. 70–80.

———. trans. "The King of Samadhis Samadhi, Dogen's Shobogenzo Sammai O Zammai." *The Eastern Buddhist,* vol. 7, no. 1 (May 1974), pp. 118–23.

———. trans. "'One Bright Pearl' Dogen's Shobogenzo Ikka Myoju." *The Eastern Buddhist,* vol. 4, no. 2 (October 1971), pp. 108–18.

———. trans. "Shobogenzo Genjokoan." *The Eastern Buddhist,* vol. 5, no. 2 (October 1972), pp. 129–40.

———. (With Abe, Masao), *The Heart of Dogen's Shobogenzo*, State University of New York Press; annotated edition (January 24, 2002)

———. *The Essential Teachings of Zen Master Hakuin*. Boston, MA: Shambhala, 1994.

———. *Zen Words for the Heart: Hakuin's Commentary on the Heart Sutra*. Boston, MA: Shambhala, 1996.

Whitehead, Alfred North, *Process and Reality* (Gifford Lectures Delivered in the University of Edinburgh During the Session 1927-28) Free Press; 2nd edition (July 1, 1979)

———. *Modes of Thought*, The Free Press (February 1, 1968)

Wilber, Ken (editor), *Quantum Questions: Mystical Writings of The World's Great Physicists*, Shambhala; 1st edition (June 12, 1984)

Wittgenstein, Ludwig, *Tractatus Logico-Philosophicus*, Chiron Academic Press (January 11, 2016)

Wright, Dale S. (Author), Steven Heine (Editor), *The Zen Canon: Understanding the Classic Texts*, Oxford University Press; 1 edition (March 25, 2004)

Index

activity, 21, 37, 66, 70-71, 95, 103, 107, 110-113, 123, 125, 126, 131, 133, 136, 138, 141, 180n, 185n, 194n, 199n
actualization, 21, 26, 28, 37-38, 71, 79, 90, 107, 110-112, 115-116,, 127, 132, 133-141, 143-146, 148-149, 154, 155-157, 163-165, 169, 199n, 201n
advance into novelty, xiv, 21, 31, 37, 110, 125, 126, 136, 163, 168, 169, 187n
Aitken, Robert, 189n, 205n
autochthonous, xiv, 27, 34, 122
Avaghosa (80-150 CE), 6

being. *See* existence
Big Bang Theory, 55-56
Blake, William, xv, 110, 115, 179n, 197n, 201n, 205; quoted, 115, 155, 159, 160
Blofeld, John, 150n, 205n
bodhi. See enlightenment
bodhicitta (aspiration for enlightenment), 98, 123-126, 130, 157, 163-165
Bodhidharma (470-543?), xv, 6, 112, 196n, 210n
Bohm, David, xv, 9, 172n, 173n, 187n, 201n, 206n; quoted, 1, 7, 9, 41, 76
Bohr, Niels, 173n, 206n; quoted, 8, 13
bondage to suffering (*dukkha*), 6
buddha(s), xv, xvi, 16, 22, 29, 30, 35, 36-39, 71-75, 84-85,86,87, 90, 93-100, 101-102, 105-106, 112-113,114, 115-118, 121, 125, 126, 131, 133, 134, 136, 138, 143, 146, 151, 154-155, 157, 158, 159-161, 162-165, 167, 169; and ordinary being(s), 29, 30, 36-38, 151, 154, 159; buddha alone together with buddha (*yuibutsu yobutsu*), xvi, 29, 80, 97, 105, 112, 118, 124, 126, 135, 179n, 181n, 183n, 202n; Sakyamuni (historical buddha), xv, 71, 106, 113, 121, 136, 158, 167
Buddha-Dharma. *See* Buddhism
Buddhism, xiii, xv-xvi, 5-7, 15, 18, 31, 61, 83, 87, 90, 92-95, 101, 133, 135-137, 165, 172n,176n, 177n, 178n, 179n, 181n, 182n, 186n, 202n; doctrine and methodology, 16, 23, 28, 38, 72, 80- 90, 100, 107, 113, 130-131; doctrines, specific, eighteen *dhatus,* 68-69, 101-102; emptiness, 23, 26-27, 37, 61-76, 134, 178n, 182-183n; four noble truths, 7, 31, 172n, 186n; interdependence, 7, 23, 63, 67, 76-80, 90, 130, 182-183n; six modes, 101-104, 162, 180n, 181n; transmission, *See* buddha(s), buddha alone together with buddha (*yuibutsu yobutsu*)
Byrom, Thomas, 193n, 206n

Campbell, Joseph, xv, 206n
Chang, Garma C.C, 189n, 206n; quoted, 61

Chinul, Bojo Jinul (1158–1210), quoted, 89
Cicero, Marcus Tullius, 172n, 206n; quoted, 5
Cleary, J.C., 171n, 192n, 200n, 206n
Cleary, Thomas, 191n, 192n, 193n, 200n, 206n, 207n
consciousness, 8, 16-17, 28, 43, 52, 56, 66, 68,76, 79, 95, 101-104, 105-109, 114, 143, 147-154, 155-157, 160, 167, 177n, 178n, 180n, 181n, 186n, 189n, 203n. *See also* mind; sentience

daigo (great enlightenment). *See* enlightenment
daimei (great delusion). *See* delusion
death, 18, 128, 130, 168, 183n, 186n. *See also* great death
delusion, 3, 5, 6, 24, 26, 30, 57, 68, 76, 104, 115, 121, 125-126, 128-129, 144, 146, 168, 169, 203n; and enlightenment, 26, 30, 76, 125-126, 127, 129, 144, 161, 168, 169, 176-177n, 178n; great delusion (*daimei*), 35-36, 160, 169, 177; vs. ignorance, 5-6. *See also* enlightenment
Dhammapada, 92-93, 193n, 206n
dharma(s), iv, 15-17, 20, 22-23, 25, 27, 28, 29, 30, 33-35, 36, 37-38, 40, 61, 62-63, 67-69, 71, 72-74, 75, 76, 78, 81, 83-84, 86, 90, 94, 95, 97, 99, 102, 103, 105-109, 111-117, 121-124, 127-132, 140-141, 143-146, 148, 154, 156, 159, 161, 163, 168, 169, 174n, 178n, 179n, 181n, 183n, 202n, 203n; defined, 15-17 . *See also* dharma-position(s); existence-time
dharma-position(s), 17, 78-80, 81, 125, 126, 136, 148, 153, 156, 165, 174n, 203n; defined, 17 . *See also* dharma(s); existence-time
Diamond Sutra, 62-63, 64, 67, 78, 191n, 210n, 211n
Dogen (1200-1253), vii, xiii, 1, 4, 13, 20, 25, 44, 52, 64, 67, 70-75, 78, 81, 84, 86, 90, 93-95, 97-99, 110, 111-116, 121-125, 133-141, 143, 144-145, 151-152, 154, 160, 161-164, 171n, 174n, 175n, 176n, 181n; quoted, 6, 7, 21, 25, 46, 50, 52, 55, 61, 64, 65, 66, 67, 68-69, 70, 71-72, 73, 74, 80, 81, 83, 84, 85, 86, 87, 91, 93, 94, 97, 98-99, 103, 106, 107, 108, 113, 114, 115, 116, 121, 122, 125, 126, 131, 133, 134-135, 137, 139, 140, 141, 143, 144, 145, 149, 154-155, 162, 164, 167
dori (reason). *See* reason
dualism, 7, 8-10, 11-13, 22, 23-24, 25, 41, 42-44, 45, 46, 50-54, 56, 58, 62, 85, 90, 92, 99-100, 104-105, 108-109, 152-154, 161, 164; vs. duality, 23-24. *See also* duality; nonduality; representational theory of knowledge
duality, 23-24, 26, 71, 76, 80, 111-112, 176n, 177n; vs. dualism, 23-24. *See also* dualism; nonduality

eighteen *dhatus*. *See* Buddhism, doctrines, specific
Einstein, Albert, xv, 51-54, 55, 151; quoted, 52. *See also* General Relativity
emptiness. *See* Buddhism, doctrines, specific
enlightenment, xiii, 5-6, 21, 22, 26, 27, 28, 29, 30, 35-36, 37, 62, 66, 71, 75-76, 84-85, 86-87, 95, 98-99, 105, 108, 110-118, 122-123, 125-126, 127, 128-132, 133-

135, 136-141, 144-146, 155,156-157, 159-161, 162-163, 165, 167, 169; by oneself without a teacher (*mushi dokugo*), 95, 98, 167; great enlightenment (*daigo*), 35-36, 169. *See also* delusion; delusion, and enlightenment

epistemology, xiii, xiv, 3-4, 5, 11, 22, 25, 27, 28, 29, 39-40, 42-45, 48, 63, 67, 71, 75-76, 92, 93, 96, 101-104, 105, 106, 113-114, 124-125, 179, 181, 202n; as nondual with ontology, xiii, xiv, 3-4, 22, 25, 27, 28, 63, 67, 71, 75-76, 92, 96, 101-104, 105, 113-114124-125, 179, 181. *See also* representational theory of knowledge

existence. *See* ontology. *See also* existence-time; epistemology

existence-time (*uji*), xii, xiv, 7, 20-21, 27, 28, 34, 36, 37, 38, 50, 62-63, 70, 76, 78-80, 81, 83, 90, 91, 99, 101-102, 105, 110, 114, 122-126, 127, 128, 131, 136, 146-147, 149, 153, 156-157, 160, 162-165, 168, 169, 175n, 179n, 187n, 202n, 203n; defined, 20-21, 175n. *See also* dharma position(s); ontology; reality

experience. *See* epistemology. *See also* ontology; existence-time; experiential verification

experiential verification, 26, 27, 37, 66, 98, 203n. *See also* enlightenment, by oneself without a teacher (*mushi dokugo*)

expression, 6, 16, 18, 20, 24,29, 30, 33, 35, 37, 63, 68, 78-80, 83-90, 103, 105, 110, 112, 119-121, 122-125, 126-127, 128-132, 136, 157-158, 159-160, 163-165, 168, 179n, 181n, 182n, 183n . *See also* language; self expression(s)

foci, 23-24, 26, 28, 35, 86, 176n, 177n, 179-180n, 183n; defined, 23-24
form(s). *See dharma*(s)
four noble truths. *See* Buddhism, doctrines, specific
Frye, Northrop, xv, 171n, 196n, 207n; quoted, xiii, 110

Galilei, Galileo, 8, 172n, 207n; quoted, 5
General Relativity, 51-53. *See also* Einstein, Albert
genjokoan (actualizing the universe), 21, 26, 31, 35, 37, 38, 71, 90, 107, 110, 118, 127, 141, 145-146, 155-158, 169, 199n. *See also* advance into novelty
great death, 127-129. *See also* death
great delusion (*daimei*). *See* delusion
great enlightenment (*daigo*). *See* enlightenment
Green, James, 197n, 207n
Greene, Brian, 2, 9, 172n, 207n; quoted, 2

Hakuin, Ekaku (1689-1769), 6, 212n; quoted, 83
Hanh, Thich Nhat, 172n, 208n; quoted, 3
Heart Sutra, 64-67, 70-71, 105, 172n, 189-190n, 208n, 212n
Heisenberg, Werner, 173n, 208n; quoted, 8, 13
Hillman, James, xv, 184-185n, 186n, 187n, 208n; quoted, 46, 47-48, 185n, 186n
Huineng (638-713), xv, 6, 62, 189n, 191n, 210n, 211n; quoted, 83

Iconoclasm, 31
Idolatry, 31, 96, 184-185n, 198n
Ineffability, 100, 102, 106, 115, 146, 159-160
Interdependence. *See* Buddhism, doctrines, specific
ippo gujin. See total exertion of a single dharma

Jung, C.G., xv
Jushin, Joshu (778-897), 117, 197n, 207n; quoted, 117

kenbutsu (seeing buddha), 22, 30, 31, 37, 71, 105, 112, 114, 122-123; defined, 22. *See also* enlightenment; *kensho* (seeing true nature)
kensho (seeing true nature), 22, 112, 114; defined, 22. *See also* enlightenment, *kenbutsu* (seeing buddha)
Kim, Hee-Jin, vi, xiv, xv, 4, 18, 90, 111, 171n, 172n, 173n, 175n, 176n, 177n, 178n, 181n, 182n, 187n, 189n, 190n, 191n, 193n, 195n, 196n, 197n, 198n, 199n, 200n, 208-209n; quoted, vii, 1, 2, 4, 5, 13, 15, 18-20, 25, 44, 66, 67, 74, 75, 92, 105, 110, 111, 127, 145, 171n, 175n, 176n, 181-182n,
knowledge. *See* epistemology. *See also* experiential verification

Lakoff, George and Johnson, Mark, xv, 187n, 198n, 209n; quoted, 40
language, xiii, 3, 15, 19, 28, 30, 42-45, 86, 119-132, 137-138, 139, 171n, 179n, 181n, 182n, 185n; as nondual with thinking and reason, 29. *See also* expression; mythopoeism
Lanza, Robert, xv, 9, 173n, 209n; quoted, 9
Linji (died 866), 6
Lipton, Bruce H., xv, 209n
Lusthaus, Dan, 101-102, 195n, 209n; quoted, 101-102

meditation, 2, 68-69, 88, 89, 113, 116, 133, 135-137, 139, 141, 199n. *See also* nonthinking; practice-enlightenment; *shikantaza*
mind, 4, 7, 8, 11, 24, 25, 40, 43, 45-46, 47, 48, 51, 64, 69, 72-73, 91-92, 93-95, 96, 97, 101-104, 105-107, 108, 114-117, 131, 133, 137, 148-149, 152, 157, 159-160, 165, 167, 180n, 181n, 186n, 194n. *See also* consciousness; sensorium; sensation
mushi dokugo (enlightenment by oneself without a teacher). *See* enlightenment
mythopoeism, xii, xv, 16, 28, 29, 119-121, 128, 129-131, 135-140, 163, 179n, 199n; defined, 179n. *See also* expression; language

Nagarjuna (150-250 CE), 6, 117
Noe, Alva, xv, 210n
nominalism, 29, 34, 182n, 186n. *See also* expression; language; mythopoeism
nonduality, xiii, xiv, 12, 22-24, 26, 34, 42, 53, 69, 71, 74, 76-81, 83-86, 90, 92, 93, 108-109, 127, 135-136, 148, 167, 177-178n, 179n, 181n, 182-183n, 202n,

203n; defined, 22-24. *See also* dualism; duality; emptiness; interdependence
nonthinking, 37, 113, 158-161, 163, 184n, 199n. *See also* thinking; practice-enlightenment; *shikantaza*
normality, 24, 27-28, 29-30, 37-38, 54, 97, 124, 125-126, 128, 131, 146, 155, 159, 161, 162, 165, 178-179n, 181n, 184n; defined, 24; (as) thusness (*tathata*), 24, 54, 124, 178-179n; universal, 27-28, 38, 162, 165, 178-179n
no-self, 72, 75, 176n, 178n, 182n, 183n. *See also* Buddhism, doctrines, specific, emptiness

objects of consciousness. *See* Buddhism, doctrines, specific, eighteen *dhatus*; Buddhism, doctrines specific, six modes
Ockham's Razor, 54, 95, 96, 98, 194n
ontology, xiii, xiv, 3, 4, 22, 25, 27, 28, 34, 61, 63, 67, 71, 76, 92, 96, 101, 103, 105, 114, 124-125, 174n, 179-180n, 181n, 202n. *See also* epistemology; existence-time
other. *See* no-self.

practice-enlightenment, 21, 22, 28, 29, 35, 36-37, 66, 75 87, 108, 110-113, 130-131, 133, 135-141, 144, 162, 165, 167, 194n, 199n, 203n. *See also* meditation; enlightenment

quantum mechanics, 2, 8-10, 52-54, 56-57

reality. *See dharma*(s); existence-time; ontology
reason (*dori*), 14, 17-20, 23, 28, 30, 33, 35, 36-37, 65, 71, 75, 76, 78, 80, 81, 85-86, 113, 121, 123-125, 126, 128-130, 149, 154, 164-165, 174-175n, 178-179n, 181n, 183n, 184n; *See also* language; thinking
representational theory of knowledge, 40-45, 50-54, 58, 119, 154, 188n. *See also* epistemology

Sarton, George, 39; quoted, 39
Schrodinger, Erwin, 8, 172n, 211n; quoted, 8
science, xiii, xv, 1, 2, 3-4, 8-9, 10-12, 39-54, 55-59, 92, 96, 109,120, 126, 146-147, 150, 161, 164, 165, 184-185n, 187-188n, 194. *See also* General Relativity; quantum mechanics
self expression(s), 29, 30, 103, 121-126, 127, 130, 131, 183n. *See also* expression; language
sensation, 16-17, 43, 68, 97, 102, 104, 110, 114-116, 146, 151, 154, 158, 162, 163, 168, 178n, 180n, 181n, 189-190n, 194n. *See also* consciousness; mind; representational theory of knowledge; sensorium
sensorium, 101-103, 194n. *See also* consciousness; sensation
Sheldrake, Rupert, xv, 49, 172n, 211n; quoted, 3, 39, 49-50
Shelly, Percy Bysshe, 186n, 211n; quoted, 33

Shih-Shuang (Sekiso) 807-888, quoted, 89
shikantaza, 118, 133-141, 199n. S*ee also* meditation; nonthinking; practice-enlightenment
six modes. *See* Buddhism, doctrines, specific, six modes
sole-sitting. *See shikantaza*
soteriology, 4, 25, 44, 71, 92, 182n, 202n
speculation, 28, 34, 37, 42-44, 45, 51, 96-100, 109, 119-121, 143-147, 163, 180n, 184n, 194n
spirit, 31, 184-186n
Steinbeck, John, 189n, 211n; quoted, 57, 105
Surangama Sutra, 148
Swanson, N. Lee, xv, 41, 49, 187n, 189n, 211n; quoted, 41, 49, 55, 57
Swift, Jonathan, 172n; quoted, 6

Tarnas, Richard, xv, 12, 46, 47, 171n, 173n, 187n, 188n, 198n, 212n; quoted, xiii, 12, 45-46, 47, 50-51, 126
thinking, xii, 5, 7, 29, 41, 53, 62, 66, 97, 104, 105, 107-108, 137-137, 139, 141, 158-161, 163, 182n, 184n, 194n. *See also* consciousness; language; mind; nonthinking; reason; speculation
Thoreau, Henry David, 189n, 212n; quoted, 61
thusness (*tathata*), 19, 24, 30, 114, 124, 128, 177n, 178-179n. *See also* normality
time. *See* existence-time
total exertion [or self obstruction] of a single dharma (*ippo gujin*), 34-35, 63, 78-80, 81, 174n
transmission. *See* buddha(s), buddha alone together with buddha (*yuibutsu yobutsu*)
Tung-Shan (807-869), 211n; quoted, 75

uji. *See* existence-time
universal normality. *See* normality

Whitehead, Alfred North, xiv, xv, 10-11, 107, 123, 171n, 173n, 187n, 195n, 212n; quoted, 10-11, 107
Wittgenstein, Ludwig, 171n, 213n; quoted, viii

yuibutsu yobutsu (buddha alone together with buddha). *See* buddha(s), buddha alone together with buddha (*yuibutsu yobutsu*)
Yunmen (864-949), 6, 197n, 205n; quoted, 117
Zazen. *See* meditation
Zen (Ch'an), ancestors, see under specific names. *See also* Buddhism

Printed in Great Britain
by Amazon